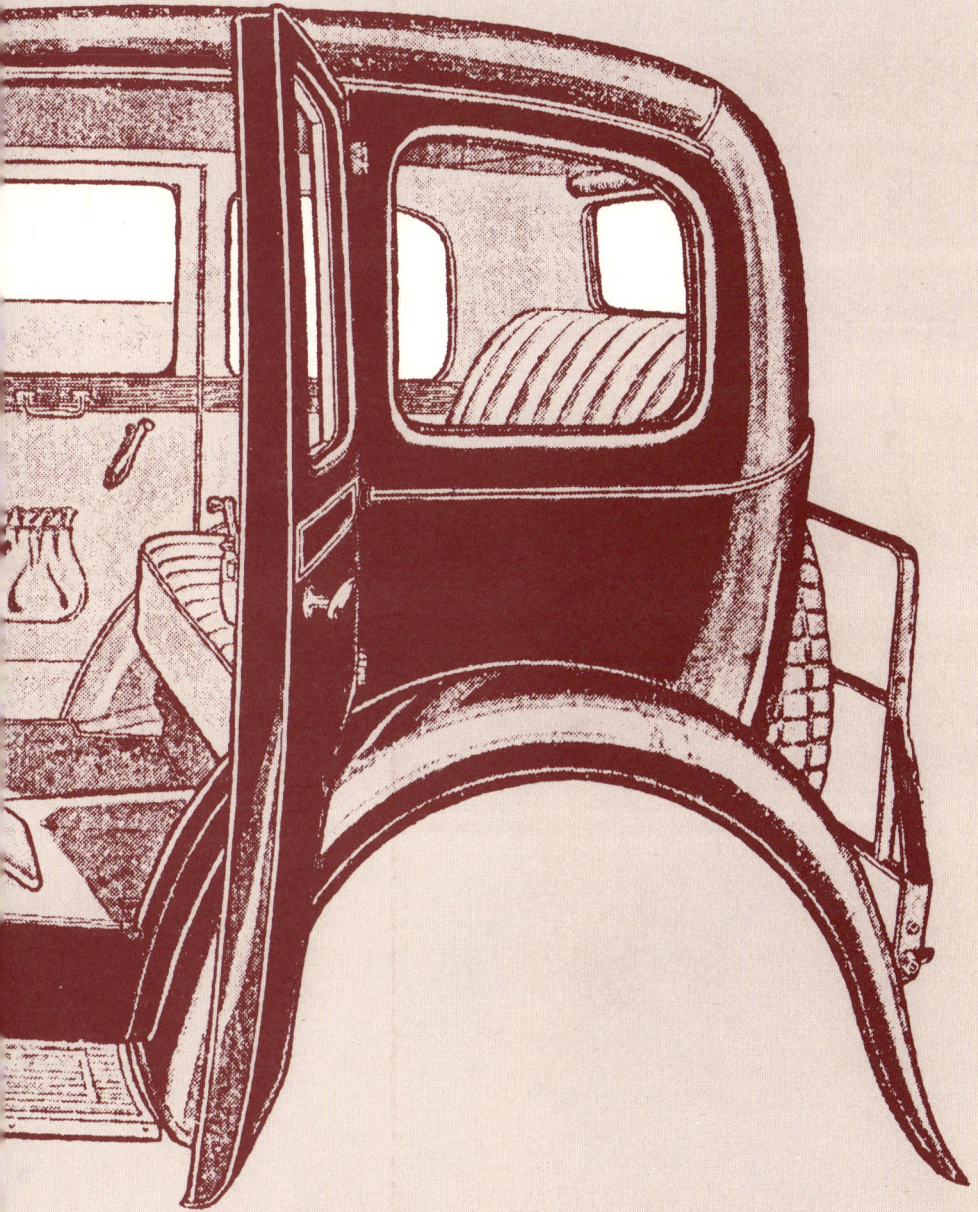

The Austin

By the same Author:

The Austin 7, 1922-1939
The Austin 7, A Pictorial Tribute
Cars — The Visual Library Series
Lord Austin — The Man (with Z.E. Lambert)
Collecting Volunteer Militaria

The *Austin*

1905-1952

R.J.WYATT

DAVID & CHARLES
Newton Abbot   London   North Pomfret (Vt)

To the Memory of Bob Burgess and Cliff Lewis

The illustrations are from the author's collection.

British Library Cataloguing in Publication Data

Wyatt, Robert John
  The Austin 1905-1952.
  1. Austin Motor Company — History
  2. Automobile industry and trade — Great Britain —
  History
  I. Title
  338.7'62'922220941   HD9710.G74A85

ISBN 0 7153 7948 8
Library of Congress Catalog Card Number: 80-68896

Typesetting by TJB Photosetting Limited
South Witham, Lincolnshire
Printed in Great Britain
by Redwood Burn Ltd., Trowbridge, Wilts.
for David & Charles (Publishers) Limited
Brunel House Newton Abbot Devon

Published in the United States of America
by David & Charles Inc
North Pomfret Vermont 05053   USA

Contents

Introduction

I first began collecting information for a history of Austins in the early 1950s, but my efforts were diverted when I was asked by Mrs Zeta Lambert to co-operate with her in producing the life of her father, the late Lord Austin — my contribution dealt with the period before 1906. Later, Bill Boddy of *Motor Sport* suggested that I should write a history of the Austin 7. With both these tasks behind me, I have been able to complete this survey of the history of the Austin from its formation until it became part of BMC in 1952. I call it a survey because had I tried to include all the information about the company that I have gleaned over the past twenty-five years, the book would have been five times as long.

I make no apologies for the fact that some chapters are longer and more detailed than others, because some passages in the history of this great British company are of such major significance that the story had to be told at some length. Brevity exists where possible, but I have not neglected detail where it is relevant. Any references are given in the text, and footnotes have been avoided, the quotations being allowed to speak for themselves.

Prime published sources have been the *Austin Magazine*, learned engineering journals, *Autocar, Automotor Journal, Motor, Light Car and Cyclecar, Motor Owner, Financial Times, Financial News, Investor's Chronicle, Motor Trader, Garage and Motor Agent, Payload, Austin Service Journal, BMC World* and my own collection of Austin catalogues, handbooks and photographs. Much information has come from the personal recollections of hundreds of people who worked at Longbridge. I regret to say that many of these excellent people have since died: J.H. Barnett and Alf Depper, who both joined in 1905; Cliff Lewis and Bob Burgess from the 1920s, and many more who became close friends. The late Lord Thomas provided much unpublished information on the shadow factories during World War II, and the late J.F. Bramley made available his copious notes on the history of the company whilst he was the publicity manager. I am also indebted to

INTRODUCTION

F.T. Henry, Arthur Waite, Sam Haynes, Roland Harrison, Anders Clausager, Mrs Zeta Lambert, Michael Sedgwick, Norman Milne, Kevin Gover, John Bowman, Alan Rayment, C.D. Murray, W.J. Oldham, Col. F. Buckley, Dick Burzi, Edgar Wren, Ron Beach, Stanley Edge, Gunnar Poppe, E.C. Gordon England, Carter & Co and Ryland, Martineau of Birmingham. I ask all the others who have helped me to accept my apologies for not having mentioned them by name: my thanks are none the less sincere for without their help this book could not have been written.

Carol Eady spent many late nights translating my manuscript onto the typewriter, and I am most grateful to her for the patience which she displayed.

R.J. WYATT
Wokingham
March 1980

No one has ever achieved eminence in any branch of human activity or attained greatness by relying on luck. It is the refuge of the weak and the inefficient. A man never drifts into success. It is obtained only by activity allied to courage, and capacity for ceaseless hard work.

Life is not a sweepstake, but a serious and fascinating business in which each one of us must carve out his own destiny.

Sir Herbert Austin, March 1930

All my life I have had a natural dislike for shoddy and unreliable work and as all my workshop experience has been in the direction of making machines or goods that have to function, the value of dependability has been drummed into my understanding. I feel convinced that what success I may have achieved is largely due to this schooling.

Sir Herbert Austin, 1935

1 The Formation of the Austin Motor Company

I started the Austin Motor Company in 1905 because I disagreed with the Board of Vickers.

Sir Herbert Austin, 1929

Herbert Austin was 38 years old when he left the Wolseley Tool & Motor Car Company Limited, and many of his old friends called him a pig-headed young fool for throwing up a good position as general manager in an established firm in order to be his own master in a hazardous new industry. But his little more than four years in this senior post with Vickers-controlled Wolseley had been marked by disagreement with the board over the merits of the horizontal compared with the increasingly popular vertical engine. In view of everything Austin had said in favour of horizontal engines — an attitude which resulted ultimately in the appointment of Siddeley to his old post at Wolseleys — it would seem reasonable to assume that he was so firm in his opinions that he would design a new horizontal engine to be marketed under his own name when his new firm was formed. This was not to be so. As he said himself: '. . . apart altogether from the trend of fashion, when the four-cylinder engine car became practicable I found that I could obtain the same advantages with the vertical as with the horizontal position. So I changed over'. In other words, he had no intention of agreeing with Vickers or Siddeley, even if they were right — typical Austin obstinacy.

Horizontal engines were the excuse rather than the reason for disagreement with the Vickers brothers; a patent taken out jointly by Wolseleys and Austin in April 1904 relating to the mounting by three-point suspension of a horizontal four-cylinder engine into a conventional chassis frame bears this out. Siddeley abandoned the patent in 1908, and Austin was not sufficiently interested in maintaining it alone, although the system of suspension of power units at three points was used on most Austin cars of the 1920s.

About two years before Austin left Wolseley, a young man named A.J.Hancock had joined him as a junior draughtsman. His work was of a particularly high standard, a fact which Austin noted. One evening in 1905, the senior draughtsman sent for Hancock and told him that he had heard of an opening which he thought would be well worth the latter's consideration. The conditions of engagement were unusual in that he would not be told the name of his employer until after he accepted the position offered. This was certainly a strange and unusual proposition to receive and, although it intrigued the young man, he asked if he could have until the morning before making up his mind. After thinking matters over he decided to accept the offer, and was then told that his future employer would be Herbert Austin, who was leaving shortly to start manufacturing for himself.

Hancock started his new job almost at once, working on designs of the first Austin car in a bedroom at Austin's house in Berwood Grove, Erdington, which had been turned temporarily into a drawing office. It was very soon realised that more help would be required and, on Hancock's recommendation, a young man called Davidge was engaged. Bobby Howitt was also appointed as private secretary, making the third member of the staff. All three men remained with Austin until he died in 1941.

Even before leaving the Wolseley company, Austin had been searching for suitable premises to open as a factory. On Saturday 4 November 1905 his wife packed a lunch basket and, with his meagre staff of three, he set out in a Wolseley 7½hp car to visit a factory he had heard about on the south side of Birmingham. They returned home in time for tea, with Austin in an elated mood; he was at last sure that he had found a suitable place. The district, seven miles from Birmingham and known as Longbridge was on the Bristol road, served by a railway branch line, and he had discovered there a derelict factory — a small works with a frontage of about 200ft and about the same depth on a site of some 2½ acres, surrounded by fields. Built in 1892, it had last been used by White & Pike Limited, metal workers, who had vacated it at the turn of the century. E.A.Olivieri, a Birmingham financier, had acquired it early in 1902, and Austin was the first serious buyer to show an interest. He calculated his capital requirements that evening. The premises, he thought, would cost in the region of £10,000 and £7,900 would be needed for additional plant. His operating costs would run at about £600 a week, and he would have to support this expenditure for the four months that it would take to produce the first hand-built chassis, after which output would be two vehicles a week.

He had the plans for a car, and a factory site, and it now remained for him to raise the capital. There was an option on some of the adjoining land, and he took the risk of including some of it in the purchase from Olivieri, the final agreement being for the factory buildings and 8 acres for which the transfer was signed on 22 January 1906 for £7,750.

The Austin Motor Company was formed with Austin and Frank Kayser of Kayser, Ellison & Company, steel manufacturers of Sheffield as co-directors and there was a capital of £50,000. Austin held £10,001 and Kayser £5,001, but the latter had already advanced £20,000 in cash. An agreement signed on 31 July 1906 allowed Harvey Du Cros of the Dunlop Rubber Company to have £20,000 in shares for cash, and to become a governing director, and to transfer £3,800 in shares to Austin and £200 in shares to Kayser for a nominal sum. Du Cros had many business interests, one of which was a Mercedes agency at 127 Long Acre in London; part of his agreement allowed him to become the sole agent for Austin cars from that address, which was later for a time to become the London base of the Austin company.

But even before all these financial arrangements were made, Austin and his staff moved into the building taking over the empty offices and, with a few deal tables and cheap chairs, a start was made. The empty room which Austin took for himself remained his office for the rest of his life. From its windows he could watch the factory, and over the years he saw it spread until it covered the surrounding district. The reason for the urgency in opening the works was the Motor Show to be held from 17 to 25 November 1905. At that time this show attracted not only all the motoring journalists and buying public as it does today, but also agents and dealers looking for new models to sell. So many firms had sprung up who had nothing more than a catalogue and intentions to offer, that Austin wanted to show that he had a factory as well as a reputation as a car-maker. Drawings were made in a great hurry so that they could be exhibited, and they were pinned onto boards and shown on a corner of Stand No 42 which was being used by Du Cros Mercedes Limited. Austin, Hancock and Davidge took turns to talk to visitors and considerable interest was shown; with only these drawings they managed to secure a number of firm orders.

This first model was a 25-30hp car. The chassis frame was made of a very stiff section, forming the engine sub-frame all in one. The four-cylinder vertical engine with a 4¾in bore and 5in stroke, had separate cylinders with 'T' heads and a detachable cover over each valve, which gave easy access to the valves for withdrawal or seating adjustments. There were adjustable

11

fingers between the cams and tappets which could be set with the engine in motion — an unusual feature which does not seem to have been adopted by many manufacturers at the time, or since. It had problems later when methods of engine lubrication became more complicated, and there were problems with oil sealing. As in all engines then, maximum speed was regulated by a governor, and the unit was designed for a modest maximum of 900rpm. The first car was chain-driven, and had four forward speeds with the gear-change lever and brake control on the right-hand side of the driver. Austin soon realised that a more silent drive was needed and so, as an alternative, a bevel-geared axle was developed. By the standards of the time, the chassis was excellent; there was nothing unconventional about it but it was of first-class quality with high reliability. These early models were efficient and dependable, and established the foundation upon which the Austin reputation was built.

The first prototype was on the road in April 1906. With Austin at the wheel, it was driven out of the factory gates and up into the Lickey Hills on its first test run, on a day when the press had been invited to Longbridge to celebrate the launching of the first Austin, and the official opening of the factory.

Between the completion of the prototype car and the presenting of the first set of accounts in October of that year showing a net turnover of £14,772 only about 23 cars can have been sold. The press were told later that in the first year of operation 123 cars had been completed and that 270 men were employed. I refer elsewhere to the difficulties experienced in arriving at correct production figures, and all that can be said with certainty is that the number of Austins produced in the first year was not only small in itself, but minute as a proportion of the output of the British motor industry.

It was to be some time before Austin was to become a major producer with sufficient output to make an impact on the demand pattern, but it is useful at this early stage, while he was still struggling with the problems of forming his company and in gaining a reputation for the Austin car, to consider various aspects of the industry which he and William Morris were to dominate in the two decades between the wars.

We have first to consider the style of engineering that was current at the beginning of this century. The machine-tool industry was by no means new and, although it may appear somewhat unsophisticated to the present-day engineer accustomed to the modern production line, a system for repetitive mass-production of interchangeable parts was already well established at

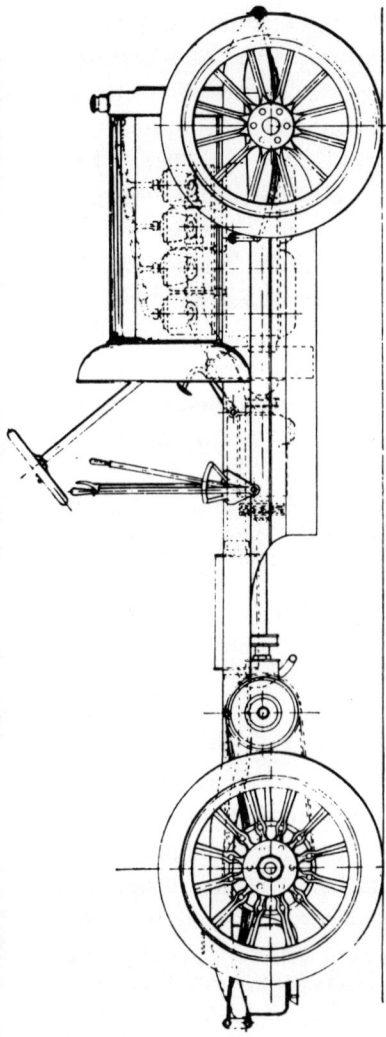

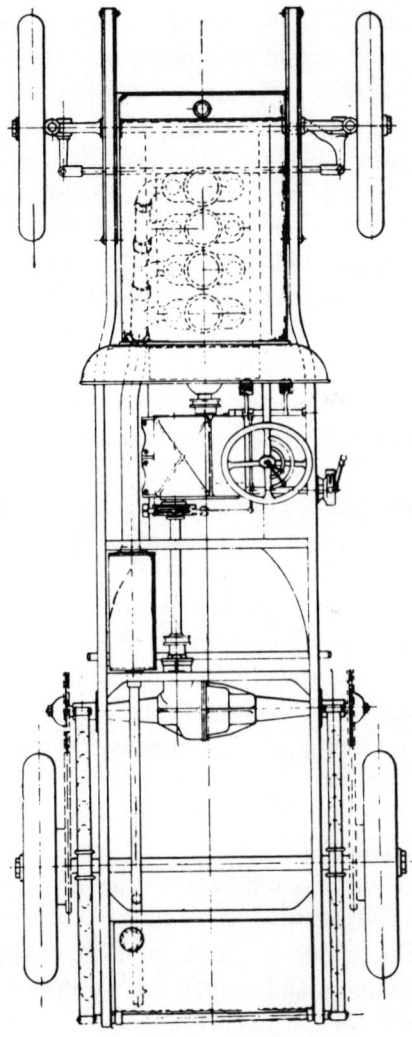

Chassis drawing from the first Austin catalogue, 1906

the birth of the motor industry. Colonel Colt had produced his famous revolvers both in America and at Pimlico in London whilst Britain was fighting the war in the Crimea in the 1850s, and by the end of that decade the Royal Small Arms Factory at Enfield produced the first British rifle — the 0.577 Enfield — with the aid of mass-production techniques. Advanced machinery, that the motor industry in this country did not adopt until after World War I, was in use at Enfield. Every similar part of each rifle was identical and capable of being interchanged with any other similar part, allowing speedy production and the assembly of finished products in huge quantity. Henry Ford was a notable exception. His British assembly plant in Manchester brought over American techniques, and there was an important similarity in that quantity was the feature in common between the Enfield rifle and the Model T Ford. Skilled manpower was expensive, but so was special machinery. Given a heavy demand for a product, the theory of mass-production worked. It reduced the labour content of manufacture and, if the quantity was sufficient, the capital cost of the machinery could be written off quickly and the unit cost of the product reduced.

Henry Ford thought in terms of hundreds of thousands of cars a year; the largest British firms thought in hundreds, never more than a few thousand a year. Like the rest, Austin began by virtually producing single cars to order when he was with Wolseley. He knew about machinery but, to begin with, a small team of skilled men was all that he needed; there was little point in setting up production lines to make a few cars a week. Anyway, he did not have the capital for rapid expansion.

Another point to remember is that the style of engineering in which Austin had been trained was inclined towards comparatively heavy engineering. Never use a ¼in bolt if a 1½in one would do may, when we look today at one of his 1907 cars, seem to have been his principle. He was by no means alone. There were light cars which had grown on three or four wheels from the cycle industry in Coventry, which in itself owed something to the sewing-machine era in that same city, but generally speaking cars were heavy and ponderous, comfortable and expensive. The state of the roads, the current legislation and the customers all played their part in determining the appearance of the car before World War I.

In these days of motorways, 70mph speed limits and cars for all, it is sometimes easy to forget that these are all very recent features of our lives. Roads, which had been allowed to deteriorate after the stage coach was replaced by the railways in the nineteenth century, were pot-holed and consisted of graded stones covered in a thick layer of fine white dust, which became mud when it rained. The road system in Great Britain was extensive, and between 1909 and 1929 the total road milage was only increased from 175,000 to 179,000 miles. But the dust problem, which made early motoring so unpleasant and even dangerous, was only first tackled seriously in 1907 when it was decided to spray tar on the surfaces of the busiest roads. Within a year, more than 1,000 miles had been treated in this way.

Separate vehicle export and import statistics were first produced by the Board of Trade for 1902, but both in that year and for 1903, motor cycles, commercial vehicles and cars were grouped together. In the first year 3,747 vehicles were imported, 183 were re-exported, and a mere 415 British vehicle products exported. In 1903, imports had nearly doubled to 6,134, 382 were re-exported, and there was a good growth in exports to 955. More detailed statistics appeared for 1904, and cars were counted separately. Net imports were 4,972 against exports of 703. In 1905, the figures were 5,422 and 800 respectively. There was a slight increase in both figures for 1906, a year in which 23,192 private cars were registered in Britain — for an industry which produced less than 8,000 cars, of which about 1,000 were exported, there were 6,000 imports.

Proportions like that sound all too familiar. The fact was that foreign cars could be imported freely into the UK without the payment of duty, whereas most countries would not permit British cars to be imported without a levy. Only three British firms exhibited cars at the 1905 Paris Show, namely Argyll, Star and Wolseley. Charles Jarrott, one of the major car factors and importers, said that the demand for English cars abroad was small; some in the industry argued that this was primarily because of our inability to compete on price with foreign cars in their own markets because of duty. The strange fact pointed out by Jarrott was that the Italians in that same Paris Show were represented by more than a dozen firms, and sold a considerable number of cars under the same impositions. This applied to a lesser extent with Belgian and German products. France managed even to carry on a successful business in the USA, where 95 per cent of the cars in use were made in that country, and where a 45 per cent duty was imposed on imported cars. Thus, Jarrott argued, it was not the imposition of a duty on British-built cars which prevented their sale abroad and, this being so, what was responsible for their not being sought after?

Others saw the problem in a different light. After all, the duty into France was not very high, only about £20 on a £500 car. Charles Sangster, a leading light in the Coventry cycle trade, warned of his own experience with trying to export bicycles to France, where the duty was proportionately much higher at £1 10s a machine. He attempted to negotiate a contract to export 5,000 from Birmingham to France in 1905, but the negotiations fell through for one reason only — the deliberate policy of the French government not to admit anything manufactured abroad which could be made equally well in France. As soon as the imports of a particular product increased, duty would be increased, so there was little point in trying to alter the pattern of French trade by increasing exports to France. Her protective measure would in the end reduce the competitiveness of imports.

Jarrott did not think that the trouble was a lack of advertising or that British products were inferior in any way. In fact probably the low rate of exports of cars from Britain resulted from an accumulation of several factors: fear of restrictive duties; a slightly inferior product which is hardly surprising considering the early advantages gained in Europe and the slow start in Britain caused by speed limit restrictions placed on motoring; and a general lack of interest in being involved with the bother of exporting.

There was a clash of interests in this country between the car manufacturer and the car importer. Foreign cars were better in many respects, they were more advanced in most areas of automobile engineering and production and, without an import duty, very competitive. It was argued that if a duty was imposed, or anything else that would restrict foreign sales here, the manufacturers would overcome this by setting up their own factories in this country. Henry Ford is an example of what a volume producer from abroad could do if he had to. We imported 6,000 cars in 1906, but car parts came to another £2 million. No doubt some of these went into British cars, but much of the value of imported parts finished up in complete foreign cars assembled here. Against that, we were only able to export parts valued at some £200,000. Today we do not like such a high proportion of UK car sales to be Japanese importations, but if we were to impose prohibitively restrictive duties on Japanese imports, Japan might ruin our balance of payments by refusing to take our exports of other goods, or at least making them uncompetitive by a high rate of duty. Even when their so-called quota for a year looks like being exceeded they, and their British agents, make sure that there is sufficient stock held to ensure continued success. And vested interest applied no less in 1906 than it does today. Jarrott himself was very active in selling imported cars in Britain.

This then was the technical and economic background against which the newly formed Austin company had to consolidate and develop.

2 The First Eight Years: 1906-1913

In that first financial year of 1906, as already mentioned, the net turnover for the eleven months was only £14,772 and 23 cars were sold between April and October. Most of them were 25/30s, but there were a few of the smaller 15/20 cars, a cheaper version with the same engine with smaller cylinders — the bore was only 4in, ½in less than on the bigger and more popular car. In 1907 the 25/30 was continued and the 15/20 became the 18/24 with a 4⅛in bore, which continued with slight modifications until 1913. In 1911, the bore was again increased to 4⅜in with the stroke remaining at 5in, which increased the bhp at 1,000rpm to 35. Nearly £100,000 was turned over in the year ending 31 October 1907, and 147 cars were sold.

Austin realised the value of publicity. The first car had been launched in front of the press, and that same vehicle was entered in the 1906 Scottish Reliability Trial, making a 3 day non-stop run. The second car built won the 100 Guineas Dunlop Challenge Cup in the Irish Reliability Trial, and another early Austin won a hill-climb at Wolverhampton. In 1908 a private limited company was formed by Austin, Kayser and Du Cros, and for the 11 months to 30 September 1908 the net turnover was £119,744 and 254 cars were sold; the 18/24 remained but the 25/30 engine was bored out to 4¾in and simplified to become the 40; the complicated adjustable tappets and the impossible ignition system were also replaced. In the first 25/30 car dual-ignition was used. An accumulator and coil, working through a distributor, supplied power to high-tension sparking plugs — the conventional system still in use in most cars in 1980 — but in the first Austins this was supplemented by a separate low-tension ignition in which a 50V dynamo supplied current to all the cylinders through complicated plugs which opened and closed inside the inlet-valve caps to create a spark. In the 40, these two systems were replaced by the much more reliable magneto.

S.F.Edge, the leading light behind Napier cars, had been successful with the new six-cylinder cars, a fashion which Austin could not ignore. He added two more cylinders to the new 40, and it became the 60, continuing in production until 1910, being used in the company's first attempt at motor racing.

Motor racing using limited fuel was never popular, largely because of the effect it had upon the drivers who never knew whether they were going to complete a race with the huge racing cars of the period on the regulation allowance. For the 1908 Grand Prix which was to be run on the Dieppe circuit, cars were not permitted to weigh less than 1,100kg and engines were limited to 155mm cylinder bore for a four-cylinder engine, or 127mm for six cylinders, but there was no limit to the amount of fuel that could be used.

Three British Weigel cars were entered, with four-cylinder engines and overhead camshafts. Charles Napier began to prepare a team of powerful six-cylinder cars based on experience gained after nearly a year's strenuous work racing at the recently constructed Brooklands track. All the Napiers were to have the new Rudge detachable wheels, but the regulations for the race prohibited these on the grounds of safety. The detachable rims had already come off and killed several people, and there was fear of even worse disasters if detachable wheels were adopted. Also the organisers felt that to change so important a component as a wheel would open the door to people who wanted to change engines. To them, wheels were as much part of a car as an engine and if competitors were allowed to change one it would be difficult to argue that they could not change the other, and this would not be acting in the spirit of Grand Prix racing. By all means change a tyre, but changing a component such as a wheel would be going too far. S.F.Edge was so annoyed that he withdrew the Napier cars, which were proving difficult to complete in time anyway, so the controversy may have come as a blessing in disguise.

Austin decided to enter a team as early as January 1908. Four cars were made with six-cylinder engines with a bore and stroke of 127mm, four forward speeds with direct drive on third, 4ft 7in track, 9ft 9in wheel base and fixed wheels with Dunlop detachable rims and tyres. Two had propeller-shaft transmission and the other two used side chains, and a maximum speed of 92mph at 1,500rpm was intended. The drivers were to be Dario Resta of the Putney Automobile Club, who had raced a Mercedes at Brooklands in the previous season, and Warwick Wright, a successful driver of a 100hp Darracq and an aeronaut and balloon owner: A.C. Barnes was also considered and, as J.T.C Moore-Brabazon wanted to race a Napier, so also was K. Lee-Guiness. Resta bought his car from the company so his position as a driver was secure, Warwick Wright was also a certainty and, when the Napiers withdrew, Moore-Brabazon was given the third place. He was well qualified; also an aeronaut and balloon owner he had built and designed an aeroplane and had been racing motor cars since 1906. He won the Circuit des Ardennes, the principal Belgian race of the year in 1907, becoming the second Englishman to win the event by covering 375 miles in 374 minutes — a remarkable achievement when one considers the unreliability of tyres and the condition of the roads. It would be difficult to cover 375 miles at 60mph in a modern car today on our class A highways. S.Hands, an old Wolseley racing driver who had been C.S.Rolls's (of Rolls-Royce) mechanic in the last Gordon Bennet race, was selected as reserve driver.

Resta took his car over to France in March and drove over the circuit, and Austin secured the Hotel du Cygne at Eu, the most northerly point touched on the Dieppe course, and no less than sixty people from Austins were to be accommodated there. A special race for the Austin cars was organised at Brooklands in May. Three cars, two with chain drive and the other with a live axle, the fourth live-axle car being retained as a spare, were driven around two inner laps by Resta, Wright and Moore-Brabazon with two tyres being changed on each car at the half-way mark. On completion of the first lap, Resta and Wright drew up level to change tyres, Brabazon overshooting and having to reverse. Resta was first away, Wright following after a long interval with Brabazon close behind. Resta won the race easily, mainly because he had managed to change two rims and tyres in 3 minutes. Only two makes entered for the Grand Prix — the Austin and Porthos teams — were using six-cylinder cars and, as the Napiers had been withdrawn, the Austins looked as if they might have a chance. However, the engines were the conventional Austin 6s which were only 40hp cars with two extra cylinders bored out from 121 to 127mm, and Austin regarded the Dieppe circuit as a 'third-speed course' and had designed the cars with that in mind.

The four cars were shipped over to France a couple of weeks before the race and as it was forbidden to practise on the course any testing had to be done on the other minor French roads. All the drivers suffered from what was called a 'slight superiority' by some of the works' mechanics; the one allocated to Resta had been left to walk home when he had been induced to get out to look for some fault at the back of the car. During another test run Resta crashed into a horse and cart which was travelling on the wrong side of the road, and the Austin turned upside down in a ditch, on top of driver and mechanic. The two men were rescued unhurt, but were very nearly mobbed by some infuriated villagers, being saved only by a long and tactful speech from Moore-Brabazon who arrived behind them in his car and suggested adjourning to a local *estaminet*. Everything was going well when Herbert Austin arrived. A new misunderstanding arose and the row began all over again, Resta was hauled off to prison and had to be rescued very much the worse for wear. On the following day, he began practising with the spare car. Tearing along at 80mph he met yet another cart, this time crossing at a crossroads, but managed to avoid it by swerving into a ditch. Both men were picked up unconscious, no bones were broken but Resta suffered from shock. Out of the remains of the two cars that he had destroyed, with spares rushed over from England, they managed to build a complete machine.

On the day before the race, the three cars were modified slightly. Larger fuel tanks were fitted, bigger radiators given higher filler caps to put the overflow as high as possible, valve covers were flanged to help with engine cooling and one of the two magnetos was replaced by a distributor for HT ignition.

At 6am on Tuesday 7 July the first Austin in the green English racing colours, and driven by Resta, set off around the 47.8 mile course followed by the rest at one-minute intervals. Each car had to cover the course ten times. Resta unexpectedly completed his first lap while a string of others were waiting to start in the centre of the road opposite the grandstand, which considerably disconcerted the starter. Warwick Wright ran out of oil and before anything could be done his engine seized after four laps, but the other two Austins although unplaced succeeded in finishing the course, Brabazon in 8 hours 42 minutes 50 seconds and Resta in 8 hours 46 minutes 50 seconds — average speeds of over 54mph. Moore-Brabazon's car suffered from water in its fuel, the carburetter having to be dismantled twelve times. His mechanic, Lane, had his goggles smashed by a stone and was suffering from tar spray, while Brabazon had a bad cut on his head caused by another flying stone. Tyres proved to be the biggest problem for all cars in the race, and although the two that finished had proved to be mechanically reliable, they were no match for the Mercedes which Lautenschlager drove to victory at an average speed of 69mph. The French dominated the motor industry at that time, and were not at all pleased that two successive French Grand Prix had been won by foreign cars. Racing giant cars on minor public roads was also both unsafe and expensive and when the entry list for 1909 opened only nine entries were received, so the

Grand Prix was abandoned. All three Austin cars were converted to tourers and sold to private owners, Jack Johnson the boxer being one. Only one car survived and has been preserved — still in running order.

No further attempts at motor racing were made by Austins until after the war, but one or two private competitors were successful with sporting versions of standard Austins. Oscar Thompson, a motor sport enthusiast of the time, took delivery of a 40hp touring car in 1907; for the first nine months it was used only as a tourer, during that time covering about 10,000 miles. Thompson was so pleased with its reliability and performance that he decided to try racing it at Brooklands but, before doing so, the car was fitted with a new 120 x 127mm 40hp engine, different gear ratios, a special carburetter and a two-seater body. At about the same time the car was named *Pobble* after Edward Lear's toeless creature. In May, Thompson entered the car in a private race at Brooklands against N.G.Nalder on his 35hp Berliet, and Nalder won by a length. On its second appearance on 8 June it came first in the second heat of the President's Cup race with a speed of 71mph; the following month, Thompson's sister Muriel drove the car to victory in the Ladies Bracelet Handicap. By this time, *Pobble* had such a public following that it was recognised as one of the main attractions of Brooklands. Between 1908 and 1909 it made 36 appearances, collecting 11 firsts, 6 seconds and 6 thirds. In July 1909 Thompson entered the car for the Shelsley Walsh hill climb at which, driven by Hands, it made the fastest time of the day. Thompson repeated the performance himself a year later, competing against two six-cylinder cars. In 1911, after more tuning, *Pobble* caused more excitement by lapping Brooklands at 91mph. It made only one more appearance after that in the hands of Muriel in 1912, ending five extremely successful racing years for what was nothing more than a slightly modified ponderous production car — a record of which Thompson was justifiably proud.

Austin's 40hp car had proved so successful that in 1910 it was decided to enter one in the Russian International Tour. Harold Kendall, Austin's experimental road-test and competition driver at the time, was chosen to drive in the event. The race began on 30 June in appalling conditions with some of the roads being no better than ploughed fields; the route taken was through St Petersburg and Kharkov to Moscow, a distance of 2,139 miles and there were 46 starters. Only about half-a-dozen cars finished without mechanical failure such as broken springs, broken steering gear and bent axles. One of the survivors was Kendall's Austin which won the St Petersburg Automobile Club trophy. Austin was highly delighted with the performance and widely advertised the fact that an Austin car had run non-stop in an event considered to be the most severe trial on record.

Another car worthy of mention is Percy Lambert's *Pearly III*. Based on a 15hp chassis, the engine was modified considerably with a special crankshaft and connecting rods, steel in place of cast-iron pistons, twin Claudel carburetters and a double-spark Bosch magneto with two plugs to each cylinder. The steering column was set at an angle in the frame to be within reach of the centrally mounted single driving seat; it had a cowled radiator, disc-covered wheels and a pencil slim body with an external exhaust pipe. At its first race at Brooklands in June 1911 it did not win, but managed to get up to 70mph. It did win a race for private cars there a month later; was successful at several other events, doing a flying kilometre in 26 seconds at a race in Nottinghamshire; and after fitting a Solex carburetter won an Allcomers Handicap at Brooklands and in October came third and second in other races there.

Things continued to go well at Longbridge; net turnover in 1909 reached £169,821 and 402 cars were made, still the 18/24, 40 and 60hp engines but also a new, cheaper 15 with a much smaller engine of 3½in x 4in and a three-bearing crankshaft. This was unusual as far as Austin was concerned, because it was the first — and only — pre-war Austin which used a single casting for the cylinders. They had a great deal of trouble in casting the monobloc, with its complicated water passages, and abandoned the 15 at the end of 1910. Its replacement in 1911 had a 3½in x 4½in 19.6hp engine, but was still called a 15, with the conventional five-bearing crank and single-cast cylinders; it continued until 1915. Whilst it was current, however, it was used as a basis for the town carriage and the light van of 12-15cwt capacity; it was also intended for use as a taxi but the authorities would not allow it to ply for hire. Its leading feature was the driver's seat, placed centrally and over the engine. However, this caused some problems with the steering which used a bevel and pinion; the driver of the first test car got something of a shock when he first took the vehicle out of the shop — he found that when he turned the steering wheel to the left, the vehicle went to the right! This was soon put right, and two of these unusual cars still exist. No further attempts were made at central or forward control, and individual cylinder casting continued until 1919, years after almost every other manufacturer had turned to casting monobloc or in pairs.

Another unusual departure as far as Austins were concerned occurred in 1910. Austin designed a very small car using one cylinder-block from the 18/24 engine as a basis for a tiny single-cylinder engine in a very light frame. At least one car was made at Longbridge and it, together with the drawings and what patterns there were, was taken to the Swift works at Coventry and put under the control of R.H.Every. He said many years afterwards that they set up a separate department there to make the cars and although Austin designed them he was so busy with his successful four-cylinder models that Harvey Du Cros, who controlled Swift in addition to his many other motor-trade interests, allowed the new 7hp cars to be made in Coventry. The single-cylinder cars which sold for only £150, were not a great success, and within two years Swift had their own two-cylinder motor to replace the Austin single. It appears that most of the cars made came out as Swifts, but at least one in single-cylinder form has survived, and Austin production figures suggest that there were 162. During the two years in which they were available, altogether 1,030 were produced.

A new small 10 was announced at the Motor Show in November 1910, with a bore and stroke of 2½in x 3½in to cater for the demand for smaller, cheaper cars on the continental market. The car was not available for sale in Britain until late in 1911, and it was discontinued in 1912. It was said at the time that both Austin and Daimler, who had just produced a small 12, had been compelled if not quite to withdraw such models, at least to curtail production to cater for the rush of orders for their higher-powered models.

As early as 1908 Austin first recognised the possibility of an entirely enclosed body. The potential of the saloon body had not at that time been grasped and Austin introduced one with revolving doors with windows in the upper half between back and front seats. When the owner was driving the doors were thrown back and back and front seats were in communication, but at other times the doors could be drawn together and the driving seat cut off from the back of the car. This was a very advanced design for 1908 as there was only one door on each side, access to the front seats being gained by a passage between them. It was altogether ahead of its time and the first enclosed limousines did not begin to gain favour until 1910 or 1911. Austin, who was unusual in that he built his own bodies, had several limousines to offer, but there was not much demand for them.

In 1910, 576 cars were made, and the turnover reached £209,048. Steady progress in 1911 increased net turnover to £276,196 and production to 664. That same year saw the first issue of one of the first car manufacturer's monthly journals, the *Advocate*, later to become the highly respected *Austin Magazine*, which was to remain in existence for over fifty years until it was axed with all the other BMC house journals. The first editor was H. Welsh-Lee, who had worked for an excellent magazine called *Car Illustrated*.

23

Two years later, Austins became involved in speed-boat engines. In 1912, Tom Sopwith, in a boat called *Maple Leaf IV*, won the Harmsworth Trophy, the first and only time that this premier race was won from the Americans in American waters. *Maple Leaf I*, *II* and *III* had been built for the financier Mackay Edgar with that object in mind, to regain the British international trophy. Each boat had failed to come up to expectations, although *Maple Leaf III* had two huge V12 engines of 425hp each designed by the New Orleans Company, who however made only one of them, the second being constructed to the same design by Dixon Bros & Hutchinson Limited of Southampton, who also had to design and construct new cylinders and pistons for the New Orleans engine. Mackay Edgar was not satisfied with *Maple Leaf III*, so he had *Maple Leaf IV* constructed by Saunders of Cowes, and approached Austin to do something about the engines. J.W. Kinchin, who later owned Solihull Motors, was in charge of this work at Longbridge and was at Cowes during the tests.

The engines were stripped down, and as there had been trouble with the cooling, Austin designed and made new cylinders with greater space for the coolant around the water jackets. Pistons were lightened, strengthened and ground, the valves and valve gear were improved, and a pressure-fed oil system was designed and built by Austin which worked at 20lb per sq in. The exhaust system was altered and the carburation improved, each block of six cylinders having a separate manifold and carburetter. It was widely thought at the time that these two V12 engines with single overhead camshafts and a bore and stroke of 7in x 7½in were of Austin manufacture. Austin was certainly responsible for major modifications which resulted in the boat winning the trophy but, as several people who were involved in making the originals were quick to point out, they were engines that had been modified and adapted by Austins, and were not built by them in the first instance.

In order to beat the Americans, it was necessary for *Maple Leaf IV* to run reliably in excess of 40 knots, a remarkable speed for a motor boat in 1912. The trials attended by Kinchin proved a huge success and on her first six runs, three with the current and three against, over the Thorneycroft mile in Southampton Water, she averaged 45 knots. America was challenged and on further tuning up 52 knots was reached, a record speed at the time. Before the boat was sent to America she was raced in Southampton Water against Hucks in a biplane, the finishing post being the royal yacht on which were the king, queen and other members of the royal family. In September 1912, Tom Sopwith took her to America where she lost the first race, but with Sopwith's seamanship and the consistent running of the engines gained the second and third races, and won the trophy for England. Not to be outdone, *Maple Leaf IV* won it again in English waters in 1913.

On the strength of the 1912 success, Austin decided to enter the marine field in earnest. A prototype 15hp motor was installed in Harvey Du Cros's 25ft Saunders-built boat *Nitsu* and there followed a 10hp engine and a 30 with, for the first time for an Austin, an overhead camshaft, no doubt as a result of what had been seen on *Maple Leaf IV*. All of them were adapted to run on either petrol or paraffin and they all had surprisingly long strokes for Austins of the day: the 10 was 3in x 4½in, the 15 was 3½in x 5in and the 30 was 4⅜in x 6in.

In the summer of 1912 an Austin car was entered for the 2,000 mile trial held by the Automobile Club of Russia from St Petersburg to Riga and Moscow. The car chosen to compete was the near-square 40 with a bore and stroke of 125mm x 127mm, a streamlined body with a tapered bonnet and a radiator with curved edges, called the Defiance. It had the new Austin-Sankey detachable wheels which used a novel method of central fixing without studs and nuts, being a sophisticated version of the wheels used on the 20s of 1919. It performed so well that it was regarded as a certain winner of the czar's cup for the best performance on the circuit, but an accident put it out of the competition. The car was in no way faulty, in fact it made the fastest time in every speed test; at St Petersburg it covered the flying kilometre in 28 seconds — over 80mph — with three people on board and fully loaded with two spare wheels, spare parts and luggage.

As far as Narva the roads were fairly good for Russia, but between there and Revel the cars had to use rough tracks and forest roads where two cars could not pass each other and in which there were ruts two feet deep in the mud. On each side of the track there were deep ditches. At Riga the Austin again made fastest time in the speed trial. On the next section, to Warsaw, the cars had to drive through dry sand up to their axles in the boiling sun in first and second gear. Fastest time was made yet again at Warsaw. Towards Kiev the roads improved, and the Austin won the hill climb on that section. By the time Gomel was reached the roads were described as perfect; up to then the car had suffered only two punctures, but from there on it ran out of luck. As soon as one puncture was repaired another occurred, and when flying along a narrow level road with a sharp camber and a ditch, a tyre burst. Kendall who was driving at the time tried to keep control, but the tyre came off the rim, and the car knocked down a telegraph pole and turned over. Kendall was badly knocked about, but soon recovered. The

Russian observer, Bell and Taylor the mechanic did not come off so lightly, and the last we hear of them is that they were doing as well as could be expected.

Following the Russian trials and particularly the success of the 40hp Defiance, and in view of what Thompson and Lambert had done, Austin decided to start a racing and experimental section. C. Hornsted, an experienced Brooklands driver who had driven *Pobble*, was put in charge with the stated object of producing a record breaker.

The year 1912 was the most successful for Austin so far, net turnover reached £354,209 and in the year ending 30 September 886 cars were sold, 1,800 people were employed, and in July the showrooms were moved from Long Acre to 479-483 Oxford Street. Anyone in London was invited to visit the new premises where they were welcome to make use of the club rooms available for Austin owners, consisting of reading, writing and dressing-rooms. At the back, in North Row, there was plenty of garage space and well-furnished club rooms for chauffeurs. At Olympia in November 1912, Austin cars were displayed on stand 82: an 18/24 cabriolet; the new 40hp Defiance which was a facsimile of the Russian trials car with its distinctive tapering bonnet and streamlined body contour, Austin-Sankey detachable wheels, electric lighting, curved glass screen and rounded radiator; and 10hp and 18/24hp chassis. Bare chassis exhibits were rarely seen at shows before World War I. Not many of the owners of the larger cars of the period drove themselves, but an increasing number who bought small and medium-sized vehicles either could not afford to employ a chauffeur or preferred to do their own driving. It was considered quite a novel idea to let them see what the innards of a car were like. The 10, introduced at the end of 1911, had not been altered much, the three-speed gearbox having been replaced by one with four; the 15 and the 18/24 were the only other models to sell in any quantity.

A new 30hp car was first shown at the Paris Show in December 1912; the engine had enclosed valve springs, an aluminium dash, dynamo charging, the Defiance radiator and a torque tube encasing the propeller shaft, articulated so that it was free to move laterally with respect to the rear axle. There was a new method for supporting the sub-frame on which the engine, clutch and gearbox were carried. At its front end it was bolted to the front cross-member of the main frame at two points, and its back end rested on a circular rubber pad carried by the middle cross-member, the object being to deaden the noise from the gearbox and to prevent vibration getting to the frame and body. There was also a new 20, not simply a 15 with a stroke ½in longer, but a completely new model, in effect a scaled-down 30.

By September 1913 it was realised that it was much more profitable to concentrate on fewer models, so all were withdrawn except for the 30, 20 and a new small 10 with a 3in x 3½in engine, called a 12 for the overseas market. They were highly successful and of the 882 cars made in 1913, 495 were 10s. The year was a highly successful one again with a net turnover of £425,641.

Towards the end of 1913 Austin, Du Cros and Kayser decided that they would form a public company to be called The Austin Motor Company (1914) Limited. With net turnover at over £400,000 for the year, and after allowing for all expenses, depreciation and for the cost of developing the 1914 models, a healthy profit of £41,130 had been made. Liabilities were a £3,000 mortgage, a debenture of £100,000, and £15,459 for directors' fees and commission, and dividends at the rate of 5 per cent on preference shares and 17.5 per cent on ordinary shares. With 2,000 employees, 118 acres of land for future expansion, an output approaching 1,000 cars a year and prospects of a turnover of £550,000 with profits of £64,000 for the coming year, there was a need for more working capital. After preliminary expenses and underwriting, £99,041 was left for the additional capital, the purchase price being £399,993 payable in fully paid £1 ordinary shares, good-will being valued at £228,874, five times the average profit for the last three years. Liabilities were guaranteed not to exceed £261,047.

All the 399,993 ordinary shares went to the vendor company's directors, Austin getting 186,663, Du Cros 186,663 and Kayser 26,667, and of the £15,459 due, Austin received £7,054, Du Cros £6,884 and Kayser £1,521. Austin was given a five-year contract as chairman and managing director at £3,500 a year and 2.5 per cent of the net profits in each year, over and above the amount required to pay the dividend on the preference shares. Directors and subscribers of the new company were allocated shares as follows: Austin, Du Cros, Kayser, Albert Ball and H. Marks got 250 preference and 1 ordinary share each; F.S. Goodwin and P.H. Carter got 1 ordinary share each. The issue of the balance of 250,000 £1 7 per cent preference shares was a resounding success.

At the first meeting of the company, held on 16 April 1914, it was stated that 2,000 ordinary shares had been sold for 9s each as a result of a misunderstanding on the part of a friend of Kayser. It appears that he mentioned to his broker that he was willing to sell some of his stock at 9s premium, and during his absence in America the shares were sold at 9s instead of 29s. Somebody had a lucky purchase and Kayser lost £2,000. It did not seem to bother him, and the other holders of Austin ordinary must have been delighted to learn that it was an error and that their £1 share were worth not 9s but 29s!

Five English cars were entered for the Austrian Alpine Trial in June 1914: an Austin, a Vauxhall, an Armstrong-Whitworth, a Rolls-Royce and a Wolseley. The Austin was a new 20, OA4133, driven by Harold Kendall with Vernon Austin as his co-driver. It was a standard car apart from a deeper radiator, and resembled closely the 1919 Austin 20, even to the shape of the flush-sided body. The course was for 1,800 miles from Vienna through twenty-five Alpine passes and the 20 succeeded in completing the course, being timed at 61.6mph on a speed test on the last day, covering in all 7,000 miles without a mechanical breakdown. A development of this car, the 20 of 1915, (already with a 95mm bore, like the Brooklands sports model) was, except for the engine and gearbox, virtually a 1919 car. By June, just before World War I started, the 30 was to be abandoned and there was to be only one car to supplement the 20, the 10 which was to be called the 12/14. This did not survive and, as will be seen in the next chapter, all efforts were to be put into the famous 20.

3 Munitions to Mass Production: 1914-1919

The years from 1914 to 1919 were of great importance to the firm's development and growth in the next decade, the ability to expand during the early 1920s stemming, to a great extent, from experience gained and new techniques employed during World War I. Mass production of the Austin 20 cars in 1919 had its origins in the lessons learnt in the large-scale production of munitions. It is necessary, therefore, to examine this period in detail.

From a small firm employing 2,638 in the spring of 1914 and producing only 882 cars a year, in three years the company became one of the largest munitions factories in the country. At one period in 1917 there were as many employees at Longbridge as there were in the 1960s — over 20,000. Prior to the outbreak of war in 1914 this small factory produced excellent cars; the name Austin was reputable and, with a large number of orders on hand for its new models, there was no reason why the company should not look forward to the future with every confidence. Profits earned from the 1913 turnover were not outstanding but it was a comfort to the shareholders to know that a great deal of the capital was tied up in valuable stock, plant and machinery and that thousands of pounds had been spent to bring the factory up to date. Although some of the £100,000 additional capital raised with the share issue was available to ensure that the company could grow as orders increased, there was no thought of mass-production on the American scale at this stage. The number of cars involved hardly warranted it; but Herbert Austin was certainly not behind the times, in spite of his insistence upon the continued use of individually cast cylinders. As we have seen, he had tried monobloc casting, without much success, and abandoned the practice although the trend in the industry had been in that direction for a number of years. Individual cylinders were easier to make and at that stage there seemed no particular reason to change. Austin's policy was dictated by the fact that the company did not undertake its own casting; it was not considered a practical proposition to run a small foundry because, unless it was working to full capacity, it would not be economical. There were many large foundries — especially in Staffordshire — concentrating on work for the motor industry and most manufacturers prior to World War I bought in their castings, particularly the aluminium components.

Difficulties in obtaining sufficient skilled labour prepared to travel to and from Longbridge each day affected the choice of machinery used in the factory. One could either have many skilled men and few machines or hundreds of machine tools and a proportionately small number of expert craftsmen, relying largely upon one's ability to train sufficient semi-skilled and unskilled workers as machine operators. The object at Longbridge was to simplify the work to such an extent that a machine could be set up by a skilled man and attended to by a labourer. The machine shop was in the centre of the works, new buildings to the east were used for engine and chassis erecting, and the body-building shop lay to the south. Offices, including the 'old man's', were on the west side of the south works facing the main Bristol road. Many of the machines employed were of Austin's own design; his patent 'Victor' lathe, for example, was used to machine the cylinders. In order to save time, he devised a method of milling crankshaft journals rather than having the shafts turned in lathes.

Great emphasis was placed upon inspection. Each finished engine was set up and run for a number of hours in a small cubicle, a group of which were arranged along an outside wall. Every cylinder block and crankcase was measured and much care was taken to ensure that the crown-wheel and pinion teeth were meshed correctly. After machining, each pair was ground in by hand. Engine flywheels were balanced dynamically, but the shafts themselves were only dealt with statically on a pair of knife edges.

The declaration of war in August 1914 had an immediate adverse effect upon the motor industry. One large firm told how it had closed for the Bank Holiday with 700 orders on its books and a week later only 70 remained. Orders, particularly those from overseas customers, were cancelled, with the result that the 'pleasure car' industry as it was called practically ceased to exist overnight. There was panic at Longbridge. Other firms in better positions geographically could resort to the common practice of standing off a large proportion of their staff. Such a course of action could hardly be adopted by Austins, because the chances of getting the staff back again to such an out-of-the-way place when conditions improved were likely to be remote. Appeals for other classes of engineering work went out, anything to keep the machines going, and a letter was sent to the press headed 'Business as Usual' which told of the way in which the company was endeavouring to keep as many men in work as possible and that, already, arrangements were being made to fit suitable commercial bodies to existing chassis in an attempt to increase commercial vehicle trade. Owing to cancellations there was 'a fair number of chassis on hand'.

Commercial vehicle manufacturers, on the other hand, had plenty of work; the government had taken up all the subsidy vehicles for which it had been paying retainer fees to private owners and, in addition to War Office orders, the commercial industry was being called upon to replace the subsidy lorries. Albion Works for example were working night and day, even with the cancellation of orders brought about by the cessation of export trade. Both the Thornycroft and Straker-Squire companies were also very busy.

Austin's appeal for orders for machine tools, petrol-driven electric-lighting plants, small engineering work and subcontracts had fair results but even so, and in spite of the fact that a number of staff volunteered to serve in France, it was still found necessary to give notice to some of the non-skilled employees in August.

September 1914 saw a slight improvement in the situation. With the successful blockading by the Royal Navy which kept the German Fleet within its home waters, it was possible to lift the embargo previously placed on exports. Some of the completed orders which had been delayed since the prohibition were despatched in the summer and some cancellations were restored. Work also began on a new venture. Because the company was prepared to 'have a go at anything' and was fortunate enough to have a large quantity of ash and oak in stock, a government order was secured for 700 wooden limber-wagons and 200 horse-drawn ambulances. Towards the end of the year the War Office commandeered ten lorries from the works and ordered an Austin-Curtis aero-engine; a trickle of orders followed which was soon to become a flood. Ambulances were being made, not only for the army but also for private individuals, as it was a common practice for wealthy, public-spirited people to present vehicles to the nation and ambulances were needed in ever increasing quantity. Patriotic motor owners were offered a service whereby the bodies from their own cars could be removed and stored at the works, where the chassis could be fitted with canvas ambulance tops for only £30. Ambulances had a very short life at the Front, and it is clear that very few of them were returned to their original owners for, in an advertisement dated 1919, the company offered for sale 'a number of car bodies which have come into our possession', no doubt from the cars donated five years earlier. Oscar Thompson fitted out *Pobble*, the

31

ex-racing car, as an ambulance and gave it to Section 3 of the British Ambulance Committee in September 1915, and someone else gave a 40hp Austin called *Quangle*. Even Sir F.M. Edgar offered his Austin-engined boat *Maple Leaf IV*, but the navy found that it used far too much fuel to be of any practical value.

The British government signed a contract for one hundred 2-3 ton lorries and a number of 20hp ambulances, but the most important activity at this period was the trade agreement entered into with Imperial Russia. Austin had been selling cars to Russia since 1906 and his products had earned for themselves great respect amongst a number of influential Russians, so that when it was decided to introduce a mobile section into the czar's army, the company was given the opportunity of providing some of the initial equipment. The Imperial Army had a mere 679 vehicles at the beginning of the war; 418 of them were lorries and only two were motor ambulances. To supplement their military transport they requisitioned 475 cars from private owners and placed orders with British firms for lorries and aircraft. Although there was a great deal of British capital invested in Russia — for example Vickers held most of the shares in the Tsaratsyn Arsenal which was owned nominally by the Russian Artillery Works Company — vehicles were not considered as important as an abundance of home-produced munitions, ordnance and ships, and as a result no outside capital was used to build up the vehicle and aircraft industries. Britain and France supplied the necessary transport and in order that supplies might flow freely Russia made an agreement with them which resulted in Britain becoming the headquarters from which all decisions concerning Russian vehicle purchases were made. Russia undertook to buy only after consultation with the British government and a committee was appointed to ensure that British interests were protected. Credit was set up in London, amounting to some £102 million up to September 1915, after which the power to purchase was increased by a further £25 million monthly until September 1916. This was extended again and continued until the Bolshevik coup d'état in October 1917, having then reached the incredible sum of £569 million. Hundreds of orders were cancelled on 26 October 1917, including one for 1,000 2-3 ton Austin lorries.

But, to return to 1914, perhaps the largest single contract which had ever been secured at any one time by a British motor manufacturer was then signed between Austins and the Russian government, valued at £½ million with an additional agreement to purchase £50,000 of spare parts. The bulk of the first part of this consisted of 48 armoured cars, 18 equipped workshop vans, 16 20hp tank wagons (the tanks were divided into compartments for petrol, oil and grease), 8 binned spare-parts lorries, 120 4- and 6-stretcher ambulances (bodies of which were to be fitted in Russia), 20 12-stretcher heavy ambulances and 100 2-3 ton lorries. This substantial order was completed and shipped to Petrograd just before the winter of 1914, three months after it was received — a remarkable feat. A small group of technical experts accompanied the shipment because there was a shortage of trained drivers in Russia and, as the quality of Russian roads left much to be desired, it was necessary to be a mechanic as well. This made it essential to recruit staff to train the operators and to help maintain the vehicles. Donald Gooch, the company's representative in Russia, was sent to serve as an officer in the czar's army and was given the job of looking after and running the Austin 2-3 ton lorries and armoured cars. It proved a formidable task as 200 vehicles were in use by January 1915, mostly with the 10th Automobile Regiment, and it was with them that the 50hp armoured cars were employed successfully for the first time when they supported the Russians around Prasnysz in the retreat from East Prussia.

Austin armoured cars (in all 480 were built) served later in nearly all theatres of war and some accompanied Allenby's army to Palestine. The first models were built on 30hp Colonial chassis which, in spite of weighing 3 tons, could travel at 45mph when being driven with pneumatic tyres on good roads. As the scene of battle was approached the detachable rims holding the inflated tyres were removed to an armoured compartment and replaced by what were known as KT solids. These were rims onto which were fixed two rows of large rubber blocks, rather like cotton reels. The 50hp armoured cars, the type used by the Russians, housed a crew of six. Two sat in the driving compartment, two pointed rifles through holes in the armour and the others sat in revolving steel turrets — heavy plate constructions built up on cast-aluminium bases, each armed with a Vickers machine-gun. Rapid movement into and out of action was assisted by an additional steering wheel at the back linked up to the existing gear on the front wheels.

Just before Austins changed over to munitions production, a personal tragedy occurred that was to affect Herbert Austin more than any other single event in his life — the loss of his only son, Vernon. Vernon was born on 21 November 1893, and began his schooling at Malvern. Later he became a probationer scholar at King's School, Canterbury, where he studied in 1906 and 1907 before going to Sweden and Germany to complete his education. After finishing his training at Bulford as a Reserve Officer he went to France and spent his twenty-first birthday in November 1914 on the battlefield with his unit, 22 Battery, 34 Brigade, Royal Field Artillery, with which he took part in the battles of Mons, Marne, Aisne and Ypres. He fell whilst fighting at La Bassée on 26 January 1915. Vernon was a clever young man, very fond of horses and a keen golfer, but although he enjoyed motoring he showed no great interest in practical engineering, having neither his father's inventive genius nor an insatiable desire to make cars. However, Austin saw in his son someone to whom, some day, he would be able to hand over his share of the business and retire from the everyday running of the factory. Any hopes he may have had were shattered on that sad day in January.

With regard to Austin car production, the company's intentions for the coming year were outlined in November 1914. No new models were announced; the 10hp (later referred to as the 12/14 from January until discontinued later in 1915), 20hp and 30hp types were to continue with only a few minor alterations. Perhaps the most important feature was the development of the 20 into the Brooklands sports-type phaeton, a few of which were sold in 1914. This gave a foretaste of what was to come in 1918. Although individually cast blocks were still used, the cylinder bore was increased from 89mm to 95mm, lighter pistons and connecting rods were fitted, a higher lift camshaft, larger valves and a larger carburetter; in addition, the steering box was moved forward in the chassis frame. The resemblance between the flush-sided tourer, with its Austin patent detachable wheels, its new narrow radiator with rounded edges, and the 1918 prototype 20 turned out to be striking.

Financially, however, there was nothing to excite the ordinary shareholders when, in February 1915, the directors recommended declaring a dividend amounting to 2 per cent per annum for the previous fourteen months. £1,750 was appropriated to reserve, a further £6,000 reserved for losses on continental accounts — money owed, no doubt, by customers in countries on the other side of the Channel; £7,354 was allowed for depreciation of plant and to premises, but the very large sum of £23,218 for maintenance and repairs during the period left a credit of only £413 to be carried forward.

Austins still advertised cars in 1915, but by November were only able to complete an odd chassis or two and intending purchasers were advised to put their names down on the waiting list. To all intents and purposes, now that the 'pleasure car' industry had ceased to exist the whole motor industry was devoting itself to the supply of munitions and to making the 60,000 lorries, nearly 35,000 cars and 41,000 motor-cycles handed over to either the War Office or the Ministry of Munitions between the end of 1914 and 1918.

As on most other occasions, Britain was totally unprepared for war. The army was hopelessly behind the times, its equipment obsolete and its generals out-dated in their approach; the current military imagination according to Lloyd-George, made up in retentiveness what it lacked in agility, and one of the results was that the 3 million unfortunate recruits who had responded to Kitchener's moustache and accusing forefinger were receiving inadequate training because of insufficient small arms and artillery. Generals insisted that two machine-guns per battalion were sufficient — the enemy used sixteen. Initially, the provision of munitions was in the hands of the War Office, and they were firmly of the opinion that the high-explosive shell — being used with deadly effect by the Germans — was still in the experimental stage. Shrapnel had been good enough against the Boers in 1900, so what small manufacturing facilities existed were used to produce shrapnel shells. A similarly backward approach existed with regard to the artillery itself, anything larger than a 4.7in gun being out of the question. The enemy, however, were using 5.9in howitzers which shattered the nerves of our troops. What we needed to compete with them was 8in and 9.2in ordnance. Many examples can be found to illustrate this backwardness but suffice it to quote this description of the inefficient way in which shells were produced. David Lloyd-George visited Woolwich Arsenal at the end of 1914 and saw stacks of empty shells being filled tediously one at a time by hand; in his *War Memoirs* he says, 'The production of the fuses for detonating the shells was governed by the same lack of imagination and, consequently, there was a similar deficiency in output'.

War Office red tape and its mistrust of businessmen added to the difficulty. Hundreds of firms wanted to help but the authorities simply referred them to concerns who had for years been supplying the army so that they might offer to subcontract for supplies. The fact that the traditional firms were far too busy to organise a larger group of subsidiaries never occurred to them. Then some of the businessmen became greedy and took on too many Russian orders; consequently, when the time came, they were unable to cope with the demand from either our own or our Allies' forces.

'It is on the supply of ammunition for artillery that the future operations of the British Army will depend', said Sir John French in November 1914, but already by September shell stocks were dangerously low. In October, Lloyd-George persuaded the Cabinet to appoint a committee to examine the problem and this led, eventually, to the formation of the Ministry of Munitions in May 1915. Lloyd-George resigned as Chancellor of the Exchequer to become its first minister and within a short space of time the manufacturing resources of the country were directed along the lines which made victory a possibility. The minister visited the Midlands and northern factory areas in June 1915, spending a day at the Longbridge works. He made a tour of inspection and gave one of his usual inspiring speeches; he discussed also, with Austin, the firm's ability to expand. Austin was hardly a jovial man but he had a sense of humour which expressed itself in a dry wit, and the incident which follows is supposed to have taken place during Lloyd-George's tour of inspection. The war leader enquired about production, Austin quoted the numbers of certain articles which had been produced and added 'and 10,000 cigarette lighters'.

A few months before Lloyd-George's visit a contract for a small number of shells had been secured, and when questioned about the firm's wartime activities in 1919 Austin remarked: 'We demonstrated to the War Office our ability to produce them (the shells) of better quality and at much lower costs than had recently been thought possible.' Probably he was justified in claiming this of the early days of the war, but once the Ministry of Munitions' National Shell Factories were in full operation by 1916 they were turning out shells much more economically than any private firm. But, of course, by then quantity was a more important consideration than cost. Although the company's earlier munitions orders may have been obtained on the score of cheapness and superior quality, their geographical situation, combined with the fact that there was ample room for expansion as clearly demonstrated to the minister during his day at Longbridge, resulted in the Ministry of Munitions virtually taking over complete control of the works and making immediate growth possible with the aid of substantial government subsidies. It seems incredible that in less than three years a small firm housed in one building could grow to employ, and to a large extent provide living quarters for, over 20,000 workers and produce more than 8 million shells.

As regards factory buildings, two new works — the North and the West — were erected by Austins upon the instructions and at the expense of the government while the existing works was extended and paid for by the firm, from then onwards being referred to as South works. Expansion began on the latter site in 1914 with the erection of two structures, one for the manufacture of 18lb shells and the other, which also contained the forge, for 9.2in shells. In the same block there were also the stamping and No 2 and 3 machine shops. As soon as they were finished the bond-room was built in which the shells were stored for gauging for acceptance and, later, filling. There were various assembly bays and in 1915 a large building known as No 9 was erected. The press shop, which contained the 9.2in forges, started in April 1916; by June its output was 2,000 a week and by the spring of 1917 it was able to cope with 5,000 shells every 7 days.

Some very ingenious improvements on established practice were devised to simplify the work. Every operation was streamlined, pneumatic valves were attached to the tongs used to transfer the red-hot billets from the furnace to the forge and from the forge to the trolley, which enabled one man to manage where two had been necessary. A patent Austin lathe saved time in the machine shop by turning and boring the shells simultaneously, other machines were employed for screwing up adaptors, pneumatic riveters were used for facing and riveting the adaptors into the shell, and there were new, improved ways of turning the copper driving bands. Much difficulty was experienced in the construction of these shops on the rising ground and about 150,000 cubic yards of hard sandstone had to be excavated to obtain a level surface. Block No 6, the final addition, comprising sewing rooms, dope rooms and the aeroplane erecting shop, was completed in 1917. Further to the south there was an engine-running test bay and the 73 acre circular flying ground for which it had been necessary to remove the top of Cofton Hill. In all, these extensions alone doubled the size of the original works.

North works was commenced in July 1916, on a site on the Birmingham side of the railway line, and the same building is still used today. In its original form it consisted of a machine shop measuring 850ft x 270ft with beside it a long supplementary structure housing the forge, on the other side of which was a mess-room seating 4,000. The machine shop was finished by Christmas and the forge started to operate in March 1917. In addition, two long bays were devoted to the manufacture of 4.5in guns — OQF 4.5 howitzers (Land Service); 650 were made in all. Within twelve months of the site's being marked out the output of 8in shells exceeded 12,000 a week, rising to a maximum of 20,000 forgings and 15,000 complete shells each week.

An 8in shell weighed 174lb and most of the machining operations were carried out by women; there were 5,000 in this section of the works. The skilled men set up the machines which, from December 1916, were kept going day and night. The forgings were placed in cradles and wheeled to the lathes by labourers, who then took away the finished shell and brought up the next. At one stage 15,500 were delivered to the bond room in one week. These 'munitionettes' came from all over the country, many being attracted by the high wages earned on piece-work; after a short course of training they became competent, proving that women could cope if need be with long periods of boring repetitive manual work, even if it did involve them in trades not tackled by women before.

Building of the West works commenced in December 1916; again it is still used today. Situated on the opposite side of the Bristol Road it was completed by June 1917, the 5 acres under cover containing a machine shop 660ft by 330ft. There were 5,000 hands and 1,000 machine tools driven in groups by electric motors arranged on three sides of 23 bays running across the shop, which were soon turning out 100,000 18lb shells per week. Some 80,000 tons of steel bar were used to produce the 6½ million shells made on the site; in one working day of 9½ hours the record number produced reached 13,000 and in a 106 hour week as many as 104,000. During one period the output was so great that it swamped the transport system which was unable to move the shells to the filling factory quickly enough. Each day 1,200 tons of steel arrived in two special trains, one of which returned with a complete load of swarf.

In all this building up of the works the greatest possible speed was needed, the North and West factories — each capable of employing more than 5,000 people — taking only six months to complete. This was a remarkable achievement accomplished only with difficulty, especially since construction began during the exceptionally hard winter of 1916. For five weeks the earth was frozen to a depth of eight inches and had to be blasted with small charges of explosive placed in the ground at intervals of a few yards. Excavation went on day and night, flares being used to illuminate the scene.

Accommodation was a serious problem which had to be faced. Being so far from a town and bringing in some 15,000 men and women from outside the area, something had to be done to house them. In September 1917, three large hostels were built and later, to the north of the factory, a more permanent estate for 7,000 people, including 252 prefabricated wooden buildings brought from Canada; they are still in use today.

Training was another important aspect of life at Longbridge. Nazareth House, on the west side of the Bristol Road, which had originally been a nunnery and later housed the women munitions workers, was converted into the Austin Engineering College. At this apprentice hostel free education was available for all employees under the age of 18 and at a moderate fee for an adult. Seventy-five apprentices lived there and, like so many of the other buildings used during World War I, it still stands today. Boys over 14 of 'good education' were taken on as apprentices. No premium was required, but during the first three months no wages were paid; after the probationary period, 12s a week was allowed. All boys were given time during working hours for technical education, the amount depending upon the ability of the apprentice. The period of indenture was 5 years, reduced to 4 years for boys over 16 who had matriculated or passed school-leaving examinations. A minimum of 4 hours a week had to be spent in the school during working hours, and an equal number of hours spent during the student's own time. 'Boys of a good type' living at a distance from Longbridge could become residents at 18s 6d a week inclusive and 'all the usual advantages of a public school life' were provided.

Austin's personal reward for his tireless devotion to the needs of the nation came on 27 September 1917, when he attended Buckingham Palace to be invested with a Knighthood of the newly created Order of the British Empire. Some other well known people in the motor industry were honoured too: Arthur Stanley, chairman of the RAC; Alfred Herbert, the machine-tool maker; H.T.Vane, managing director of Napiers; and P.Perry, head of Ford's branch in this country. Back at Longbridge, the new aeroplane shop was cleared and everyone stopped work at 5pm to welcome Sir Herbert and Lady Austin home; 20,000 men and women cheered and 'stirred to the depth of his being', he went on to say, 'I appeal for every ounce of co-operation to continue the good work of delivering the goods and suggest that the present is no time for a bean feast to celebrate the honour which has been conferred upon me. I am marking this occasion by giving a large sum of money to build facilities and buy equipment for recreation purposes.' In 1919 he was made a Commandeur de L'Ordre de Leopold II; and in October 1918 was appointed Honorary Commandant of the 3rd Volunteer Battalion Worcestershire Regiment, with the honorary rank of Lieutenant Colonel in the Volunteer Training Corps.

Throughout the war good labour relations were maintained. The only serious breach occurred early in 1918 when over 10,000 workers went on strike for a month over the alleged victimisation of Arthur Peacock, one of the War Munition Volunteers. Peacock, an East Anglian, had been employed as a fitter by the Ministry of Munitions about three months before and was soon after appointed Chairman of the Works Committee, a body not recognised by either the firm or the ministry. He applied to be transferred to a job nearer his home, and in the midst of a dispute with the management over the operation of the bonus system he was moved, perhaps rather conveniently, to a firm in Lincoln. This removal of their leader at what they looked upon as a crucial point in their fight was regarded by the workers as victimisation. The day-shift downed tools, followed by those on night-work, and Austin and the ministry both refused to discuss the matter until work was resumed; but after ten days they had to give in and Peacock was reinstated. Apart from holding up munitions at a difficult stage of the war, the damage that a strike of such proportions could cause was reflected in the price of the £1 preference shares on the Stock Exchange, which fell from 24s 3d to 18s 7½d.

Perhaps not unnaturally Austin had little sympathy for those who took the law into their own hands. He tried to make it known to all employees that their troubles could be brought to his notice either collectively or individually, claiming that he was sympathetic to any but frivolous requests. His ability to settle a practical argument regarding for example piece-work rates, by setting up a machine and doing the job himself much more quickly than the operator, may well have upset his workers, but at least everyone realised that wool could not be pulled over 'Pa's' eyes! As he was always to be seen in some section of the works, both day and night, very little happened unnoticed. On one occasion he approached the works engineer who was supervising a gang and said, with a glint in his eye, 'You have the cleanest lot of navvies working here that I have ever seen.' 'Oh-er-yes!' replied the engineer, suspiciously. 'Yes', retorted Austin, characteristically pushing his bowler hat back, 'every time I come along they are either scraping their spades or cleaning their boots — sort it out,' after which he stalked off.

Austin was liked by the majority of his staff; they appreciated his strictness, respected his superior knowledge and skill and, above all, liked him for his modesty. At a quarter to six on the evening of 8 November 1916, men from every section of the works followed A.W.Jones, the company secretary, into the chief's office. It was Austin's fiftieth birthday, and to show their regard the work-people had subscribed for a silver salver and a dressing-case which were presented following a speech by Jones in which he attributed the growth of the firm primarily to Austin's own skill and resourcefulness. There was a long pause while the great man regained his composure; then he thanked them for their gifts, praised their loyalty and unselfish assistance over the years and modestly endeavoured to place the bulk of the credit with others. 'A lot of high compliments have been paid me for work which I have not touched and the wonderful developments which mark the progress of the Company are events which it is not possible for one man to carry out without the help and co-operation of his staff.'

The engineering unions were powerful and they regarded some of Sir Herbert's ideas with suspicion. Prior to the commencement of the war many industrialists were against payment by results, and even where bonus schemes were in operation it was a general rule to hold back production to prevent anyone earning more than 25 to 50 per cent more than the basic rate. Later, if a particular job was seen to be highly profitable to the operative the basic rate was refixed, a system much more difficult to apply in the face of trade union opposition than one of simply curtailing requirements of the part involved.

Austin realised that this lowered overall efficiency and that the indirect result was to hold back the work done by people paid other than by results; in fact it produced a general lowering down to one agreed level of production. Clearly then, this levelling had to be changed. The way to do it — the Austin way — was to grade labour so that the most skilful and diligent were given the opportunity to maintain, and even increase, their productiveness. There would be a rising scale of rates of minimum standard pay, and different piece-work rates, with an efficiency bonus for both day and piece-workers who exceeded an agreed standard output. Men, he argued, should be paid on results and one way of increasing production would be to dispense with a system of limiting output to suit the capabilities of the slowest worker. In spite of a certain amount of criticism, he put these ideas into practice after the war.

When speaking of future prospects in April 1918 he said, 'It is somewhat difficult to say anything in detail, as the war appears to be going on for at least another two years and by that time all present prospects of business in the future may be entirely upset.'

The end came in November, sooner than he had anticipated; government contracts came to an end and the plant ground to a halt. There was plenty of money for munitions production was a profitable business, and the gross value of the total output amounted to £10 million. Shortly afterwards the company exercised the option to purchase the North and West works from the government and with their one-model policy and one prototype Austin 20 faced the future in a 'land fit for heroes' — and it proved to be the most desperate struggle in their history.

WAR PRODUCTION FIGURES, 1914-1918

These official Ministry of Munitions figures were released about December 1918, and include the total of all war materials used by British and foreign governments. The period covered by military contracts dated from October 1914 until the last part of the final contract was delivered some few weeks after the Armistice in November 1918.

18-pounders		6,500,000
15-pounders		100,000
13-pounders	Shells	25,000
9.2in		350,000
8in		980,000
210mm		60,000
Guns		650
Aeroplanes		2,000
Night tracers		506,399
Percussion tubes		682,808
Burster containers		167,791
Shrapnel heads		47,768
Lorries (2-3 tonners)		2,000
Armoured cars		480
Ambulances		148
Touring cars, light vans, etc.		750
Switchboards and resistances		4,422
Electric generating sets		4,762
Pumping-equipment trench		40
Aeroplane engines		2,500
Electric motors		25
Workshop trailing wagons		25
Searchlight sets		20
Cable-drum outfits		54
Limber wagons (horse-drawn)		1,603
Lewis-gun carts		2,000

In addition to the above completed units, there was a large quantity of spare parts for lorries, aeroplanes and other vehicles.

MUNITIONS TO MASS PRODUCTION: 1914-1919

Military orders on hand mentioned in a letter from Austins dated 29 June 1916, and
signed by Jones the company secretary

	£
Spares for War Office cars, biplanes, RAF engines, etc.	84,802
General orders and repairs	5,000
1,000 sets of RAF gears	7,350
120 RE7s	154,800
83 limbered wagons	6,080
120 limber hooks	91
Wood plugs	200
Night tracers	10,238
VS tubes	18,525
2,000 bodies for MG carts	28,000
1 aeroplane trailer	265
Russian spares	1,000
9 12/24hp chassis	2,104
12 12/24hp cars	4,268
78 20hp chassis	335,858
22 20hp cars	14,462
52 2-3 ton lorries and lorry chassis	32,193
2 5 ton chassis	1,510
100 Russian chassis and spares	68,315
40 Russian lorries and spares	42,067
471 RAF 1a engines	210,450
231 propeller bosses	1,328
6 18kW generating sets	2,311
12 3kW generating sets	1,620
5 8kW generating sets	992
6 trench pump equipments	3,083
19 8kW searchlight switchboards	136
117 3.5kW mobile workshop engines	12,870
117 3.5kW mobile workshop engine spares	479
4 5kW generating sets	643
15 wireless controllers	221
1 stone-crusher switchboard	95
1 1¾hp mine and sapper lighting set	83
104 charging resistances	158
83 mobile-workshop switchboards	861
Private orders for lighting sets	2,000
Spare parts for lighting sets	2,500
25 230hp engines for the Admiralty	32,750
18- and 13-pounder shells	503,933
13-pounder shells	10,000
	1,303,641

4 The Car with a Wide Appeal: 1919

If I am to make a profit of £1,000 I would sooner it were £10 each on a hundred cars than £100 each on ten cars. I will make a car that has a wide appeal.

Sir Herbert Austin speaking at the end of 1918.

In 1918, Austin, already in his mid-fifties, entered perhaps his most prolific and certainly the most important phase in his career as far as design was concerned. It culminated in his greatest accomplishment, the introduction of the Austin 7 in 1922. He presented, in four years and under very difficult conditions, three of the most successful British cars of the 1920s: the 20, the 12 and the 7. The 20 was eclipsed, to a certain extent, by the other two as the demand for a 3.5 litre car decreased; but there is no doubt that the 12, and to a lesser degree the 7, owe much to their larger brother. Unfortunately, historians and vintage car enthusiasts have neglected it — enthusiasts regretting this too late, because very few examples have survived.

As soon as the war ended there was an enormous demand for new cars, yet production was at a very low level. Protection from American competition was afforded by the McKenna duties — a 33⅓ per cent levy introduced during the war which safeguarded the industry until repealed for a short time by the first Labour government in 1924. This prevented a flood of foreign cars entering the country during the immediate post-war boom and, in theory, should have enabled our own manufacturers to regain some of the ground which had been lost in what Sir Herbert called 'the four years of idleness'. The slump which began towards the end of 1920 followed a period of artificial prosperity made possible, in spite of soaring prices, by the amount of money in circulation due to high wages, unrestrained credit and cash available in the form of service gratuities and accumulated pay. The consequences of such a false situation were inevitable. Prices began to fall and in many cases products had to be sold at a loss, while intending purchasers held off in the hope that prices would sink still further.

Unemployment increased — there were already more than a million out of work by the spring of 1919 — stability was lost, and by 1921 it became clear that there was no hope of sustaining what, at first, had looked like becoming an industrial revival. Materials were scarce and expensive. Iron, steel and aluminium had doubled in price, and wages rose to a level more than twice the pre-war average.

Industrial unrest had reached a dangerous level by the summer of 1919. By September, 50,000 moulders had downed tools, and almost every member of this trade so vital to the motor industry was idle for months; the disagreement cost the union £140,000. Austin had this particular dispute in mind when, in November, he said: 'Supplies are pretty well exhausted and there can only be one sequel, unemployment all round. I might be compelled to close down completely in a fortnight. So far this year strikes have cost me between a quarter and half a million pounds.'

During this period of industrial unrest a number of industrialists stood for Parliament. In July 1918, Austin had been adopted as the Unionist candidate for the Kings Norton Division of Birmingham, a constituency which included the districts of Selly Oak and Northfield, where most of the Longbridge workers lived. He supported the Coalition in the 1918 election, at which he was returned to Parliament with a majority of some 4,000 votes. About a hundred MPs, led by the representatives of the industry, formed what they called the Parliamentary Road Transport Committee. Austin served on the executive panel of this body which proved itself to be singularly unsuccessful in bringing about any positive benefits for the motorist. Its members were unable to prevent the implementation of the Finance Act of 1920, which raised car taxation to £1 per hp or to stop the Chancellor from hoarding the Road Fund instead of spending this revenue entirely upon the improvement of roads.

There was some substance in the argument put forward by the opponents of these 'MPs for Motoring', in which it was suggested that the amateur politicians would be far better employed in putting their own business houses in order. Not one of them excelled as an orator, in fact very few of them spoke more than a word or two in the Chamber and they never succeeded, as a body, in bringing any influence to bear upon the Cabinet. Gradually they drifted away; Sir Herbert Austin was defeated in October 1924 by a Socialist who gained a narrow majority over him of 133 votes, and apart from some expressions of his opinions in speeches he made to the Austin shareholders later on in the twenties he took no further part in politics.

Against the background described earlier in this chapter, it is hardly surprising that the motor industry found itself beset with difficulties. As it had been virtually impossible to buy British cars for three years, most pre-war owners were anxious to replace their existing vehicles quickly. In addition, a new generation had grown up, creating an even greater demand, particularly for vehicles in the £200 to £300 price range. It was estimated that in the United Kingdom demand exceeded supply by about a ¼ million cars. In 1913 there had been more than 30 makers with outputs of over 500 vehicles a year who, together with a host of smaller firms, turned out nearly 40,000 cars. In 1919, about 10 companies were organising their factories for outputs of between 3,000 and 6,000 cars a year, and some of the larger ones were rash enough to broadcast it as their aim to exceed the latter figure. But during that year fewer than 35,000 cars were completed amongst which were more than 17,000 British-built Fords. From this one can see the impact of the cheap American mass-produced £250 car upon the British market, this being particularly marked because of the lack of serious competition.

Hundreds of British manufacturers had announced their plans and issued specifications. Admittedly one or two had built prototypes, but as late as September 1919 it was claimed that those actually turning out cars could 'be counted on the fingers of one's hand'. Even they were hopelessly behind with schedules because of the shortage of raw materials and the lack of sufficient skilled labour. Another great problem was how to transfer the huge productive capacity left by the war into the active manufacture of private cars. The war had meant a vast increase of assets by way of enlarged factories and plant, but an excess profits tax had not allowed the accumulation of sufficiently large liquid assets for the plunge into quantity production to the extent necessary, and at the speed required, for immediate commercial success. Mass production meant more machine tools which were very expensive, and this high initial outlay necessary was likely to remain unprofitable for a considerable time, as can be seen from the following example. Before the war it would have been difficult to produce a five-bearing crankshaft in less than sixty hours because the small number of machines used made it necessary to reset them for each process. To avoid delays caused by this method the post-war Austin 20 crank was made by no less than nine different machines, all pre-set for their various functions. Consequently, the component could be turned out in twelve hours, but nine machines were needed where formerly two had been sufficient. Thus production could not keep abreast of the increased demand for transport.

Wealthier customers bought American but the others, the vast majority, had to content themselves with expensive second-hand cars and war surplus vehicles which commanded high prices at public auctions. New cars were to be seen on the roads, but to all intents and purposes they could not be bought by the general public in the early part of 1919. The situation did not improve for some time, and there were many people prepared to pay well over £1,000 to secure a new car listed at less than £700, delivery of which was not expected until 1920.

With one or two exceptions, the British cars of 1919 closely resembled their 1914-15 counterparts, whereas the Americans, who had benefited from continued production and development, were two years ahead. Their factories had an enormous lead and an immense amount of cash on hand from the vast number of cars sold between 1914 and 1917. Ford, as the supreme example, had just paid a 200 per cent dividend on his $2 million capital and retained a total accumulated surplus of $100 million in undistributed profits. Austin saw that there was a demand for a utility car that was not only cheap, but reliable and efficient, qualities which did not necessarily go together. He also felt that if one intended to make cars in great quantity it was logical to base one's designs on those which others had proved were adaptable to economic production. Our rivals across the Atlantic had been making cars extremely efficiently for a number of years and only a very short-sighted man indeed would not have looked very closely at the methods which their experience had shown to be the most profitable.

Sir Herbert ran a Hudson Super Six during the latter part of the war, maintaining that his own company was not producing cars at that time and that the Hudson was the only satisfactory vehicle which could be bought. A careful study of both its design and construction was made. The Hudson was a fairly typical American car and there is no doubt that Austin was influenced by what he saw. It would be wrong to suggest that the four-cylinder 20 was a copy of this particular model but there is a resemblance in basic principles. The chassis frames are similar. In plan view they both have straight side-members which taper to the front, without being stepped at the point where the power unit is located. It was customary British practice for the dumb-irons to curve down to the rear shackles, but in these cars the members run straight back to the rear spring mountings after rising up to clear the rear axle. Other points of similarity exist in the use of a monobloc engine casting, a separate sheet-metal cowling over the radiator core, a centrally operated gear change, unit construction of engine and gearbox, and a host of smaller points such as the adoption of coil ignition — albeit only on the two prototype Austin chassis, Watford magnetos being used in production — and the use of the word 'gas' on the hand-throttle control. Austin was about to show, yet again, his ability to study what others were doing, sum up his customers' requirements, and then design to his own high engineering standards, having learnt sufficient from the experience gained by others after a close examination of their work.

The prototype Austin 20 chassis, known as the Pl, was laid down in the chassis-erecting shop at Longbridge late in 1917. This prefix P denoted 'post-war' and was used, in conjunction with car numbers, for identification purposes on all four-cylinder 20s. It seems that only two Pls were made, the tourer OB6912 and the landaulet (which first appeared in December 1918). Both were used for experimental and demonstration purposes only. One highly touched-up photograph of a coupé was supplied to the press but it is unlikely that this car existed outside the drawing office at this stage. That the post-war policy had been formulated some time before 1917 is evidenced by the following words from an Austin advertisement which appeared in June 1916: 'The Austin car of the future will be found to be a distinct improvement on its already well established predecessors.' By the end of that year a series of advertisements appeared in the motoring press which stated: 'Our post war policy is fixed. It will be a one chassis output at a substantial reduction in price.' An abridged specification appeared in the *Advocate* in September 1917, but it was not until September of the following year that precise details of the experimental car were released.

At the end of 1918 journalists were invited to examine the chassis and made a trial run in OB6912. They were told that, although in general the cars to be offered to the public at about £400 would remain unaltered, minor modifications would have to be adopted. In fact, these included the replacement of the distributor and coil by a magneto and the transfer of the carburetter from the off-side of the engine to a position beneath the exhaust manifold. A small circular disc on the steering column with the three control levers at 120 degrees replaced the older type of quadrant, and aluminium pistons were used. The final drive ratio was lowered from 3.75: 1 to 3.93: 1, but in most other respects the production car was identical to the prototype. A full description of this, the P2 is given at the end of this chapter. Austin's agents were invited to lunch at Longbridge in January 1919, shortly after which Edgar Wren, Austin's test driver at that time, took OB6912 on a nationwide tour. Later, he came to London where he

"Essentially high-grade in every detail — yet moderately priced."

Advertisement for the 1919 Twenty

managed the old Austin showrooms in Oxford Street; the building was pulled down in 1962. Shortly before he undertook his journey one of the company's sales organisers, Alfred Dupuis, set sail on a Commonwealth tour. He obtained thousands of pounds worth of orders with nothing more than some photographs and a description of the car. At home the tourer proved extremely popular, drawing large crowds wherever it appeared. Orders, together with cash deposits, came in quickly in spite of the fact that no firm delivery dates could be given; customers were told not to expect to receive their cars before August. Prices were fixed at £395 for the chassis, the tourer was £495, the coupé £595 and the landaulet £625. These figures were calculated on an initial demand for cars valued at £4 million which it was thought might well rise to £10 million. It would have been necessary to produce at a rate approaching 25,000 units a year to satisfy this fantastic requirement, but in 1919 the company was never even organised to turn out more than 150 a week. This bore no relation at all to the orders taken and thus costs had been calculated on a completely false basis. In fact, commitments had already reached £6 million by July 1919, so during that month it was decided to accept no more orders for delivery in 1920.

It would have been all very well if production could have met the demand, but insufficient capital, lack of materials and staff, and the four months lost through various strikes made it impossible to relate one to the other.

49

Consequently, in October 1919, the company reluctantly placed what it called a temporary surcharge of £100 on each complete car and £75 on the chassis. This action caused a terrific outcry and clients were given the option of cancelling their orders. Many of them did so, and this was probably fortunate from the Austin company's point of view because only 534 Austin 20s left Longbridge between July 1919 and July 1920. A very small number, possibly six, of 1914 10hp chassis were also built in the repair shop in 1919, presumably out of surplus parts left over from before the war.

One gets the impression, when studying this period, that cheaply made mass-produced cars were not accepted without some qualms by traditional Austin customers. At the annual dinner of the Institute of British Carriage Manufacturers in September 1919, Sir Herbert said that in a short time he had tried to organise for the speedy production of cars, not on the American plan because he did not think that this country was prepared to take 'American tin boxes'. He went on to say: 'I am trying to build carriage work on mass lines and at a very moderate figure.' Certainly he achieved this, but there is no doubt that the post-war Austin 20 resembled the 'American tin boxes' so closely that one wonders if anyone was gullible enough to be taken in by what he said. Austin may have used a few panel beaters instead of presses for shaping the body panels at this stage, but this was through necessity rather than preference. He would have been delighted if he could have afforded enough presses to cope with his entire body production. The only resemblance to the old-style carriage work lies in the fact that Austin 20 bodies were built up of steel sheets on wooden frames, but from the outside appearance, for all that, the car looked very much like the American counterparts upon which it had been modelled.

The author owned one of the first Austin 20s for a time. It had suffered the fate of most survivors — after having served its purpose as a touring car for nearly twenty years the back of the coachwork had been removed and replaced by an open truck body. A crane had been fitted to the platform and it was used by a garage as a breakdown vehicle. One of his most cherished memories is of a weekend spent driving this car from a garage at Kirkby Stephen in Westmorland, down to London. Once in top gear, sailing along at 40mph, one was aware of a sensation of great strength and solidity; the 3.6 litre engine had only to be run at about 2,000rpm due to the high final drive ratio of 3.6:1 and yet the engine was so flexible that third gear only had to be resorted to when climbing a steep hill. Unfortunately, this car, the earliest vintage Austin known to exist, and the eighty-seventh to have left Longbridge after the war, seems to have disappeared.

In a statement shortly after the signing of the armistice, Austin summed up the firm's policy. The object was to invent, develop and design well in advance of current engineering practice. There was to be complete standardisation, not only in engine construction, but also in every part of the chassis and body building. In mass-production parts were to be kept to a minimum, each individual component being machined to fine limits and reproduced identically so that the elaborate and costly hand-fitting of parts, due to the inaccuracy of machining, could be eliminated. In all, 2,873 separate pieces went into the 20 and although this is high compared with the figures achieved later in the 1920s, it shows that Austin shared Laurence Pomeroy's (of the *Motor*) view of the virtue of the 'fewness of bits' and maintained, as he did, that it was immoral to use four parts if two would do the job.

Once it was ensured that a design was suitable for economic manufacture, machine tools, jigs and machinery were ordered or designed by the jig and tool drawing office. Works engineers were responsible for laying the machines out on the shop floors in the correct order and the entire production department was controlled by the production manager and the chief inspector, the latter constantly watching the work being turned out and rejecting that which fell below the required standard. There was a service department; experimental, sales advertising and commercial sections; and the 'necessary evils' — those offices dealing with secretarial, labour, welfare and accountancy problems. Sir Herbert said of them: 'They pursue their useful labours within the Works and contribute to the general result.' His 'secret of organisation' was that 'every man should do with his whole heart and strength the job for which he is best fitted. To the effort to set men to work on these lines and to the spirit of cordial good fellowship which have happily become growing traditions at Longbridge, I attribute such success in manufacturing processes as we have attained'.

By 1919, with the largest automobile works in Great Britain, the firm was ready to expand though, as already seen, such expansion in the social and economic conditions prevailing was far from untroubled. All the government buildings were bought for £240,000 and the work of reconstruction began. The first task, undertaken in January 1919, was to lay out the West works for the manufacture of car bodies; 1,000 machine tools were removed and storage sheds, timber-drying kilns, sawmills, a boiler house, paint-spraying and drying rooms, as well as a new heating and ventilating system, were installed. When production commenced, rough timber was brought into a new railway siding alongside the loading bay and placed on specially designed narrow-gauge trucks. It remained on them until reaching the sawmill, after which it was reloaded to be taken to the drying kilns. When this process was completed the trucks took the timber to the end of the main building which was arranged as a wood-working shop, to be worked into its final shape. Even the wood-shavings and sawdust were utilised. After being removed by an automatic extraction plant they were deposited in front of the boilers in which they were used as fuel. Completed body-frame sections were taken to the stores where they were made up into 'kits' for each car, placed on a trolley and pushed to the assembly shop. After a body had been made and the panels fitted, it was transferred to the spraying room for painting, varnishing and drying. All post-war Austin cars were spray painted; one coat could be applied in 20 minutes as against the 3 hours necessary for the more common brush method. Altogether 6 coats were given and the surface was rubbed down between each.

From April the North works were rebuilt, new buildings there housing 900 new machines. The shell forge was dismantled and converted into a steel foundry costing £80,000. As many as 350 new electric motors were installed in South works; the old shell press-shop was dismantled and replaced by drop forges and a new smith's shop, and the new hardening shop, which cost £34,000, was the most modern of its kind in Britain. Expansion was very costly. Profits on the £10 million turnover for 1918 were small — only £358,000 — and the firm's capital remained at £650,000. A further issue of £1 million shares was made, but controlling rights still remained with the ordinary shareholders — Sir Herbert and Harvey Du Cros. However, holders of the new preference shares had the option of converting a third of them into ordinary shares in 1922, hence the new offer, with the ordinary shares at £1 10s, was heavily oversubscribed at £1 each. Two new directors, H.Drew-Anderson and S.Van den Bergh, joined the Austin board.

Specification of the 1919 Austin 20

ENGINE

Four-cylinder vertical type with cylinders cast *en bloc*, forming with the clutch and gearbox the combined power unit; 3¾in x 5in bore and stroke, developing 45bhp at 2,000rpm. The whole engine unit carried on three points, one bracket at the front forming a trunnion, and two brackets at the rear, supporting arms from the crankcase, thus insulating the unit from frame distortion on the road.

CRANKCASE
Of aluminium, divided on the crankshaft centre line, the bottom portion carrying the crankshaft on 5 white metal bearings, with separate caps, also forming the oil reservoir. A large cover at the bottom gives access for cleaning. The top half, carrying the camshaft, simply forms a distance piece between the bottom half and the cylinder block. Removing this part, together with the monobloc, enables the main bearings to be removed for adjustment and replacement without taking the whole unit out of the chassis. Large doors are fitted to the upper portion of the crankcase, enabling inspection to be made of the bearings.

CYLINDER BLOCK
Of special-quality cast iron, with a detachable head which makes the combustion space of the cylinder more uniform, and gives better balance and sweeter running of the engine. It also gives access to the piston heads for removing carbon deposit.

CAMSHAFT
Of case-hardened steel and driven by silent chain, means of adjustment being provided whereby any slackness can be taken up. The cams solid on the shaft and accurately ground.

CONNECTING-ROD AND PISTON
The piston is aluminium and of exceedingly light design; the connecting-rod is alloy steel, machined all over, enabling the greatest acceleration and sweetness of running to be obtained.

LUBRICATION
By means of a gear pump driven by skew gear from the camshaft. Situated at the bottom of the crankcase and accessible by removing the crankcase-bottom cover. The oil is fed through passages drilled in the crankcase to the underside of the main bearings, and then through the hollow crankshaft to lubricate the connecting-rods. A strainer is attached to the bottom of the crankcase and, by means of this, oil is strained before being circulated. A strainer is also fitted to the oil filler, which is provided on the top half of the crankcase.

IGNITION
By HT magneto driven by silent chain.

COOLING

By thermo-siphon. A large radiator is assisted by a high speed fan, with eccentric adjustment to adjust the linked 'V' belt.

CARBURATION AND FUEL

An automatic Zenith carburetter is used. The inlet pipe is combined with the exhaust manifold, to give ample heating. An extra air-valve is fitted, controlled from the three-position quadrant on the steering wheel, the other two positions being a hand throttle and an ignition control. Petrol is fed to the engine by gravity from an Autovac secondary tank, which draws petrol by manifold suction from a 16 gallon tank supported on brackets attached to the cross-member in the centre of the frame. A filler cap of ample dimensions is supplied under the driver's seat. A petrol-level indicator is fitted alongside the filler cap, and a plug provided at the bottom of the tank for draining.

STARTING AND LIGHTING

CAV self-starter and lighting equipment, with a large 12V battery and all necessary switchgear, and a detachable starting handle for use in case of emergency.

CLUTCH AND GEARBOX

Ferodo single-plate dry-friction clutch. Four-speed and reverse gearbox with ratios of reverse 13.3:1
1st 17.0:1
2nd 9.7:1
3rd 6.2:1
4th 3.93:1 (direct drive)
All shafts carried on ball bearings. The speedometer is gear-driven from the change speedbox, which is operated by a lever through a gate which, with the hand-brake lever, is fixed in a central position.

REAR AXLE

Of 'live' semi-floating type, the outer casing carrying the rear wheels on ball bearings thus relieving the transmission shaft of the chassis weight. Main driving gears are of helical bevel type, ensuring silent running.

FRONT AXLE

The 'I' section front axle, swivel and swivel arms, are forged of high-grade steel, tempered to resist fatigue. The front wheels run on roller bearings with ball thrust.

STEERING
Of worm and sector type, with a stationary outer column supported from the scuttle, and fitted with a 17in wheel, with the throttle, ignition and extra-air levers on a stationary quadrant.

SPRINGS
Road springs semi-elliptic, the rear being underslung and 60in long, the front 36in long. Special provision made to prevent rust between leaves.

BRAKES
Metal-to-metal internal expanding shoes on rear wheels and contracting shoes faced with Ferodo, which close upon the drum mounted on the third motion shaft at the rear of the gearbox. The handbrake operates this brake, and a foot pedal the brakes on the rear wheels.

WHEELS
Austin wooden artillery detachable wheels 820 x 120mm with a spare housed in a covered compartment at the rear. Not fixed with studs and nuts, but by a patent Austin design.

There are three styles of body. A four-door, five-seat tourer with a novel cowl at the rear to house the hood; a seven-seat landaulet; and a four-seat coupé. All models have a cover for the spare wheel.

5 Confidence and Consequences: 1920-1922

I feel frankly that our works have not got their equal in this country, at any rate carrying out the class of manufacture that we do; that we have got exceptionally good prospects, everything that we could wish for in the amount of trade, and the ability to do it.

Sir Herbert Austin's speech to shareholders, 21 January 1920.

Although, on the whole, 1919 may be regarded as a successful year for the Austin company, events were to nullify many of the advantages which had been gained. Most of the initial difficulties had been overcome, and factory reconstruction was complete. Unfortunately, however, due mainly to the strikes and the other factors which had made manufacture so difficult, only a few cars were produced. An establishment prepared for production at the rate of 150 cars a week could not be operated profitably if sales scarcely exceeded 500 a year. This, in itself, would have led to trouble even without taking into account the effects of the slump.

All the money which had been accumulated in munitions production, and the finance raised at the beginning of 1919, had been spent in making the works capable of reaching a level of activity which circumstances made it impossible to achieve. But there is no doubt that the year was one of the most important in the firm's history, and benefits were to come later. The decision to reorganise on a massive scale allowed Austin products to gain a leading position in the 1920s, and the company to weather the storm of the coming financial crisis. This could not have been accomplished by the use of monetary resources — there were none; success depended upon the ability to turn out cars that would sell.

Accounts for 1919 were not published until June of the following year and showed that there was a credit balance at the end of 1919 of £1,656,000, more than half of this sum representing net profit for 1918 which had been brought forward in the profit and loss account in January; added to this was a further trading credit of £238,000. After the dividend on ordinary shares at the rate of 15 per cent for the 13 months ending 31 December 1918 amounting to £65,000 was deducted, approximately £829,000 remained, £67,000 of which went in payments to the preference shareholders. A further £88,000 which had been expended in issuing the B preference capital was written off together with the value of the flying ground which had cost £35,000 to build. Preference shareholders had to be given their dividends in cash — ordinary shareholders could be treated differently. In this case it was decided that they should receive no payments in cash, so a further 200,000 £1 ordinary shares were issued and distributed on the basis of one bonus for every two held. This made it possible to put the bulk of the capital — £475,000 — to general reserve as a provision for excess profits duty and other Inland Revenue liabilities, as well as to allow for future cash requirements.

Preference shareholders wield considerable power in the running of a public company and the following example shows how they can try to force their will upon a business although, with Sir Herbert, they were up against a strong-willed adversary who was fighting for the company's very existence. The dire need for more capital at virtually any cost in 1918 has already been mentioned, but in order to increase the company's borrowing power by this issue of debentures or debenture stock from £100,000 (a level which had been written into the Articles of Association in 1914) to £1 million, three-quarters of the preference shareholders had to give their consent. An extraordinary general meeting was called in January 1920, but only 170,000 of the 187,500 voters necessary acceded and in no way could any more be induced to support the board of directors. Faced with failure in getting the company's borrowing power increased, on 18 May Austin, Du Cros and R.G.Ash, who had been elected to the board in 1918, bought the number of shares needed. It cost them £11,533. Had they not done this the company might well have had to close down. In 1923, when it must have been clear to all concerned that the action of the three directors had been in the best interests of the company generally, a resolution that the three men should not incur a loss personally was strongly opposed. In the end, the proposition was upheld, in spite of belligerent opposition, and the money was refunded — it took more than a committee of 7 per cent preference shareholders to get the better of Sir Herbert.

The year 1920 began with a bank overdraft of nearly £1 million and a similar sum owed to creditors either as payment for materials supplied or as deposits which had been received from customers. With contracts valued at £13,375,070, on which initial payments of £162,961 had been made, once again it was necessary to seek more money from the public. Austin estimated that £2½ million would be required, so the company's capital was increased to £5 million in January 1920 and, on the strength of this extra being raised and in view of the orders on hand, large stocks were purchased on account. The Beecham Trust acted as underwriters for £1½ million 10 per cent £1 preferred ordinary shares. They were offered with an even more attractive dividend than the earlier shares, but were non-cumulative, which meant that the holders would not be entitled to dividends in arrears if profits were not sufficient to give them returns in any particular year. This issue was almost a complete failure; £1,361,066 was paid to the company but most of it had to be met by the underwriters. The general public had no money to spend on securities and even if the speculators had been attracted they were not in a position to lay out any of their funds. By July the new issue stood at a 50 per cent discount on the Stock Exchange.

There were several reasons for the financial disaster in so far as it affected industry generally. By the middle of 1920 the ready cash that had helped to create the boom in the previous year had been spent. The Chancellor of the Exchequer said that it was government policy to deflate the currency, and the restriction on borrowing imposed by the banks inevitably caused a slump in the commodity market as purchasing power fell. It also effectively increased the value of paper securities, such as war loan stock and, conversely, reduced by upwards of 60 per cent the value of manufacturers' stocks and other assets. Any capital raised, therefore, was spent when prices were high and as a direct result of the deflation principle referred to it became necessary to write-down the stock, tools and assets.

High taxation soon began to make itself felt after the Budget, which raised the excess profits duty from 40 per cent to 60 per cent, many manufacturers maintaining that this burden was beyond the economic limit. It was reduced in the following year because industry was slowly being strangled. And although the marked decline in business activity during the early twenties was mainly because of the general falling-off in world trade, there is no doubt that financial policy accelerated the recession. Austins suffered badly — almost to the point where it was impossible to continue.

Sir Herbert was still without sufficient capital to carry out the programme to which the company was committed, without borrowing more from the bank and keeping the creditors waiting. The £1,850,000 ordinary shares which had been authorised at the beginning of 1920 were on offer at par until 31 March, and he had high hopes that the proportion not already earmarked for a very important undertaking would soon be taken up. One of the ways in which manufacturers can overcome the effect of import duties is to assemble their cars in the country in which sales of imported vehicles are restricted. It was this that had prompted Austin to open the Liancourt tractor factory in Paris. The Americans had plenty of capital available to expand into overseas markets, and early in 1920 representatives of the American General Motors Corporation, with $1,000 million behind them, came to visit British factories and naturally Longbridge, where American production methods were being employed, particularly attracted them. They approached Sir Herbert in an attempt to negotiate for a large block of Austin shares; the directors announced that proposals were being considered for an alliance, and £1¼ million of the ordinary share capital was reserved for this purpose. Austin's £1 ordinary shares climbed 6s and were in great demand at 36s for a time. In June a statement was issued pointing out that 'the proposed amalgamation with a United States combine is still being discussed'. Austin thought that such a combination would be beneficial and would remove some of the potential competition both at home and abroad. Luckily the board failed to come to terms with the Americans but General Motors did not give up easily and were to return to the attack again in 1926.

While their proposals were being considered the American firm offered to buy out Sir Herbert's own interest. He refused to sell. In an obituary notice for Sir Herbert in 1941, 'Contact' of the *Motor* reported that he had spoken to Austin at the Scottish Motor Show some time after and the unhappy Sir Herbert had told him, 'To think that I was offered £700,000 in cash for my interest in the Austin business and that I could have retired and lived in comfort for the rest of my days.' In fact, he could no more have retired then than if his son Vernon had returned in 1918, and in spite of many later offers which would have provided enough for him to live in idleness he carried on working until illness prevented him from continuing twenty years later.

The General Motors proposed merger was not the only attempt made in this direction; earlier there had been reports in the press of a possible link between the Austin and Humber companies. Although preliminary discussions may have taken place it is difficult to see how any great benefit could have accrued from an amalgamation between these two concerns, both of which were in a poor position financially. But Austin's records for the period contain a number of references to Humber's finances and from a study of these documents it is clear that mention of an outside organisation's activities was a rare occurrence, unless there was something in the air. In late 1919 Humber owed their bankers £110,000 and showed a credit balance of only £90,000, with the usual army of creditors, so again it is probably just as well that any negotiations failed to progress beyond the exploratory stage. More definite discussions took place between the two firms some ten years later, again without any results.

During the first half of 1920 Austin car production increased splendidly as markets began to expand. In January, 34 cars left Longbridge; in February, 201; March, 324; April, 326; May, 403; June, 506 and, at the height of the season in July, the number rose to 641. This meant that the estimated rate of output had been reached in spite of the fact that again it had been found necessary to increase prices, the chassis to £550, the tourer to £695, the coupé to £850 and the landaulet to £875. Net sales had risen from £72,760 in January to £469,014 in June and in the summer, to mark the attainment of the proposed production level and the likelihood that it would be possible to carry out the programme of manufacture known as C134 (producing an estimated sales turnover for 1920 of £6½ million), 250 of the most important shareholders were invited to the works for a celebration. But the hopeful anticipation which had brought about these festivities was not fulfilled and although 4,319 cars were made in 1920, to have realised £6½ million, even taking into account tractor sales, it would have been necessary to turn out almost twice that number. The turnover was below £4 million and the profit in 1920 fell to £217,500 compared with £238,000 in the previous year. Sir Herbert summed the period up retrospectively in a letter to shareholders in March 1923, when he said:

> ...had the demand for the company's products kept up, the results achieved by the middle of 1920 might have overcome the difficulty, but, as is common knowledge, first the export and then the home markets suddenly collapsed and, by late autumn, output had to be restricted to a point which could not support expenses, in fact, the latter part of the year not only wiped out the profits made in the earlier half (as certified by our Auditors, and by independent investigation) but incurred a loss.

Because it was difficult to ensure a steady supply of materials and components large contracts were negotiated for months ahead for, amongst other things, chassis-frame pressings, CAV electric lighting equipment and tyres; 20,000 tyres were ordered from the North British Rubber Company — the firm founded by W.S. Bartleet, the cycle pioneer, who had patented the beaded-edge tyre in 1890. Half of them were to be the famous Clincher Cross covers for use on the rear wheels and the remainder were to have plain treads which, since brakes were not fitted to the front wheels at this period, were often supplied with new cars on the score of cheapness.

This, combined with the disgusting condition of most of the roads in the country after the war, shows why the company went to the trouble and expense of providing two spare wheels. When orders for cars decreased later, in many cases the contracts which had been entered into could not be cancelled. Stocks built up to enormous proportions — their value at the end of 1920 exceeded £2 million — and creditors began to press for payment.

Greatness however, often seems to triumph through adversity. Amid all the worries attendant upon this situation, which to any ordinary person would have seemed insurmountable, not only did Sir Herbert confidently struggle to solve the financial problems, but he designed yet more cars to capture the wider markets he felt sure would exist in the near future. He had not the daring of Morris, who could slash his prices by £100 overnight; anyway the Austin 20 was not the car to appeal to the type of purchaser he had in mind. He went home and designed two cars that would. One was to remain in production for nineteen years and the other revolutionised motoring by bringing it within the range of the 'man in the street'. But then he was above all a designer who was seldom without a pencil and notebook and, if he was, would scribble designs on odd scraps of paper, tablecloths or his shirt cuffs. The illustration on page 161 of a letter dating from the 1930s typifies this inveterate sketching, and the attention which Austin always paid to even the smallest detail. It was very kindly made available to me by Mr R.Burzi, who worked closely with Austin and became one of the company's senior designers. Sir Herbert was on his way to a board meeting in London and Jack Gethins, his chauffeur for many years, drove him from the Grange to Snow Hill station in Birmingham. Whilst waiting for the train to arrive Austin grabbed a pencil and paper and made a most detailed diagram of an important idea which had struck him during the journey from home. Jack was told to rush the paper back to Mr Burzi so that the idea could be considered for incorporation in the final planning for a design alteration. Austin exercised complete control of car design until the mid-1930s although one or two models were introduced with his sanction but against his better judgment — they were unsuccessful.

To return to the early 1920s — disaster finally struck the company in 1921. Pay days were delayed and each day's post was eagerly awaited in the hope that enough cheques would arrive to enable money to be drawn from the bank to pay the workers. A number of men are reported to have declined to accept their wage packets until the situation improved. Indeed those who had been with the 'old man' since 1905 would very likely rather have gone without sufficient food than lose faith in his ability to pull the firm through.

The vast majority however probably regarded him as just another wealthy business man whose only saving grace was that he was providing them with employment.

Now that the borrowing power under Article 47 of the 1914 Articles of Association had been increased to £1 million every effort was made to provide additional funds by the issue of short-term, well secured debentures for this amount. At the last moment the attempt failed because no one could be found to underwrite it, although the original proposed return of 7 per cent was increased to 10. By February 1921 pressure from the creditors reached its height, and on the 24th of the following month the debenture holders sanctioned an increase in the permissible debenture stock from £1 million to a maximum of £1½ million.

In desperation, £150,000 of short-dated 10 per cent mortgage notes were issued to the Eagle Star & British Dominions Insurance Co Ltd and then, to give time for the board to evolve a scheme of finance, the note-holders were asked to appoint a receiver. An action was taken against the company and the bank in the Chancery Division of the High Court, and on 26 April Sir Arthur Whinney was appointed receiver and manager of the company's affairs. Simmons & Simmons, the London solicitors, issued the following statement:

> It is generally known that negotiations for finance for the Austin Motor Company Limited have been in hand for several months, but it has been very difficult, in view of the continued stringency of the money market, to arrange matters on a satisfactory basis. Negotiations are still proceeding, but in the meantime, it has been considered necessary to conserve the interests of the business by the appointment of a Receiver. He will carry on the business pending the formulations of proposals for the reorganisation of the company's finances.

The *Automotor Journal* for 5 May 1921 commented:

> It appears that Sir Herbert Austin has been managing to carry this huge concern during the past few months under such conditions and in such a way as stamps him as not only a great organiser but a born business man.

Two petitions for the compulsory winding-up of the company were presented but adjourned and, on 15 May, the receiver called a meeting of creditors. Sir Arthur Whinney suggested that the creditors might be paid by issuing them with 2nd debentures paid off out of profits, and estimated that in this way the whole of the debt could be settled in five years. After lengthy discussion the following resolution was passed:

That this meeting is of the opinion that the business should be carried on to enable a scheme to be submitted under Section 120 of the Companies Act (1908), and in the meantime that the petition for the compulsory winding-up should be adjourned.

The following representatives were appointed to a committee of unsecured creditors:

F.R. Wade	Chairman, C.A. Vandervell & Co
W.H. Maudslay	Birmingham Aluminium & Casting and Midland Motor Companies
A. Beck	Metallic Seamless Tube Co
Colonel H.J. Higgs	Ransome & Marles
L.M. Bergin	Dunlop Rubber Co
A. Johnson	North British Rubber Co

Wade incidentally knew Austin very well, for he had been his works superintendent at Wolseleys until they both left in 1905.

A complicated financial situation now existed and a list of major debts, together with a summary of the final arrangement made with the creditors, appears at the end of this chapter. The first thing to be done was to secure £200,000 cash in exchange for the new 1st mortgage debentures — the entire issue was taken up by Sir John Leigh, Bt, in November 1921. Sir John had inherited large interests in the Lancashire cotton trade from his father, gave away £300,000 to aid the disabled during the war and was created a baronet. During the post-war boom he sold out his holding in the family firms which left him in control of an enormous fortune; in fact he was one of the wealthiest men in the country. In addition to his financial interest in the Austin concern he was able to make some of his most profitable investments in shares and property at a time when money was short. Support from a man of his standing gave renewed confidence to some of the less hopeful shareholders in 1921; not that Sir John was risking much as a 1st mortgage debenture holder, but to have such a wealthy man associated with the business was encouraging.

Throughout the year numerous discussions took place between the board of directors, the receiver, the preference shareholders and the debenture shareholders which resulted, early in 1922, in the acceptance by the creditors of the final scheme of arrangement. On 16 March 1922, a year after the receiver had been appointed, a Court Order was made approving the scheme which placed the affairs of the company in the hands of the directors once again, albeit with some new blood on the board. H. Marks, S.

Van den Bergh and Sir Reginald Brade (who had become a director in June 1920, after thirty-five years at the War Office, having held the post of Secretary to the financial department since 1914) resigned. Of the previous directorate (H. Drew-Anderson having already been dropped), this left Sir Herbert as chairman, Harvey Du Cros as deputy chairman and R.G. Ash. Taking effect from April 1922, the new directors were:

Sir Arthur Hardinge	Formerly British Ambassador at Madrid
A.T. Davies	Chairman of Charles Hatton & Co metal merchants, and a director of several other companies
T.D. Neal FCA	
C.R.F. Englebach OBE	
E.L. Payton	

The last two, one a brilliant production engineer and the other a clever financier, were largely responsible for the growth and development of the firm over the next few years.

Austin car production amounted to a mere 2,246 in 1921, but not only the manufacturers of comparatively expensive cars suffered. Morris only sold 3,077 but, in this case, this was an increase of some 40 per cent on the previous year against a 50 per cent decline in Austin 20 sales. What is more important is that Morris was able to make a profit which, on a sales turnover of £1,227,056 for the year ending September 1921, amounted to £144,902. He increased the demand for his car because he was brave enough to adopt a policy of decreasing his prices dramatically at just the right moment. Austin, on the other hand, believed that any increase in costs, unless there was a substantial increase in the number of orders, should be passed on to the customer immediately. It is easy to criticise him for this, but it must be remembered that the future demand for the Austin 20 was not likely to be so great as it was obviously going to be for Morris's products. Austin realised this and knew that he would have to cater for the needs of those requiring much smaller, cheaper transport, and he had his two excellent plans on the drawing board.

When the accounts for the two years ending 31 December 1921 were presented to the shareholders in February 1922, a dismal state of affairs was revealed. The profit and loss account read as follows:

	£ s d
Amount brought forward, 1 January 1920	13,995 4 9
General reserve at 1 January 1920	475,000 0 0
	488,995 4 9
Less preference dividends for six months ending 30 June 1920	38,750 0 0
	450,245 4 9
Less debit balance of profit and loss account for two years ending 31 December 1921 including £123,824 0s 6d, the normal depreciation, but before providing for depreciation of stock, tools etc	381,922 14 4
	68,322 10 5

Thus the loss for the two years of more than £380,000, and the dividends which had been paid, cancelled out most of the funds held to general reserve. And in the above summary only 'normal depreciation' is considered; a great deal more had to be written off — the value of the stock and tools and the debt owing by the French subsidiary, amounting in all to the vast sum of £1,951,923 10s 5d. Furthermore, although on the balance sheet liabilities were offset by assets, the figures were all based on values calculated during late December 1919. Had they been reassessed the situation would no doubt have appeared much worse. However, the directors thought it necessary to depreciate the investments and the Longbridge estate to the extent of about £300,000, their intention being to review the value of assets when conditions improved. There was not much point in dealing with the losses unless the capital structure of the company could be revised but this could not be done until creditors were paid off, and they were owed more than £2 million.

It is interesting to see how shares in the motor industry fell in value during this period. Austin's £1 ordinary shares dropped alarmingly in common with those of most other motor manufacturers: 27s 6d in January 1920, 18s by June, 7s 3d in December; 4s 3d in June 1921, 2s 6d in November; and eventually crashing to 1s when the accounts were presented in March 1922.

When considering their products in the light of consumers' requirements, two aspects influence car manufacturers to make design alterations: styling changes brought about by turns of fashion or in order to introduce innovations, and changes to correct faults brought to their notice by the regularity of warranty claims. Apart from these, there are changes which they introduce for their own convenience. Sir Herbert certainly had no intention of deviating from the ideas which he had decided to adopt in 1918. The 20 had proved to be a sound car with few serious competitors in its price range and, apart from the shape of the rear hood-trap — which in spite of its apparently obvious advantages was never received with enthusiasm by the motorist — there were no revolutionary principles which could be adopted to give the car either a wider market, or better performance and reliability.

Although he was obstinate when it came to changing the outward appearance of a model that was selling well, there was no question in Austin's mind when it came to correcting mechanical faults or saving money and time in the factory. Cast-iron flywheels with a tendency to disintegrate, which were used on the earliest P2s, cost the company both money and some loss of face. However, this cheap but rather dangerous practice was stopped after a very short time and all the early cars were called back to the works where the flywheels were replaced, free of charge, by new steel components.

In basic concept then, the Austin 20 had not changed since its introduction, but certain defects which existed in the P2 were corrected during the latter part of 1920. As stated in the new catalogue issued in November: 'Nothing which can be classed as an alteration of design has been found necessary this year. However, some interesting improvements in minor detail have been made, intended to meet the convenience of owners.' The triangular-belt drive used for the fan and the dynamo constantly gave trouble; if the belt was adjusted tightly enough to prevent slipping, the water-pump spindle was forced to one side which caused uneven wear on the gland and resulted in a leaking pump. To relieve the pump of the strain imposed upon it by the belt, in the new cars the drive was taken from the crankshaft by means of separate belts to the dynamo and the fan. A sight oil-level indicator on the side of the crankcase proved inefficient because the glass became covered internally with oil; initially all cars returned to the works for repair were fitted with a brass level-cock, but in the P3 engine an oil dipstick was placed beside the oil filter. This had also been moved because its original position, below the exhaust manifold, prevented lubricant being poured in from the normal type of oil-can. Among the other minor changes made, in addition to those which could be advertised as 'meeting the convenience of customers', were those which met the convenience of production. Machining and fitting of the P2 crankcase, which divided at the crankshaft centre line, were facilitated by redesigning the component as a one-piece casting. At the same time the starter motor was removed from the side of the crankcase to engage with the flywheel ring from a new position beside the gearbox. This one change saved four hours production time on each car.

With regard to the other models available in 1921, the company's policy was to cater for the growing demand for individuality in coachwork. The complete range and prices in May 1921 were: chassis £550, tourer £695, coupé £850, landaulet £875. New models with white metal radiator cowls were: Ranelagh coupé (similar to the standard coupé but with a fixed, curved leather top) £895; Mayfair landaulet £950; improved tourer with leather upholstery £750 (available also with sports body at £795); sports tourer £975 (available also with standard tourer body at £870 but reduced to £845 in June 1921).

It is not surprising that a sports tourer was added to the Austin range. In all about fifty of these chassis were produced in 1921 and 1922; they were capable of an extra 20 or 30mph top speed and were based upon the standard chassis with the refinements which had been adopted in Scriven's car (see Appendix 4). Unfortunately this excellent car and its capabilities have been eclipsed by the sporting achievements of the 7s which followed it almost immediately, consequently it has been forgotten, but the author is in the happy position of having once owned what is probably the only sports 20 still in existence. Having driven examples of the standard tourer as well he finds it remarkable how the minor modifications made transform what is merely a good touring car of the period into a very lively sports car capable of cruising on a motorway, in spite of a vast frontal area which acts as a wind brake, at 75mph with the engine turning only at 3,200rpm (the top of the windscreen stands over 6ft above the ground, the car having been fitted originally with a coupé body). As in Scriven's car the sports engine had a carefully balanced crankshaft, pistons and connecting rods, higher compression, a higher lift camshaft and dressed and hand-filled gas ports. A 32mm Claudel-Hobson carburetter was attached to a polished aluminium water-heated inlet manifold. Rear shock-absorbers and Rudge-Whitworth wire wheels were also fitted.

As well as the falling-off in car sales due to the slump in the motor industry, and the financial difficulties in which the firm was involved, another important contributory factor kept production of Austin cars at a low level in 1921. After the war and until 1920, motorists paid 6d duty on each gallon of petrol and a relatively small annual tax, depending upon the horsepower of the vehicle, which rose from £2 for engines not exceeding 6.5hp. The Austin 20 was classified as 'not exceeding 26hp', for which the duty was £6 6s a year. Suddenly the situation altered; the Finance Act of

1920 provided for the removal of the fuel tax but — commencing in 1921 — a new basis was to be introduced for motor taxation. A fee of £6 a year was to be levied on all cars rated up to 6hp with £1 for each additional hp; this increased the annual duty payable on the Austin 20 from £6 to £23. For the first time, in addition to fuel consumption and the initial cost, taxation became a factor which could have an effect upon a purchaser's choice of car. Consequently, the demand for the larger cars decreased and greater interest was taken in vehicles with small and medium-sized engines. An anomaly in the new scheme — the use of the RAC rating as a basis for payment (which took into account only the bore of the engine, not the cubic capacity) — led to a tendency for the industry to produce small-bore, long-stroke engines.

The importance of overseas trade to British producers at this period must not be overlooked, and one of the results of the new regulations was to make it even more difficult to produce a single model able to appeal both at home, to satisfy new demand, and abroad where the larger-bore, more powerful, engines were favoured. W.G. Aston summed up the likely indirect results of the situation admirably in an article which appeared in the *Autocar* on 1 January 1921 when he wrote: 'Domestic taxation impels the British designer to make smaller engines in order to reduce the taxation responsibilities of buyers at home and in so doing, he almost certainly reduces the possible demand from buyers abroad.' (This is borne out by the export figures: in 1920 4,294 private cars were sold abroad but this fell to 1,966 in 1921). One of Aston's friends from overseas told him at the Motor Show in 1920 that a four-cylinder engine of less than 80mm bore would not interest him unless it were put on the market at something less than the price of a typical motor-cycle combination. If it wished to compete with American cars abroad the British motor industry had to make either a large, powerful car — which might not sell at home — or a small cheaper car with the power of a larger one.

Austin's answer to the problem was to produce another model by scaling down the Austin 20 and producing the Austin 12. He had been aware for some time that there would be a demand for a smaller, cheaper car and, as early as January 1918 when introducing the prototype 20, Sir Herbert had said, 'If another model is turned out it is likely to be a lighter type with a 12hp four cylinder engine.' Austin knew that it was essential to produce the new model, one which would appeal to a different class of motorist — a lighter more economical car for 'every man' — without delay but to do so was going to be expensive; the factory would have to be altered, and more machines and tools were needed to say nothing of staff. The receiver could not sanction expenditure, so a small amount of cash was raised by selling unwanted plant and stock and the first 12s were built on this capital.

As early as May 1920 advance information on what was then to be called the Austin 10 was made available to the press, the first motoring journalist to discuss the new car being 'Omega' of the *Automotor Journal* in the issue of 23 June. Austins had announced that the 10 would be 'practically a replica of the 20 on a smaller scale' but 'Omega' felt that the 20 was not 'the sort of car which, by mere dimension reduction would make an ideal voiturette'. But he was not to know that the 10 — later known as the 12 — would not be the smallest Austin. It was not a voiturette but a 'small large car'.

Sanction was given to go ahead with an experimental car in the middle of 1921 and plans were made to produce a prototype so that the new model could be introduced at the Motor Show in November. The chassis was not built until September and even at that date only the sketchiest of arrangement drawings existed and there was no provision at the factory for quantity production. In fact, very few Austin 12s left Longbridge before the receiver handed over the company's affairs to the board of directors in March 1922; one which the author once owned, which was first registered on 10 July, was the ninety-eighth tourer to be sold. In order to publish the first review in September, the *Motor* had inspected the car before the first body was finished. The engine had only been run on the bench for ninety minutes but Captain Waite, Austin's son-in-law, was able to demonstrate the outstanding flexibility of the 12 in top gear; smooth acceleration from 7mph to 46mph was possible, due largely to the well chosen 5.18:1 final drive ratio. The *Motor*'s verdict on the bodyless car — 'the transmission appeared to be astonishingly silent, while the springing should be very good when a body is fitted. The car is flexible, silent and sturdy, and we predict that it will attain great popularity'. As an indication of the thorough, perhaps by modern standards extravagant, way in which the 12 was designed, the fan spindle was supported on two large double-row self-aligning ball races. And there was the five-bearing crankshaft. After describing the chassis the *Motor* admitted that '. . . no designer can put pen to paper and evolve an engine which, when built to his specification, is incapable of improvement'. Sir Herbert Austin could. Even allowing for the fact that the new car was based on the 20, it says a great deal for the care with which the prototype was conceived that, with the exception of the increase in stroke in 1926 to give more power to carry heavier bodies, the engine remained with scarcely any alterations until the last utility cars were made for the War Department in 1940.

Indebtedness in 1921

Major debts in December 1921:

	£	s	d
Government advance, secured by a 1st mortgage dated 1 July 1919, on the North and West works' buildings (repayable by nineteen half-yearly instalments commencing 1 January 1922)	240,000	0	0
A similar advance, dated 27 July 1919, on the Longbridge housing estate and other land (repayable by 30 annual instalments)	75,000	0	0
10 per cent 1st mortgage notes, secured by mortgages on other property not included above, under a trust deed in favour of the Eagle Star & British Dominions Insurance Co Ltd	150,000	0	0
2nd debentures deposited with the London Joint City & Midland Bank Ltd (the amount owed to the bank, including bank charges and interest, at 8 October 1921, was £234,850 2s 1d)	250,000	0	0
Total	715,000	0	0

In addition there were the following unsecured creditors:

	£	s	d
The Crown for income tax and excess profit duty	161,000	0	0
Fees and other money due to the receiver (at 8 October 1921)	51,551	3	1
Agents rebates (at 31 October 1921)	44,442	10	4
Deposits on cars (at 31 October 1921)	49,852	19	0
Other unsecured creditors (approximately)	1,016,117	0	0
Total	1,322,963	12	5
A total secured and unsecured indebtedness of:	2,037,963	12	5

There were also certain contingent liabilities in respect of guarantees on cars delivered but these were not dealt with by the Scheme of Arrangement.

70

Summary of scheme of arrangement with the creditors dated December 1921

1 Creation of a new issue of £200,000 8 per cent (tax free) 1st mortgage debentures, repayable by 10 half-yearly payments of £22,000 each, commencing on 23 September 1922. The company reserving the right to repay the entire sum outstanding at any time.

2 Increase of the 2nd debentures from £250,000 to £285,000.

3 A release from the government of its existing 1st mortgage for £240,000 on the North and West works upon their acceptance of a payment of £8,000 due for the 9.2in shell factory and a 3rd mortgage debenture for £248,000 repayable by eight annual instalments of £31,000 each, commencing 31 December 1924.

4 Creation of a new issue of 4th debenture stock sufficient to meet the sum outstanding to the unsecured creditors, carrying no interest until 30 June 1923, but thereafter at 6 per cent per annum, payable half-yearly. This sum to be secured by a trust deed in favour of F.N. Tweedale and A. Maitland as trustees as a floating charge on the company and its property, ranking subject to the prior mortgages. The main provisions were that the Longbridge building estate should be sold together with all excess stock not essential for carrying on the business, at the discretion of the 2nd debenture holders, in order to provide capital for the unsecured creditors.

The 2nd debenture holders also had the right to sanction such payments as they thought fit from current trading profits, any such money to be payable to the trustees for the redemption of the 4th debenture stock, no distribution to be made of less than 5 per cent of the original issue and to be made on an equal basis to all creditors. The trustees were empowered to invest the capital until such a sum was realised. They were also entitled to attend all board meetings of the company, without voting, and to examine all the Austin books and records.

If the company failed after seven days to pay over in full outstanding sums to settle the 4th Debenture, having been handed the authority necessary from the 2nd debenture holders by the trustees, or if for three months the sums were, in the opinion of the trustees, insufficient, or if the trustees disapproved of any expenditure by the company or any decision made by the board to incur expense or make a mortgage charge or security on any of the company's assets, and if it was thought that these might be detrimental to the 4th debenture stockholders, the trustees were to notify the unsecured creditors who were empowered to call in the principal of the 4th debenture stock which would then be payable by the company forthwith. It would also become immediately payable if:

1 default was made in payment of interest on the 4th debenture stock for six months after it was due;
2 a receiver should be appointed of any parts of the company's assets;
3 the company were to be wound up;
4 there was any distraint upon any of the company's property unless it was paid out within seven days; or
5 the company were to commit a breach of any trust deed covenant or stipulation.

The company had to procure the whole of the issue of £200,000 1st mortgage debentures subscribed at par and paid up in cash, and to procure the bank to accept the increase in the 2nd debentures from £250,000 to £285,000 as security for the overdraft.

From the sums provided by the issue of the 1st and 2nd mortgage debentures, and from part of the net proceeds of the sale of excess assets and any cash balance, the company were to make the required cash payments to the 4th debenture holders. Any balance to be paid to the company by the receiver on passing his final account could be kept by them as working capital.

The company were to pay in full, in cash:

1 £150,000 and interest at the rate of 10 per cent per annum, plus costs and expenses to the trustees of the trust deed dated 7 January 1921, and recover the properties and assets mortgaged;
2 any preferential creditors (other than the Crown for income tax and excess profits duty, but including the receiver's expenses) not already paid by the receiver;
3 all unsecured creditors for amounts of less than £20;
4 £1,514 1s 6d due to various railway companies, the accounts of which were guaranteed by some of the directors;
5 overdue interest on all loans and advances and debts due to the government and the bank, amounting to about £30,279 14s 9d;
6 all costs of the Scheme of Arrangement.

The Inland Revenue had to agree to accept payment of indebtedness to them (about £160,000) for income tax and excess profits duty up to 5 April 1920, at £2,000 a month, and the company were not to pay any dividends until such debt was fully settled out of the sale of excess assets and current trading profits in priority to any payments made to the 4th debenture holders. The 4th debenture stockholders were not to be entitled to the residue until the Inland Revenue debt was met.

Claims by agents for deposits on cars were to be settled by the delivery of cars and rebates due to agents by cash payments.

Unsecured creditors for sums of £20 and more were to be issued with 6 per cent 4th debenture stock, the interest to date from one month after the dates that the amounts became due. Odd shillings and pence were to be settled in cash.

When the Scheme was to become operative the receiver was to apply to the court for leave to give possession of the company's property and assets to the company upon payment of all the 10 per cent mortgage notes, retaining a 1st charge and lien upon the property and assets in favour of the 1st, 2nd, 3rd and 4th mortgage debentures and the cost of the action.

The two compulsory winding-up petitions were to be dismissed and the company to pay the costs. The Scheme was to become operative when:

1 a court order was issued sanctioning it;

2 all parties approved;

3 the debenture stock and debentures were sanctioned by the original preference shareholders; and

4 responsible persons or companies paid, in cash, for the £200,000 1st mortgage debentures.

The court order approving the Scheme was dated 16 March 1922, and an advertisement to this effect appeared in *The Times* on 25 March 1922.

6 Saved by the 12 and the 7: 1922 and 1923

I have over 300,000 of the Ordinary shares, and have never sold one of them.

Sir Herbert Austin, letter to shareholders, 6 March 1923

In March 1922 the share capital was as follows:

£250,000 cumulative 7 per cent A preference;
£1,000,000 cumulative 6 per cent B preference;
£1,500,000 10 per cent preferred ordinary;
£600,000 ordinary.

There were still £200,000 1st mortgage 8 per cent debentures, £285,000 2nd mortgage 7 per cent debentures issued to London Joint City & Midland Bank to cover their loan, 3rd mortgage debentures of £248,000 taken by the government in exchange for the previous 1st mortgage on the North and West works, and £1,600,000 4th mortgage debentures issued to unsecured creditors in place of their debts. Interest on these at 6 per cent was not payable until July 1923.

The full balance sheet and profit and loss account for the year ending 31 December 1922 was not issued to shareholders until 26 September 1923, and it showed a gross trading profit of £198,835. After adding earlier reserves and interest received and deducting profit and loss account charges, there was a credit balance of £18,564. Any likely improvement in profits would depend upon a turn round in the motor trade, and Austins would need to have cars of the right type and in sufficient quantity to meet any increase in demand.

The picture painted by the financial statements was not as bad as it looked. Only £55,000 a year was required to pay the interest on the first three debentures, and the 4th would not require interest until July 1923; so that with any revival in trade the A and B preference shares, with their accumulated arrears of dividends, looked likely to be good medium-term investments. The preferred ordinary shares, together with the ordinary shares, stood at only 2s and 1s each respectively, and this reflected their investment value. Advice from financial journalists to holders was to lock them away for three years.

For 1923, it was decided to revert to the pre-war practice of ending the financial year in September, so the accounts published in December 1923 were for the nine months ending 30 September. They showed a gross trading profit plus reserves of £410,764; less profit and loss charges a credit of £205,459 was carried forward, reducing the firm's debit balance to £1,599,578. During the year, the first three debentures had been reduced, and the estate mortgages cleared, the total reduction in indebtedness being £510,000. The gross trading profit had doubled in the first nine months of 1923, largely as a result of the success of the Austin 12 and the introduction of the 7.

In 1922 nearly 320,000 cars were registered in Britain. Total car production approached 55,000 of which only some 2,000 were exported. On the other hand, almost 20,000 foreign cars and car chassis were imported. Between November 1921 and October 1922, 1,394 Austin 20s were produced, a fall of some 80 per cent over the previous year, but against that 1,165 of the new Austin 12s were produced, giving a total Austin production of 2,559 vehicles for the year. In the early 1920s there were still hundreds of makes of car on the market, a situation which was to change as the few successful firms grew and ousted the smaller concerns. In March 1922, Lookers, the Manchester Austin agent, ordered cars worth £517,500, the largest order ever given by an English agent for an English car; it represented about 600 Austins.

Austins works was now the largest motor factory in the British Empire — with the buildings erected during the war, the total floor space was over 58 acres. The total area in the South works was 142.5 acres, with 32.5 acres of floor space; West works had 43 acres with 12 acres of floor space; and the North works covered 18 acres with 14 acres of floor space. The South works housed the administrative offices, works engineer's office, drawing office, design, jig and tool, experimental and research departments. A large power station between North and South works, close to the railway sidings so that coal could be unloaded direct into the boiler house, used twelve 8 x 30ft Lancashire boilers which provided steam to drive three 1,500kW generators. This power drove 500 electric motors of 0.5 to 500hp. The foundry had a capacity of 250 tons output a month on single day-shift operation. Press shops in the South works covered 2,700sq ft, the five main presses being capable of producing 500 bodies a week, each Austin 20 body requiring 24 separate pressed panels. There were more than 4,000 machine tools, from grinders to wood-working machines, in constant use. Accommodation for many of the workers was provided in the 120 acre Longbridge housing estate in which there were 200 wooden bungalows and 50 semi-detached brick houses catering for a total population of 1,500.

Manufacture of the prototype Austin 12 — the scaled down Austin 20 — began at Longbridge in July 1921 and the car, albeit unfinished, was tested by a motoring journalist in September. In order to achieve this scoop, the test was made at the factory in the bare chassis, before a body had been fitted. Two weeks later, the car was complete and shown to the rest of the motoring press. It had a four-door, four-seat touring body and ran on unusual Michelin four-stud wheels with 760 x 90mm beaded-edge tyres. The 20's 4ft 8in track was reduced to a very narrow 4ft and the engine was scaled down to 1,661cc (72 x 102mm). Weighing only 16cwt it was described by Austin as 'a car of moderate dimensions which would fulfil ideals of service previously only obtainable in high powered cars of 20hp and over'. After a test drive, one writer commented upon the top gear acceleration from 20mph, a notable feature of the very flexible Austin 12 engine which, with its five main-bearing crankshaft, was always particularly smooth in top. Drivers were to find this an important feature, because it required a great deal of practice to manage an Austin 12 gearbox. Once completely mastered, however, it was only necessary to used the clutch from a standstill. Although no great top speeds were noted on the test runs — 45 to 47mph and the odd burst at 50 — fuel consumption was good, with 30mpg to be expected. The smooth-running short-stroke four-cylinder monobloc engine with a detachable head had a stroke of only 102mm, much shorter than was usual with a 72mm bore in the early 1920s. The result was quite a high-revving engine for the period, assisted by the use of light aluminium pistons, and though the official RAC rating was 12.8hp, 20hp was developed at 2,000rpm.

By January 1922 when the cars were shown for the first time at the Scottish Motor Show, three body styles were offered, the four-seater tourer and the two/four seater at £550, and the coupé at £675 or £695 with leather hood and choice of colour. All these had six-stud wooden wheels, and in the first year 809 tourers and 305 coupés were sold and 51 chassis. These latter were supplied to other coach and body builders, and perhaps a few of them went to the Sizaire-Berwick company to be converted into 13/26s. The two/four seater had the two bucket seats, as in the tourer, which moved backwards and forwards in the well of the body, but at the rear of the well were two small folding seats, one in each corner, 'which can be utilised

1922 Twelve 2-4 seater

when the front seats are pushed rather more forward than usual'. This meant that to take anything much more than infants in the back, the driver's knees were brought up to touch the steering wheel. The object was to cater for housing four people under the hood and the back could be used as a luggage area when weather permitted the passengers to sit in the dickey seat.

The Austin 20 range at the time was more comprehensive. To the existing styles were added some special models designed to be the last word in comfort and distinction — the Grosvenor limousine and landaulet, the four-door Ranelagh coupé and the Westminster folding-head coupé. There was also an alternative touring car for those who preferred a hood and spare wheels carried outside the body. With the exception of the standard coupé and landaulet, which had painted radiator cowls, every other 20 had a radiator cowl in white metal. Standard model colours were royal blue, grey or green; the tourers with leather upholstery and the enclosed cars with Bedford cord. Special models were finished in the purchaser's choice for paint and trim. January 1922 prices were: chassis £550, tourer £695, special seven-seater tourer £755, coupé £850, Westminster coupé £895, Ranelagh coupé £925, Marlborough landaulet £950, Grosvenor limousine or landaulet £1,145, sports chassis £700, sports model £945, sports chassis with standard body £870, standard chassis with sports body £755. There was also a range of seven commercial bodies at £675. Rationalisation of this complicated variety of body styles came in preparation for the 1923 season.

Reasons for Sir Herbert's and Harvey Du Cros's involvement in the near defunct shell of the Sizaire-Berwick company in September 1922 are obscure. Perhaps they were both hedging their bets and preparing an outlet for the two popular Austin models under another name in a new company controlled by themselves should the Austin scheme of arrangement fail. Or

77

perhaps there was nothing more under the surface than the story given to the press by the Austin company at the time that: 'The company has agreed to supply Sizaire-Berwick Limited with certain parts of Austin chassis, to be completed with a greater variety of coachwork than is covered in the Austin models. Two Austin directors are on the Sizaire-Berwick board and Austin agents will be offered first choice of Sizaire-Berwick agencies.' Not a very convincing statement when there were four different Austin 12, and six Austin 20 body styles.

F.W. Berwick had registered his first company in Britain in October 1911, and in 1913 came to an arrangement with Maurice and Georges Sizaire of Paris to market in Britain the new Sizaire 20hp chassis under the name Sizaire-Berwick. A limited company of that name was formed on 19 March 1913, with nominal capital of 1,000 £1 shares, Berwick and A. Keiller as sole directors, and an office at 18 Berkeley Street, London. Three chassis were built by the Sizaire brothers, one of which was sent over to London in September to be exhibited at Olympia as the first Sizaire-Berwick car. Basically conventional, the car had a four-cylinder 90 x 160mm 4,070cc monobloc 20hp engine. Sizaire-Berwick held a patent for the steering gear which consisted of a pin, with two independent conical rollers on ball bearings, fitted into the threads of the worm. The worm had two tracks, an outer one with which the larger roller engaged, and an inner one for the smaller roller. The conical rollers were pressed into the thread by a spring, which took up the backlash; the wear in the worm being taken up automatically. Adjustment allowed for five different steering-wheel positions. Good use was made of aluminium castings, not only in the engine but for the dashboard and the brake shoes; possibly the first time that aluminium had been used for them.

With Sizaire-Berwick and H.J. Mulliner bodies, the cars gained a high reputation for quality during 1914. Sizaire's Courbevoie works were taken over for war production late in 1914, and the last chassis were rushed to the coast and shipped to London. These were driven by Jack Waters, later to become famous as Jack Warner the film star and actor, who worked for Berwick and had been sent to France by them to gain experience in Sizaire methods. After serving in the army and the Royal Flying Corps, he was appointed experimental engineer to Sizaire-Berwick at Park Royal in north London, the chassis testing and repair shop being under his control.

The Park Royal site had been acquired after the company obtained a government contract, and work was started on a factory there which was used for the production of aircraft and engines. But in 1919, like Austin, the company had a large modern empty factory. The board met on 25 April to increase the share capital to £10,000, and in October to create a public company with a capital of £600,000. Sir David Dalziel MP became chairman, and C.J. Ford, chairman of the Edison Swan Electric Company Limited joined the board. With 16 acres of buildings on their valuable Park Royal site worth over £800,000 and orders for cars worth £1½ million, all seemed set for a good future. The works were capable of producing between 1,000 and 1,250 cars a year, a contract for René Durand to make and sell Sizaire-Berwick cars in France and Italy was signed, and Berwick was paid £41,250 in cash and £82,500 in shares. The rest of the shares sold well and the broker handling the issue took up only a small balance of some £16,000. But the adverse economic situation proved to be too much for the firm. A receiver was appointed in October 1920 and Berwick resigned in February of the following year. A few cars were sold, not with the flat Rolls-Royce radiator in use before the war, as Rolls-Royce had come to an arrangement for the shape of the Sizaire-Berwick radiator to be altered to maintain the exclusive Rolls image for themselves. The big, powerful 4½ litre post-war car had a very small market; with an open body it cost £1,500 and as a saloon £1,700, and like most similar firms at that time, Sizaire-Berwick had to fail.

When Austin and Du Cros came on the board in September 1922, the 25/50hp car was still listed, and the 13/26 and 23/46 models were added. These were merely the Austin 12 and the Austin 20 with Sizaire-Berwick radiators and somewhat superior coachwork. Examples of all three were shown at the 1923 Olympia show and were available until the end of 1924. With the 13/26 costing £590 against £450 for the equivalent Austin 12, it is surprising that any were sold, but a dozen or so new and secondhand 13/26s were offered for sale in the *Autocar* in 1923 and 1924. Car Mart still had a late-1923 car for sale in May of the following year for which they would have accepted £365 against the original £550 retail price. By then, Austin had lost interest in the company. His own firm was flourishing, the 12 and the 7 were both successful, and Sizaire-Berwick was only a defunct enterprise which ceased to carry on business in February 1924. The assets were restored to the Austin company in April 1925, when all that was left was a complicated set of accounts and the valuable Park Royal site.

Listed among the other three models in the Sizaire-Berwick catalogues for 1922 was a mysterious 26/52hp car. It is described as one of Sir Herbert's Austin designs and had a six-cylinder engine of 81.5 x 102mm and a three-speed gearbox; none survive, and it is even doubtful that other than a prototype ever existed. It sounds very American in design and although there is no evidence now to support the view, it could just have been an extension of Austin's vague plan to make a six-cylinder car based on the American Hudson. The Austin company did not try a six-cylinder car again until 1927.

The story of the Austin 7, already mentioned as being so successful by the mid-twenties, owes much to Stanley Edge. Edge left school at the age of 14 in August 1917, and entered the Austin car drawing-office at Longbridge. From then on he spent every waking moment studying cars and engines. As the assistant to Jack Clarke, the engine designer, Austin got to know him quite well, and must have been impressed with his knowledge and standard of his work. One day in September 1921 Hancock, the chief designer, called Edge to his office, just as Hancock himself had been summoned in 1905, and asked him to sit down. This he did with trepidation, thinking that an invitation to sit down was likely to lead to an invitation to quit the company. When he was asked to leave to go and work at Lickey Grange, which was now Sir Herbert's home, he was not at first reassured, but when Hancock went on to say 'Sir Herbert has asked me to find out for him, and if you agree he will give you all the details himself', Edge agreed, and next day Sir Herbert asked him to see him at his home on Sunday morning. He stayed there working for the next eight months. Arrangements were made for him to lunch and dine at the house, and to sleep at the lodge during the week.

Edge found that at Lickey Grange, Austin was a completely different character from the tornado which used to tear around the works and offices at Longbridge. Austin gave him instructions by a few sketches and word of mouth, but as his own drawings of the 7 took shape it was these which were discussed and modified again and again. The sketches — rough full-sized semi-freehand drawings but nevertheless reasonably accurate and containing a fair amount of detail — must have been prepared by Sir Herbert himself, perhaps on the billiards table which was large enough for a full size drawing of a small car. This may account for the billiard table legend, but Edge never made a drawing or a sketch on the table all the time he was there.

These drawings at the start did not resemble the final 7; they more nearly resembled the Rover 8 with its air-cooled horizontal twin engine and worm-drive rear axle, probably the most popular and successful light car of 1921. Sir Herbert had borrowed a Rover from the chief cashier at Austins and had gone over it very carefully taking measurements. Between September and December 1921, Edge spent twelve or more hours a day on the drawings. Austin was not at home every evening, but when he was they would pore over the drawings, sometimes starting before dinner then breaking for the meal and continuing afterwards until about 10pm. Edge found Austin's alertness to design problems after having spent all day at the factory, coupled with his ability to concentrate well into the night, remarkable.

No finalised designs were available by January 1922, and many possibilities had been explored; for example four wheels in a diamond pattern and rear-wheel steering. For a time after abandoning the horizontal twin, Sir Herbert wanted three cylinders, and this was studied from all possible viewpoints. Stanley Edge knew Austin better than almost anyone else who worked at Longbridge, and gives this interesting insight into their relationship:

I feel sure that at that particular period I was as up-to-date as Sir Herbert on engine matters because I read everything which was available, Government publications, the *Automobile Engineer*, papers by Harry Ricardo etc, but on how engines could be connected to road wheels, how the whole lot were put into a frame and a body mounted thereon I was educated by Sir Herbert. In his teaching he was always painstaking and kind, and when I felt I had something worth while he would always listen. In fact our whole relationship was an extension of my first Sunday morning at Lickey Grange. My picture of him at this time is of a portly gentleman, wedged against my drawing board, talking and sketching with a stub of a pencil, or looking straight at me while I tried to say what I thought. Often after dinner he would ask whether I had enjoyed it, and at times he would bring in some chocolates or crystallised fruits.

At sometime early in New Year 1922 we had decided on the sort of car to be made, and from then on the production of the detail and final general arrangements lay with me. Sir Herbert would at times have second thoughts and make modifications, but my general attitude was to say, 'If you wish me to complete these drawings we must stick to what we have decided upon.'

If Sir Herbert and I had parted company in 1921 my picture of him would have been of a man of abounding energy yet nevertheless essentially a kindly father figure, but as I have said there were people who saw him in a different light. As my work continued into 1922 I came to know these different aspects. I had a sensitive disposition, but this is perhaps putting it too delicately. A lot of people I knew then were inclined to call me 'a touchy devil' and although I think I have grown more mellow with age — some people still do. Therefore, I may have fancied changes in his attitude, where none existed. In any case, I had probably overworked for four or five months without being truly aware of it, and goodness knows what pressures may have been exerted on Sir Herbert. Be that as it may, he came to ask the question in the evenings more and more as to when would I be ready with the drawings.

The first few months sketching and scheming were comparatively carefree, but the responsibility for correct details was entirely my own and I intended to be doubly careful in avoiding errors. In due course I completed details in batches, of engine, gearbox, rear axle, front axle, steering, frame work and finally the body. He kept saying, 'We really must get these finished you know', which began to sound more like, 'You must get a move on.' I still had no idea of what we were going to do with the drawings and I tentatively suggested that first the engine assembly details and then the other assemblies could be issued for manufacture as I completed them. In this way I think we could have started about the end of February. However, just before Easter I was finished completely and then he told me to bring all the drawings to the factory on the Tuesday after Easter and this must have been his target all the time. I found that men had been engaged on preparing a 'boarded-up' section of the works and North works superintendent McLellan, who had been put in charge, had been receiving the same exhortations as myself at Lickey Grange.

All the time I was with Sir Herbert I never saw him make a design calculation, nor did he ever give me results of calculations. I know he was keen on estimating weights and he would work out costs, whether correctly or not I do not know, but when I proposed a certain compression ratio for the engine he just said 'All right', and when I said the bore and stroke which we have settled on will give 696cc he simply said 'Will it?' Things like the inertia of the reciprocating parts, or the inlet and exhaust gas speeds he just wasn't bothered with. Again, because I considered myself an engine expert, I did not worry. Similarly I was quite capable of settling gear ratios, clutch dimensions and all calculations dealing with transmission of engine power, but there were questions of gear-box and axle construction, steering and brakes of which I had no experience, and in the main I scaled these down from larger cars. But even then the parts generally came out too large, and Sir Herbert would say, 'Make it like this', generally cutting down my transmission and chassis dimensions.

After Easter 1922 I worked in the private boarded-up section of the Longbridge works where the first Sevens were built. A separate office in this section had been set aside for me and my drawing board, and Mr McLellan also had a desk in there. He had been in his superintendent's position during the war years and those immediately following; an older man than Sir Herbert, I have never seen his name mentioned in the accounts of Austin affairs, but I think Sir Herbert had good recollections of Mac's work with him in the past and so selected him for the job. He was a rough and ready type, but notwithstanding had tact which was invaluable. He and I got along together very well and here I pay tribute to him because it was largely due to his overall guidance the Sevens were built according to requirements, which were to have three cars ready for Whitsuntide. I am not writing here about the work done in making the Sevens, except insomuch as this throws a light on personal relationships. Now that I was established in this works office Sir Herbert still spent considerable time at my board, but I had to share him with the rest of the section. He was not able to give his undivided attention to the designs in hand.

When Whit Monday arrived we had cars to show for our labours and I intended to enjoy the festivities, but some work cropped up and I spent most of my day in the office. During the afternoon Sir Herbert must have slipped away from the official function. He came into the office and was surprised to see me there. After a brief glance at what I was doing he told me that everything was going well and he outlined plans he had for variations on the Seven theme. This was nearly the last time I had a heart to heart talk alone with Sir Herbert. We spoke together many times afterwards of course, but there were generally others present. It was either on this afternoon or one shortly afterwards while we were talking alone, that a young man, who looked not much older than myself, came unannounced into the office and addressed Sir Herbert familiarly saying, 'So this is where you hide yourself away.' Sir Herbert replied courteously if somewhat stiffly, and they carried on talking about the car, myself supplying an arrangement drawing for Sir Herbert to illustrate a feature from time to time. Towards the end the young man spoke pontifically saying, 'My dear sir, the public will just not stand for this', and Sir Herbert replying with equal dignity, 'My dear sir, I am educating the public.' I learned afterwards that the visitor was Mr. 'Billy' Rootes of Rootes, Maidstone, who were then important Austin agents.

Perhaps not unnaturally in view of the state of the company's finances, there was opposition from some of Austin's fellow directors, some of whom were far from convinced that a new light car would solve the financial problems. The project was accepted grudgingly — surely the Austin 12 was the light car that was needed, not a bath on wheels. Austin had patented those of his own ideas which were used so the board, faced with the choice either of having the prototype produced at Longbridge or of losing it altogether, finally let Austin have his way. He was astute enough, however, to extract from them an agreement which gave him a royalty of 2 guineas for every Austin 7 sold.

Sir Herbert chose a most inappropriate time and place at which to announce the future production — the annual dinner of the Birmingham Motor Cycle Club which took place in January 1922. He had a profound contempt for motor-cycle combination makers, and had expressed this in jest after World War I when he told the chief engine draughtsman that he considered them 'only a step above perambulator makers'. As one of the guest speakers at the dinner he made an announcement to owners and prospective owners of light cars, and went on to refer to a new Austin which would, he prophesied, perhaps rather tactlessly in view of the fact that he was in the company of so many ardent motor cyclists and at least one well known sidecar manufacturer, 'Knock the motor cycle and sidecar into a cocked hat and far surpass it in comfort and passenger-carrying capacity'. He continued by saying: 'I cannot imagine anyone riding a sidecar if he can afford a car,' a statement that so enraged the correspondent to the *Irish Cyclist* that this worthy wrote, in a February issue of the magazine: 'This seems to us to indicate the frame of mind of the person who thinks that everyone should like what he likes.'

The general view at the time — as notes by Edgar N. Duffield, motoring journalist of *Automotor Journal,* show — appears to have been that the introduction of the 7, however good its design, would be the end of the Austin motor company. Many foresaw complete disaster and felt that not enough people would buy it and make its production a profitable proposition. How wrong they were, and how right Herbert Austin proved to be. The amusement and contempt with which the car was regarded by some was in no way detrimental to it and, because of its success, the humorists soon found that they must ridicule the new class of motorist for whom it provided such a practical and cheap means of transport for the first time in motoring history, rather than waste their efforts on the vehicle itself.

The first prototype 7, registered as OK2950, was built in the Longbridge experimental department workshop in the early part of 1922, and although it was reported as having been seen running in the vicinity of the factory and surrounding district in March, it was not until the following July that details were released to the press. The Austin company, like Daimler and Vauxhall, usually announced their new models just prior to the autumn London Motor Show, but Sir Herbert disliked the idea of waiting to make an announcement to coincide with Olympia. Another 7 had been completed by July and bore the registration number OK3537; this car and OK2950 were shown in all the early advertisements and catalogues. Initially production was slow because a complete section of the factory had to be reorganised, and it is doubtful if more than a few Austin 7s were on the road by the end of 1922. The original cylinder-bore diameter of 2.125in was increased to 2.2in in March 1923, starting at car number A1-101. The two prototypes were numbered CHA1-101 and CHA1-102 and the first production tourer was A1-1, from which it seems that the first car with the 2.2in bore, and built in March 1923, was the 103rd Austin 7 produced.

A typical reaction to the new venture followed the press luncheon which Sir Herbert gave at the official 'launching' at Claridges on 21 July 1922, after which the *Financial World* reported:

> Holders of motor car manufacturing shares are well aware that we have persistently and enthusiastically advocated investment in the light car issues. We are glad to note, therefore, that Austins have (at last) made up their minds to enter that field.

Although preliminary descriptions and photographs of the first car had appeared in the major weeklies earlier in July, this luncheon, and examination of OK3537 which was on view in the firm's Oxford Street showroom, gave correspondents a chance to discuss the new model with Austin. He said he was convinced that there was a large market of would-be motorists in England at the time who wanted some form of automobile that would give better weather protection than the sidecar, and yet was not so expensive to buy or run as a contemporary conventional car. The individual at whom he was aiming was the man in the street whose car must be:

A decent car for the man who, at present, can only afford a motor cycle and sidecar, and yet has the ambition to become a motorist. It is also for the vast host of motorists who realise that, owing to taxation and the high cost of living, they are paying ridiculously for the privilege of using their car.

Sir Herbert went on to say that:

In evolving this car we have endeavoured to meet the requirements of those who cannot afford motoring other than that of the cheapest kind. The powerful car, with its heavy running expenses and extensive garage requirements, is beyond the reach of many who, nevertheless, enjoy motoring quite as much as those possessing more cash, and so we have designed a car which will be put on the market at £225, or perhaps a little less.

Although motor-cycle combinations could be bought for between £160 and £180, the best available models could cost £200 fully equipped; for as little as an additional £25 the motor cyclist could have a complete motor car.

Many questions were raised ranging from the diminutive size of the 696cc engine to the four-wheel braking system. Even the *Light Car and Cyclecar* reported that the 7 was one of the smallest cars that they had ever seen, so it is not surprising that Sir Herbert was asked why he had adopted such a small engine — 2.125in bore was exceptionally small for the time. But his reply was simple: 'It is all that is necessary with so small a car.'

Car prices as a whole had to be reduced in 1923, in fact by September 1922 a number of firms had brought their prices down. The two-seater Cubitt fell £107 to £335, the Overland from 380 guineas to £350, the Buick two-seater from £435 to £360, their six-cylinder model from £625 to £495, and a two-seater Jowett could be bought for as little as £255. Something had to be done about Austin prices. Cars like the Rover 8 and the Rhode had proved the demand for a small car: four seats, four wheel brakes, 52mph and capable of 50mpg, coming from the Austin stable, and priced at a mere

£225 — even if it only had a hand starter, though at least this could be operated from the driver's seat — could not fail to succeed. The market had not been attacked seriously by a volume producer. There were other cheap large cars like the Model T Ford, but that certainly could not be run in Britain at 1¼d a mile; the 7 could.

On 22 September prices of 20s and 12s were reduced, and some alterations made to the specification to soften the blow to the company. The 12 tourer and two/four seaters were reduced by £100 each to £450, but were supplied with spare wheels less tyres, without a clock, and in one standard colour — grey. The two/four seater was reduced by a further £10 in October. A so-called 'special' model, costing an extra £40, had the spare tyre and choice of coachwork in either royal blue, grey or maroon, a luggage carrier, rear screen, clock and spring gaiters. The coupé was given a name — Harley — and reduced by £95, being joined at the same price by the Berkeley landaulet. Production data for the period to 31 October 1923 does not show that any two-seaters were made. None survived to prove that they were, and the figure must have been very small. All the early 12s with 4ft track were given the number prefix T, additional letters denoting the model: TT for tourer, TC for saloon, TS for special body and TF for fabric saloons. With each major design change, a number prefixed the T. For instance 2T, introduced in May 1923, related to an increase in the track to 4ft 4in; at the same time, with the extra 4in, the car was described as a five-seater. The first 12s were so narrow that the steering box had to be bolted to the outside of the chassis frame, which necessitated a slot being cut in the wing, covered by a shaped metal cowl. When the width was increased, there was enough room in the engine compartment to take the complete steering box.

Austin 20 bodies were now reduced to six. The old tourers with the hood trap were discontinued; the five-seater cost £695 and the cheapest other 20 was the seven-seater at £755. The Westminster two-door coupé was reduced by £45 to £850, the four-door Ranelagh coupé from £925 to £875, the Marlboroughs by £75 to £875, and the Mayfairs (replacing the old Grosvenors) from £1,145 to £975. The 12 chassis was still available at £380, and the 20 at £550; sports 20 chassis were still listed at £625 and the complete cars for £825.

In September 1922 Sir Herbert paid one of his regular visits to America with E.L. Payton and, at the Austin agents' dinner held at the Connaught Rooms, London, in November, Sir Herbert in his speech gave some of the impressions which he gained on his trip:

It is clear to my mind that we have not yet scratched the surface. There are 12 million cars in use in the world, of which all but 1½ million are in service in America. I saw nothing in the States to show that we could not do in proportion what they have done. All stages of society are using cars, and it is quite common to see bricklayers driving up in cars in their working clothes to ask for a job. There was a time, perhaps, when we had some justification for belittling American cars, but we cannot do so now. They are making reliable cars and selling them for £200 ... We appear to be lacking the confidence that inspires the motor industry on the other side.

Austin had prophesied that it should be possible to produce a small car at the price of an expensive sidecar combination. He had found that in America they could produce and sell a car at a good profit at a price which manufacturers in this country would have to pay for materials alone. There were 240,000 cars in Detroit, a city no bigger than Birmingham, the proportion being 1 car for every 4 inhabitants, including men, women and children. Roads were so thick with cars that a car could be in a line of traffic for 30 miles or more. Quite a third of the cars were garaged in the open streets. Chevrolet were turning out a fully equipped car for £110 at the rate of 1,200 a day and were planning to make 2,500 a day in 1925. Ford made 4,200 a day. Austin was of the opinion that this success story was the result of the co-operation of work people who, although not such good mechanics as our own, worked about twice as hard.

No doubt, all this gave Austin even more confidence in the future success of the 7. He announced a reduction in the proposed price from £225 to £165. In 1923, 389,767 private cars were registered in Britain, and over 71,000 cars were produced, of which about 4,200 cars and chassis were exported. Against the small increase in home production, and more than doubled export figure over 1922, imports only increased from 20,000 to 22,000. Austin production more than doubled in the period from November 1922 to October 1923: 2,064 Austin 20s, 2,417 Austin 12s, and 1,936 Austin 7s were made over the twelve months. Morris, still Austin's major British competitor, also did very well, with a 1923 production of 20,048 cars. Of the Austin 12s 1,481 were tourers, 584 coupés and 97 landaulets. Only one small alteration was made to the range of four 12s and six 20s available for the early part of 1923 and that was with the introduction in March of the two/four seater special 12, which cost £480, £30 more than the standard two/four seater.

In 1921, an article appeared in the *Motor* entitled 'Are Modern Cars Built Backwards?', which considered the advantages to be gained from mounting the engine at the back of the chassis. This design, with a rear-mounted engine driving the rear wheels in the normal manner through the rear axle, was used in the German Rumpler and the North-Lucas Radial, neither of which had any great success. Austin toyed with the idea for some time, and early in 1923 took out a patent for a novel chassis layout. In this design, the engine was placed at the back of the chassis, thus providing more body space for a given chassis length than with the engine in the conventional place at the front, under a long bonnet.

As can be seen from the illustration, the vehicle was designed for closed or semi-closed bodywork as a taxicab. The engine was slung in the chassis by three-point suspension at the rear, with the engine flywheel at the forward end. Austin's design differed from other rear-engined cars of the time, and from all later developments of the idea, in that the drive of his car was to be taken through a long propeller-shaft to a combined gearbox and final drive to the front axle. This gearbox was attached rigidly to the chassis between the front wheels with two universally jointed shafts extending outwards, attached to the front wheel in such a way that the steering heads could be pivoted. For simplicity, a single transverse front spring with torque rods was used, but semi-elliptic springs were still fitted at the back. These features would have given a lower unsprung weight for each axle.

Perhaps the most important technical advance was the lack of gears between the driving shafts and the wheels, the method used being to provide the pivot pins with sleeves through which ran short driving shafts which were attached to the differential gear by universally jointed and telescopic members. Weight distribution would have been very good, with the variable load — the weight of the rear-seat passengers — at the centre of the car, reducing the variation in weight that had to be borne by the rear springs. Most of the other advantages that could be obtained by a rear engine with rear-wheel drive would have been nullified by taking the drive along to the front wheels, and no prototype was built to test the ideas and, other than a transverse front spring on the Austin 7, no more was heard of the patent. Had the advantages of front-wheel drive with an engine at the front been appreciated at the time, we might have seen an Austin Mini in 1923.

Austin 12 prices were reduced in September 1923, the chassis coming down to £340, the five-seater and two/four seater to £450, and the Harley coupé and Berkeley landaulet to £525. The earlier economy variants were removed, and all models now had spring gaiters, luggage carriers and clocks. A new four-door saloon was introduced at £550. These alterations

Patent chassis lay-out: rear engine, front-wheel drive

Suggestion for taxi cab for rear-engine car

lasted only for a few weeks, and then the pricing was again modified with the reintroduction of the standard tourers at £375, the specials at £395, and the chassis was reduced to £300. At least these prices bore a more realistic relation to the 7 and were more in line with the major competition. The Windsor saloon was first shown at the motor show at Olympia in October, and the Austin 20s were priced at £500 for the chassis, £625 for the tourer, £750 each for the all-weather five-seater and the landaulet, and £850 for the saloon.

Five hundred guests were present at the show dinner in November at which Sir Herbert presided. He received the customary ovation from his agents, and spoke for nearly fifty minutes. He said that despite the rapid expansion of the industry, and notwithstanding the repressive effect of heavy taxation, motor manufacturers had only scratched the surface of the possible market for their cars. He thought that some measure of safeguarding the industry would be essential, and that the time had come when many people would have to sink their personal ideas on such a political matter and consider how to alleviate the suffering caused by widespread unemployment. There was no reason why purchasers of motor cars had anything to fear from protection, and he instanced the magneto trade which, despite the fact that it was a protected industry, was selling its goods at prices very considerably below pre-war prices, and at the same time, users unquestionably were obtaining a thoroughly good article. He mentioned the big increase in our export trade in the month of September, and said that the Austin share of the output was 59 per cent.

7 To Merge or to Sell: 1924 and 1925

... my only concern is to put the British car manufacturer in a position to meet foreign competition which we have not up to the present time had any experience of.

Sir Herbert Austin, letter to Morris's accountant, June 1924

Almost as soon as it was introduced, the 7 began to achieve remarkable sporting successes. After a test run at the Easter Monday Brooklands meeting in March 1923, at which he won the small car handicap at 59.03mph, Captain Waite obtained permission to take his light two-seater fabric-bodied 7 to Italy. He won the 250km race for 750cc cars at the Italian Cycle-car Grand Prix at Monza on 29 April at an average of almost 57mph, beating E. Anzani's car with its overhead-valve engine. It was the first British car to win an event on the continent since the war, and caused much interest at the time; so much so that the newly formed British Broadcasting Company made an announcement about it over the air. Another light-car racer, E.C. Gordon England, talked Sir Herbert into providing him with a racing 7, which first appeared at the Brooklands Whitsun meeting achieving a lap speed of over 71mph. Austins produced two more racing cars for Waite's team and Sir Herbert, Waite and Lou Kings, Austin's chief tester, went to Boulogne in September 1923. The results were disastrous as all three cars broke down due to a faulty lubrication system which, although adequate for the engines under normal conditions, failed to meet the demands of continual running at 5,000rpm.

Gordon England had been working hard on his racer; with its tiny single-seat body the car weighed only 7.5cwt and he set out for Brooklands on 6 September to capture as many of the Class L records as he could. He covered 5 miles at 79.62mph, 100 miles at 64.79mph and in all set up six new records. Next, he built a two-seater body which weighed only 20lb — less than the weight of the filled fuel tank — and entered for the Junior Car Club 200 mile race at Brooklands on 13 October in the 1100cc class. To everyone's surprise, Gordon England's car finished in second place at an average speed of 76.84mph. Another five class records fell to the Austin 7 during the race.

Due to the remarkable success of the 7 as a racing car, two sports models were offered for sale in January 1924, the Sports and the Brooklands Super-sports. Appearance rather than performance was the main attraction of the former, which had a standard chassis except that the steering column was at a more raked angle, and the gear lever was slightly longer. Any increase in speed over the standard cars was gained by a slightly advanced ignition setting. These attractive kingfisher-blue cars weighed 8.5cwt and the first ones were sold in January 1924 at £175, only £10 more than the tourer. The Brooklands Super-sports were an entirely different proposition. The cars were replicas of Gordon England's record-breaker, and were much more expensive at £265, each car being sold with a Brooklands certificate proving a speed of 80mph. With the exception of an attractive little 2.5cwt van, a commercial traveller's car, an experimental single-passenger taxi and the two sports cars, no other Austin 7s were available in the early years. A few modifications to the chassis were introduced, and an electric starter was available as an alternative to the lawn-mower starting device, at £9 extra. Electric starters were fitted to all cars from January 1924. Early 1924 also saw a change in tax policy as it affected the motor industry. The McKenna duties of 33⅓ per cent on all imported private cars and motor-cycles, musical instruments, clocks and watches, and cinematograph films, which had been imposed in 1915, were always renewed by Parliament on 1 May and were regarded as provisional because they had been introduced as a temporary war tax. Philip Snowden, Chancellor in the first Labour Government, renewed them at the 1924 budget, but only until 1 August of that year. After that he proposed to allow them to expire. The yield from them since the war had varied from nearly £5 million to just under £1 million a year, and for the year from August 1924 a loss of £2½ million to the Treasury was estimated. Protected as they had been from at least some of the foreign competition, the motor trade went mad — so this was how the Labour Government was going to treat them! Sir Herbert blamed the Americans for the intense haste with which they had been trying to supply everybody with cars — good, bad or indifferent. He thought that they had just about come to the point where the market had got sick of the cheap runabout and instanced the fact that the Americans were finding now a serious sales resistance to it. All this from a man who had just succeeded in making the British public accept a very cheap car! What he, and many others at the time, failed to appreciate was that America had overcome the effect of the duties to some extent by building their most popular car, the Model T Ford, in their own factory at Manchester, the imposition of any restriction to competition being always met, after quite a short period, by trading methods which reset the balance again. The truth was that America benefited from economies of scale; we were just starting to build up a sufficient demand to do this ourselves, but British manufacturers were slow to gain all the advantages open to them.

This is not to imply that the removal of the McKenna duties had no effect on British industry — it did. Imports of completed cars and chassis, at about 20,000 in 1922 and 22,000 in 1923, were about one-third the size of British car production. In 1924, British production rose appreciably, and imports fell to 18,000 or about one-sixth. With an increase in British exports, from the minimal 2,000 and 4,000 in 1922 and 1923, to a considerable 12,500 in 1924, the Chancellor's decision seems to have had the least possible effect on the motor industry. Exports in 1925 nearly doubled to 22,700, and British cars seemed to have established good markets abroad at about 15 to 20 per cent of production. With exports approaching imports, as in 1924, a time would soon come when the balance would be favourable. In 1925, however, even though the industry produced 132,000 cars, the demand for them was also increasing at a very healthy rate, and the disastrous effect of the removal of import restrictions was to push imports from 18,000 in 1924 to, in the following year, the highest figure of the 1920s — 41,000. This was unacceptable to both industry and government, and the McKenna duties were reimposed in July 1925. The effect was interesting, as we shall see, for it made General Motors look for production capacity in this country and to bid for Austin, and eventually to buy Vauxhall Motors.

To return to 1924; 482,356 cars were registered in Britain in that year, 100,000 more than in 1923. Production had increased by about 63 per cent to 116,600, with Morris at the top of the league with a huge production of nearly 33,000 cars; Austin was increasing production at a much slower pace, with only 9,673 cars. The 7.was at the top at 4,700, followed closely by the increasingly popular 12 at 4,000 while the 20, in line with all the other large cars, was decreasing in popularity with only 973 sold. Growth was at the middle and bottom ends of the market; petrol was only about 1s 7d a gallon, so the new motorists did not worry so much about fuel costs, but taxation was still based on a charge relating to hp and the wide difference in initial costs decreased the demand for large cars in this country. At the end of

1922, the average tax paid on a hp basis was £17 12s, by the end of 1923 it had fallen to £16 18s 6d, and to £16 by December 1924, largely because cars taxed had risen in the last 9 months of the period from 382,000 to 473,000 and much of the growth was in the lower hp classes. Sir Herbert proposed a new formula for taxation which took into account the cylinder swept volume, rather than the bore size only, which penalised engines with a high stroke-to-bore ratio. His system was simple. He took the swept volume of the cylinders, in cubic inches, and divided by 10, and this figure would be the unit of taxation, giving the Austin 20 a rating of 22 against the RAC 23; the 12, 10 against 13; and the 7 would become the car to gain the most from his proposal dropping from an RAC 8 to an Austin 4, halving the annual tax to £4. There is no doubt that his method was more logical, but in the light of a decline in the annual average tax and an increase in the number of cars that would benefit most, it is not surprising that the Minister of Transport declared that he would not consider any scheme which reduced revenue, and that reimposition of petrol tax was out of the question.

In 1924 great efforts were put into export trade. It cannot have been easy for the industry to raise its 1923 export total of only about 4,200 to some 12,500 in the following year. Much of this growth went to the Colonies, particularly of larger cars. In Australia for instance, an Austin 20 could be bought at the same price as in England but, on the other hand, American cars were so firmly established in New Zealand that our products had very little hope of success. The Austin 12, at £375 here, sold for £465 in that country and an American Essex 6 cost only £375; every attempt had been made to sell 12s over there, but the odds were against success. Small, cheap British cars were not yet acceptable in the Colonies; this was to come later.

In advance of the 1924 Motor Show, some minor alterations were made to the 7. Wider doors, a larger rear compartment and a higher raised hood-line helped to provide more space for passengers but, apart from adding a speedometer, an oil-pressure indicator button and improved instrumentation, it says much for the completeness of the original design that after some 4,500 cars had been sold, only relatively minor changes were found necessary, and these were more to enhance the specification rather than to correct inherent design faults. The most important alteration to the design of the 12 and the 20 was the adoption of front-wheel brakes, and shock absorbers (then called friction dampers) attached to each spring. Austin's four-wheel brake system was very simple and avoided some of the more complicated front-brake devices, and although the 12 and the 20 were never famous for braking efficiency, at least the new system was smooth in operation, and gave a distinct advantage over the puny rear-wheel brakes. All four brakes were coupled to the foot pedal, which had a combined adjuster to take up lining wear and cable stretch close to the foot pedal; the hand brake still applied two large contracting shoes to a drum attached to the propeller shaft, and must have been the best hand brake on any car of the 1920s.

Price reductions were announced in 1925. The 7 went down £10 to £155, with a further slight reduction in February to £149, which compared favourably with the prices of other similar cars — the 7.5hp Mathis was £150, the 10hp Salmson £158, the Citroën £145, and the Jowett £150 — and the Austin 7 still had the advantage over them all because they were only two-seaters. Not everyone however agreed that the 7 was capable of taking, in any sort of comfort, the five people claimed for the 1925 model with the larger body. After agreeing that it was a remarkable car, the correspondent of *Sporting Life*'s Christmas 1924 issue went on to say:

> I must however, criticise the attempt to suggest that it is a four seater, because it is nothing of the kind, and only very easy-going people, quite unaccustomed to motoring and motor cars, will be willing to regard it as a three seater for three grown-ups. Call it a two seater with a useful space for luggage behind the two seats and all is well. Used as such it is a most efficient and satisfactory little car but if one wants to give comfortable seating for more than one companion — well. I give it up, unless he happens to be Little Tich!

The 12 chassis was reduced by £30 to £270, the tourer and two/four seater by £20 to £355, and the new Windsor saloon by £75 to £475. Berkeley landaulets and Harley all-weathers were still listed, but reduced by £50 to £475; only fifty Harleys were made in 1924 and none in 1925, and the Berkeley was sold at about the same rate in 1924 and in 1925, when it was withdrawn. Demand for enclosed cars was taken up by the Windsor saloon; in its first year, 1924, 550 were made, rising to 2,500 in the following twelve months. It is interesting to see how the saloon style of body became increasingly popular at the expense of the open touring car in the 1920s; 550 saloons compared with 2,950 tourers in 1924 had risen to 5,000 saloons against 8,000 tourers in 1927, and by 1928 more saloons were made than open cars, with more than three saloons to every tourer by 1930. By 1932, the Austin 12 open car had become a rarity. Austin 20s were in a falling market, down to less than 1,000 in 1924, and even fewer in 1925, although there was a considerable increase later. They were still quite expensive. Prices were reduced for 1925; the chassis down £105 to £395, the tourer

Interior division, Twenty saloon

down £100 to £525, the new Carlton saloon — an overgrown Windsor — was £675, the old Marlborough landaulet was still listed at £675, and the Mayfair landaulets and limousines at £795.

Financially, the recovery of the company could not take place until production was at least twice the level of the 10,000 achieved in 1924, but there were signs of improvement in the accounts for that year. The following table summarises the company's finances since 1916:

	Net Profit	Pref Div	Ord Div	%	To Reserve	Other Allocations	Carried Forward
1916	227,177	17,498	40,000	10	-	-	176,125
1917	262,642	17,500	40,000	10	-	-	380,267
1918	358,272	18,958	65,000	15	43,500	20,000	591,081
1919	237,866	66,648	200,000	50*	425,000	123,000	13,995
1920-1	Dr 2,333,846	38,750	-		-	-	Dr 1,883,601
1922	18,564	-	-		Dr 60,000	-	Dr 1,805,037
30 Sept 1923	176,334	-	-		Dr 29,125	-	Dr 1,599,578
1924	161,174	-	-		-	-	Dr 1,438,404

* Paid in ordinary shares

Arrangements to settle the debts were held up for some time. Austins looked viable at last. Although it might not appear so from the above table, factors outlined already showed that it was going to be a very successful firm.

In 1924 there was negotiation between the Austin and Morris companies. Sir Herbert Austin and William Morris did not like each other very much. They were both products of the late Victorian era, and 'captains of industry', but there the similarity ended except, perhaps, in that they were both obstinate. Austin was an engineer, but not a financier in the expansionist sense; Morris was neither an engineer nor such a financier. Austin wanted to stay in business and was not bothered about wealth because he loved engineering more than money. Morris did not bother about engineering at all, but he wanted to make as much money as he could. He had no wish to extend his business just for the sake of extending it, and did not believe in mergers. Any growth had to be within his organisation, or as a direct result of what was happening in it; there was no place for any unnecessary additions. He feared, too, that someone else might wish to control him if he agreed to a merger. On reflection, it is hard to see how he and Austin could have worked together as joint owners of Austin-Morris-Wolseley, but Sir Herbert certainly wanted to set up that great corporation in 1924. Had it happened it would have created a company that, by sheer size, would have swamped any competition, and could well have given Britain a concern large enough to have beaten Volkswagen, Ford and the French.

Sir Herbert arranged a meeting with Morris and Dudley Docker of Vickers, which still owned Wolseley, in London in late May 1924. It was only a short meeting, and although Austin and Docker were anxious for the merger, Morris was not so keen, but he did agree to allow his accountant Thornton to study the proposals. Austin wanted the new combine's headquarters to be at Longbridge, but agreed that the manufacturing operations would be decentralised and under local management. Wolseley and Austin would have had a greater share after the capital reconstruction, and this would have given them a higher proportion than their current earnings warranted. Morris was making profits that were three times greater than Austin, and Wolseley was to make a loss of £21,000 in 1924 rising to £189,000 in the following year, with a debit balance of £1 million. It is not surprising, therefore, that the scheme contained little to attract Morris. Thornton wrote to Austin on 15 June saying that Morris felt that:

> ... his business is entirely his own, to make or break, to mar or improve, and he does not feel that he can give up this position of freedom to share, even with yourself and others, the responsibility which he would have to members of the public, if he joined in an amalgamation of the kind suggested ... apart from the above-mentioned considerations, which are the real reasons for his being unable to go on with the matter, he feels that there would be considerable risks in amalgamating two such successful businesses, even with the admirable plant which would be provided by the Wolseley Company, for the organisation would be so great that it would be difficult to control and might tend to strangle itself.

Austin hastened to reassure Morris about control and in his reply said:

> ... while I appreciate his reluctance to give up the freedom of sole ownership, it has always appeared to me that the future so far as he personally is concerned is so fraught with possibilities in both directions that the proposed amalgamation would be more in his interest than the other companies' ... Under the rough suggestion of figures I forwarded to you, Mr Morris would have control of all the share capital and would virtually be in command of a concern capable of meeting any competition likely to be met in the near future, and at the same time remove the two most formidable interests he will naturally have to deal with of the home manufacturers ...

Morris had a firm aversion to being responsible for other people's money and this, as in all other similar negotiations, was the stumbling block. The two men met in 1926 when, together with an American buyer, they bid for the Wolseley company from the receiver. Morris opened with an offer of £600,000, the Americans withdrew, and an auction between Austin and Morris followed. E.L. Payton, who was acting on Austin's behalf, asked Morris privately how much further he was prepared to go and got the answer, 'I am going just a bit further than you.' He did, and bought Wolseley Motors for £730,000.

Sir Herbert was still on the look-out for another way to reorganise his company. There was to be no merger with Morris, so perhaps someone would take over and buy some of his problems. General Motors, the American giant, needed a manufacturing base in Britain, where they saw good long-term prospects but no hope of large immediate gains. In a growing market likely to be dominated by Austin and Morris, and little hope of exporting large American cars into Britain, even if the McKenna duties were not reinstated, Austin seemed the most likely prospect, particularly as Longbridge was a complete factory and not, like Morris at Cowley, an assembler of bought-out parts. Mr Mooney, vice president in charge of General Motors export companies inspected Longbridge in the spring of 1925, and recommended that they should arrange to purchase the Austin company. In July, with three other officials, he returned to Longbridge and reported that he thought General Motors could buy Austin for £1 million, leaving outstanding over £1½ million cumulative preferred stock requiring a dividend of £133,000 per annum. General Motors thought they would be able to earn at least 20 per cent on the investment, and worked out a conservative estimate, after liabilities, of net assets valued at £2.6 million. Their finance committee met and approved the recommendation. Negotiations took place, but the deal was never consummated, largely because agreement could not be reached over the way in which the Austin assets were valued. General Motors withdrew the offer. Sir Herbert made no public announcement about the merger until October when, at the Austin agents' dinner at the Connaught Rooms in London, he said:

One of my friends in the Press facetiously asked why I hadn't married the American lass — well her dowry was quite substantial, but my relations did not like her, and therefore the engagement had to be broken off. I thought it would be safer for me to marry her than someone else, also that co-operation would have been better than competition. The future might prove I was right, but as the scheme has been abandoned, I have resolved to do everything humanly possible to prove I was wrong.

Neal, Ash and Payton were the three directors who disagreed with Austin and the rest of the board as they considered the American offer 'quite inadequate and the terms of the reorganisation of the capital unsatisfactory'. Had any proposals gone before the shareholders, the trio would have issued a statement recommending them not to accept the terms of the merger.

On reflection, Alfred P. Sloan, vice president of General Motors, was relieved as he felt that Austin's plant was in poor condition and its management was weak. Soon after the deal had fallen through they bought Vauxhall Motors, in the latter part of 1925, for $2½ million. This was a much smaller firm producing only some 1,500 expensive cars each year but, although it lost money to start with, proved quite useful to the corporation and gave them valuable experience in expanding into Europe. Without the support and direction of General Motors, Vauxhall would certainly not have survived for very long and may just have managed to struggle into the 1950s. And in spite of Vauxhall's very slow rate of production and poor labour relations today, General Motors seems content to allow it to continue under its own name as an outlet in Britain for the American firm's European cars.

Whilst all this negotiating was going on, the only people to benefit were shareholders and speculators — Austin ordinary shares rose from 5s 9d to 8s 7d, 7 per cent preference shares from 12s 6d to 17s 6d, and the 6 per cent preference from 8s 6d to 13s 9d. Even the debentures rose to £93.5 on the rumours.

One new Austin company did emerge in 1925. Austin had bought Walker

Horrocks & Co Ltd, lighting-plant manufacturers, in October 1915 for £3,500 to obtain three of their patents, applied for in 1909, for the generation and storage of electrical power for house lighting. The Austin lighting plants sold in large numbers from 1916 to 1925, and in January 1925 the business was taken over by a new firm, the Austin Electric Co Ltd which was to develop the sales of automatic and semi-automatic house and village lighting plants. The new company was jointly owned by Austins, British Thompson-Houston Co Ltd, Callenders Cable & Construction Co Ltd, Mirrlees, Bickerton & Day Ltd and R.B. Matthews. It was registered as a private company on 19 February 1925, with a capital of £50,000 in £1 shares, directors being Sir Herbert and senior representatives of the other companies. R.B. Matthews was a consulting engineer who was entitled to a place on the board for as long as he held 500 shares, and the managing director was C.B. Walker, an electrical engineer. Austin's interest was in supplying static Austin 7 engines to replace the old pre-war engines that had been used in the Austin plants since 1915.

In February 1925, Austin said that he was convinced that Britain was on the eve of a considerable increase and improvement in trade generally, and that the building of motor vehicles would be one of the industries that would feel the good effect of the confidence now returning to the country. The number of cars in use was rising steadily at some 100,000 a year. With 590,000 cars registered in 1925, UK production was at 132,000. The export of cars and chassis stood at 22,700 against the previous year's figure of 12,500. Removal of the McKenna duties had lifted imports to a massive figure of 40,800 but, as mentioned above, this was only a temporary setback. Morris was still the major producer with over 53,000 cars, but Austin had done very well with 1925 production, up from 9,673 in the previous year, to 16,429. Of this total, 7,043 were 7s, 8,500 were 12s and the 20 still falling off at 886. When he introduced the 7, Austin had said that it would 'knock the motor cycle and sidecar into a cocked hat' and signs of this were seen in 1924 when, for the first time, more cars were registered than motor cycles; and the proportion of motor cycles was to go on decreasing throughout the 1920s. During 1925, the British motor industry built 28,000 cars rated at 10hp and below — more than a quarter of them were Austin 7s.

Racing and sporting successes with the 7 continued in 1925. Gordon England held no less than nineteen 750cc class records, including 100 miles at 80.72mph, and a fastest lap time at 84.10mph, which prompted Waite to set out to achieve a new goal — to obtain 100mph from a 750cc car. The only way to do it was to use a supercharger, which raised the engine power from 25 to 43bhp. In April, he covered a flying start mile at 92.44mph, proving that a supercharged 7 was a practical proposition, although the company found that it was extremely difficult to get that extra 8mph to reach the coveted 100.

With the Austin 7 at £149 in 1925, the magic £100 car began to look like being a distinct possibility. It was not to come just yet, but there were signs of the beginning of a price war. Rumours, strongly denied, of a 5hp Austin at a very low price showed how the press expected the £100 car to be achieved, but in the event it was to be done by increased and more efficient production and by hectic competition. For the 1926 season, a number of price reductions were announced in September: a Morris Cowley could be bought for £182 10s, against £195; the Oxford was reduced by £25 to £260; the Clyno from £195 to £182 10s; and the Bean 14 — a sluggish cast-iron monster — from £525 to £450, and even at that price it is doubtful if many were sold. Some minor alterations were made to the Austin range, the 7 now having a speedometer and a horn button on the steering column; the 12 and the 20 had an electric-horn ring on the steering wheel, which became a nuisance after a time because it vibrated and rattled; and the new 20 Open Road tourer coachwork was introduced. Austin 12 doors were widened and the tourer was christened the Clifton, the two/four seater the Hertford, and there were two new saloons with divisions and fixed front seats — the Ascot on the 20 chassis and the Iver on the 12. Prices were £675 and £470. The 20 tourer was reduced by £30 to £495, the new Open Road tourer was £525, the Carlton was down £25 to £650; Cliftons and Hertfords were reduced by £5 to £350 and shortly after there was a further surprise reduction of another £10. A good quality saloon with coachwork by Mulliner was also introduced at £395, and there was an expensive and quite luxurious Gordon saloon at £455. All cars could be provided with the new balloon tyres which were just about to replace the high-pressure beaded-edge tyres of the day, which were retained on the rim by air pressure which forced beads on the tyre into curved slots in the rim. Wired-on tyres with rims having a deep well could be operated on about half the pressure and 20psi against 40 or more not only gave a more comfortable ride, but also burst with much less violence. A blow-out on a beaded edge tyre at 50mph could be very spectacular! A further price reduction was made in November 1925, this time to all the Austin 20 models, varying from £20 off the tourer to £80 off the Mayfair. These new prices made the 20 a much more competitive car, and led to a tenfold increase in sales in 1926.

Attempts at a merger and at a sale to the Americans having failed, something had to be done about the company's debts. Austin was not the only firm to have suffered as a result of the war and the slump that followed the boom of 1920. At the end of 1925 Vickers wrote down assets by £12½ million, Dunlop was £10½ million in debt, Crosse & Blackwell £4.6 million, British Dyestuffs £2.8 million, and Sheffield Steel £2 million, all more than Austin's not inconsiderable debt of £1,397,909.

The year ending September 1925 showed a gross trading profit of £748,890 which, after maintenance and depreciation charges, resulted in a profit before charging interest and redemption premium of £520,677, the debit balance being reduced to less than £2 million. With assets worth over £3 million, a bright year forecast for the motor industry, and three excellent cars at competitive prices, all was set for a highly successful 1926 for Austins. In the words of the catchy advertising slogan of the 1920s, it looked as if many more people were going to 'Buy an Austin and Banish Care'. It was not quite so bright for the shareholders; they still had to pay for the capital reconstruction.

8 The Six-cylinder Car: 1926 and 1927

We have not introduced the six-cylinder car for a mere whim or fancy. It was the result of the public's continual demand for increased refinement and luxury.

Sir Herbert Austin, Motor Show dinner, 25 October 1926

Car prices continued to fall throughout 1926, the 12 was becoming more popular, but the price had to be brought down more into line with the major competition. This was done from 1 March 1926, the tourer being reduced by £45 to £295, the Windsor and Iver saloons went down to £395 and £405, the Hertford to £315, the Gordon saloon, Berkeley landaulet and Harley coupé to £425, and the cheaper Mulliner saloon to £365. For the 12 and 20 models, there was a choice of four colours, royal blue, kingfisher blue, elephant grey and nigger brown, with either leather or Bedford cord upholstery. Lamps were either black or nickel-plated.

During 1926, 695,555 private cars were registered in Britain, 100,000 more than in 1925, equal to the steady rise that there had been in each year since 1923. UK car production increased slightly to 153,500, much of which came from Morris, who sold 48,330 cars in 1926. His firm became a private company as Morris Motors (1926) Limited with an issued capital of £5 million in £1 shares, being the largest share capital of any British motor manufacturer. Austins were second, Sunbeam-Talbot-Darracq a close third, but apart from them there were only two others with more than £1 million capital — Crossley and Rover — although Napier and Rolls-Royce came close to that figure. Humber, Standard and Swift were the only other companies with capital even approaching that of the giants. Vauxhall and Ford were both American owned, and Clyno and Bean, although quite large in terms of cars produced, had much smaller resources. British car exports for 1926 were maintained at approximately 25,000, and imports were well down at 16,000 following the reimposition of the McKenna duties. Austin production, although only at half the Morris level, continued

103

to increase to reach 24,900, about 14,000 of which were 7s, 10,000 were 12s and 900 were 20s. A very satisfactory figure in view of the General Strike and the coal strike which, after 8 weeks, reduced coal stocks leading to the closure of steel works and a 2 day week at Longbridge. The Midland's pits closed when 60,000 men were locked out in May and June, and money was collected in Birmingham factories to buy milk for miners' families; in one week the 8,000 workers at Longbridge gave £16 to the fund, which showed that there was not much sympathy amongst Austin workers for a group which reduced their wages to about £1 a week.

Late in 1925, reorganisation had begun at Austins, largely under the aegis of C.R.F.Englebach. The latter first became involved with the motor industry in 1900 when he joined Armstrong Whitworth who were then making the Rootes Venables paraffin-engine car at Scotswood-on-Tyne. He was works manager when they made Wilson & Pilcher cars from 1904-6, and built a special factory to make the 30hp Armstrong Whitworth cars, continuing to produce smaller examples of that make until 1914 when he was called up for service in the RNVR. After a year, he was brought ashore to take over the 4.7in howitzer department at the Coventry ordnance works where he remained until the end of the war. After a spell as general manager of a component supplier in London, he joined Austin as works director in 1922. He was a brilliant production engineer, amongst the finest in Britain, and his considerable reorganisation of the factory during the winter of 1925-6 soon began to take effect. The 1,500 machine tools were moved to new positions and many time-saving devices such as lifts and conveyors were installed. The principle was to machine each main component, and then to assemble it under the same superintendent in the same shop. Assembled components were then conveyed to the appropriate point in the chassis-erecting track along which the car was moving. Gearbox assembly was tackled first, followed by back axles and engines, with a row of test cubicles in a line parallel with the chassis-assembly track. Completed engines were tested in the cubicles, and then run out to the track for mounting into the chassis. Chassis were driven under their own power to the body shops in the West works.

Body building was also carried out on series-production lines. Jigs were used for the wooden and steel parts so that no hand chiselling was required for correct assembly. At the end of the body track, the completed body with its windscreen and all fittings was lifted by slings to an overhead runway to the mounting shop where it met the correct chassis. When chassis and body were bolted together, the car was driven out for a road test, after which it went to the finishing department for the final parts to be fitted. Coach paint had been applied by spray at Longbridge since 1919, but a gradual changeover to cellulose took place early in 1926. This was much more durable than the soft, porous coach paint and was used as a body finish almost exclusively in the motor industry for more than forty years.

A system of payment by results had already been established at Longbridge. Overtime working was discouraged and a standard 47 hour week — which was the standard for all manual workers at the time — was worked, in shifts in those parts of the factory which had to operate on a 24 hour basis. Austin always regarded overtime as a waste of money, and felt that it was much better, both for the production worker and for the company, for a man to work for only 5½ days a week. During that time he could be expected to work at his full capacity. Overtime was expensive, as the rate was 1¼ or 1½ the standard time, and a man could not give of his best in a production-line environment for more than about 47 hours a week.

Workers' interest in a company could best be aroused if it could be bound up with that of the business in such a way that the result of increased effort was immediately apparent. There was little hope of achieving this by paying a monthly or yearly bonus out of profits; it had to be clearly reflected in the weekly pay packet directly after the effort had been made, with a statement showing the cause. At Austins every employee knew exactly what he was expected to do as his contribution towards the success of the firm, and his reward for what he had done came in extra cash quickly enough for him to remember how he had earned it. Payment was on the basis of time saved, with a fixed basic allowance as the factor for comparison.

In order to fix the rate, a member of the planning department went into the shop concerned and chose what was called a 'moderate' worker, not only moderate in his speed of working but possibly also of moderate temperament, and his time for the job was recorded. This became the fixed-time rate for the job. The basic union trade rate was guaranteed, but every worker was expected to reach double the top rate, and if he could not do so he was regarded as useless to the company. Every effort was made to press the men into earning at least £4 for the 47 hour week. The earnings of each operative were recorded and the extra-efficient were entitled to an additional 'merit bonus'. There was a 30 per cent reduction in scrap and 37 per cent in small machine-tool replacements, since a man would not scrap or break a tool if he could possibly help it, because time — valuable money-making time — was lost and the equivalent cash missing from his next pay packet. High earnings were encouraged and expected and the amounts were, in theory, unlimited.

The system worked. Wages at Longbridge were high, output was good and relations between staff and management amongst the best in the country. After the adoption of the system, output increased by 52 per cent, the production cost was reduced by 38 per cent, total labour charges increased by 65 per cent and average individual wages and company profits doubled.

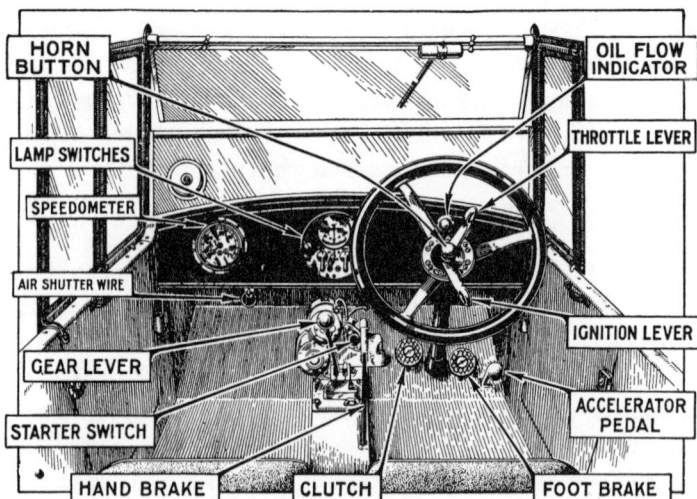

HORN BUTTON · OIL FLOW INDICATOR · LAMP SWITCHES · THROTTLE LEVER · SPEEDOMETER · AIR SHUTTER WIRE · IGNITION LEVER · GEAR LEVER · ACCELERATOR PEDAL · STARTER SWITCH · HAND BRAKE · CLUTCH · FOOT BRAKE

The 1927 Seven, from the driver's seat

From October 1926, for the 1927 season, no fundamental changes were to be made in the 7's design. The brakes were improved by increasing the drum diameter; the lamps were moved to a forward position between the mudguards and radiator, although they had to be moved back to the original place at the end of the year because they did not comply with the legal requirement; the bonnet was provided with a central hinge; a windscreen wiper and licence holder were supplied as standard fittings and the price was reduced by £4 to £145. The chassis was £112 and the new Austin 7 saloon, which was produced as a result of the great success of the Gordon England saloon, cost £165, although first listed at £169. Gordon England's little fabric saloon, said to have been the smallest enclosed car in the world, was fitted with a body which weighed 28lb less than that of the standard tourer, and at £210 had shown that there was a steady demand for

106

an enclosed Austin 7. A coachbuilt saloon body would have been far too heavy for the early Austin 7 chassis, and the Gordon England design was conceived to overcome the problem of excessive weight. But fabric bodies, developed from principles used in the aircraft industry, had a number of disadvantages when applied to motor cars, and Gordon England spent four years in developing a technique of construction which made his saloons better than many of the patented fabric bodies of the time. He used a solid plywood shell, and not a flexible skeletal frame of the type used in Weymann fabric-body framework designs. A hollow box-girder of plywood around the base of the body was attached to the frame at three points, with the instrument panel, seats and floor boards mounted independently on the chassis. This allowed the body to become an umbrella resting on the chassis by three-point suspension, and to maintain its rigidity and shape, even when the chassis was disturbed by being driven over rough roads.

Gordon England gave up racing his 200 miles' race car after 1926, but examples of the model still won races at Brooklands at 72 and 73mph. In his last 200, which he won at 58.28mph, the car used only half a pint of oil and averaged more than 33mpg. Waite held thirteen International class H records at the end of 1926 from 1 hour at 83.66mph to the 1 mile flying start at 84.29mph.

Although the 7 was unique, there were a number of other cheap cars on the market. Fords were still cheaper than the Austin at only £125, and a Morris could be bought for £148 10s, but the Ford did only 25mpg with an annual tax of £23, and even the Morris could not better 25mpg and its tax was £12. They were, therefore, in competition more with the 12 and the 20 than with the 7. This was not the case with the Trojan at £145 which, though it could only be coaxed to give a maximum speed of 36mph, could be had at even less than this price with solid tyres. The flat twin Jowett was £139, the Citroën £135; the 11hp Clyno two-seater was £160, and more serious competition was likely to come from the new Singer Junior at £148 10s. There was great interest shown in the first two cars to be offered, briefly, at £100 — the magic figure that was to become a reality in the 1930s. One was the Waverley with a rear-mounted flat twin engine and friction drive, which could be bought for £100 without a starter, spare wheel or speedometer for which essential components a further £17 10s was charged. It was a disaster, having all the worst features of the cycle cars of 1919. Waverley continued to make cars for the rest of the decade but this effort only appeared in their catalogues for 1926. The other was more conventional, the British Ensign 8hp four-cylinder Gillett. It is doubtful if more than a

The 1926 Chummy

few were built, let alone sold, and the company went out of business shortly after 1926.

Quite substantial reductions were made to the 12 and 20 prices for 1927. The 12 chassis was down £20 to £225, the tourer was £275, the Windsor saloon £350, the Gordon saloon and landaulet £395, and the cheaper Mulliner saloon cost £325. The 20 chassis dropped £45 to £350, the tourer £25 to £450, and the most expensive model remained the Mayfair limousine or landaulet at £650. Over the twelve months since the previous Motor Show, a 12 Windsor saloon had been reduced from £455 to £350 and a 20 Carlton saloon from £650 to £550. Improved production methods had helped to bring down prices to combat competition from firms like Morris and Clyno, who were selling a 12hp saloon for £250; but it was also the increasing success of the 7 that helped Austin to bring down the prices of the 12 and the 20 without a reduction in quality. Reductions were being made in the price of tyres at the same time; Dunlop, Michelin and Goodyear reduced their prices by 15 per cent in October, saving £2 on an Austin 7 and over £4 on the 12.

At the Motor Show in October 1926 a new six-cylinder Austin was announced. It had a large 3.4 litre engine with a bore and stroke of 79.5 x 114.5mm; the chassis alone cost £450, and the luxurious Ranelagh limousine, the sole model, £775. Only one of these cars seems to have been made in 1926, and that was used as a demonstration car and shown at the Paris salon and at Olympia. The outstanding trend at the 1926 Paris salon was the increase in the number of such new six-cylinder cars. About twenty-five firms exhibited them including Renault, Berliet and Donnet-Zedel, and they had been introduced primarily by the French to meet American competition in foreign rather than home markets. At Olympia there were no less than twenty new 6s, of which twelve were British.

Austin had not made a six-cylinder engine since before the war; his reason for doing so in 1926, apart from following a fashion, was his 'desire to produce a vehicle of exceptional smoothness of running and capable of carrying a body of more than ordinary capacity'. His new six-cylinder 20 certainly met his aims, but at £775 it could never become a popular mass-production car, and although over 1,100 were made in 1929 only about 7,000 were made in the twelve years that it was available. Like all other previous Austin 6s, all that was necessary to give the added smoothness to the engine was to stick two more cylinders on to the four-cylinder car. One of the problems when this was done, was to increase the length of the engine which meant either a reduction in the body space available or a chassis with a longer wheelbase. In Austin's new design, the engine length was reduced as much as possible by moving the timing gears from the front to the back, which enabled the cylinder block to be placed fairly far forward in the frame. This resulted in a wheelbase of 11ft 4in, only 6in longer than that used on the four-cylinder 20. The six cylinders were cast in a block with a detachable head, bolted to a webbed-aluminium crankcase to support the eight bearings for the crankshaft. A sprocket for the chaindrive to the camshaft was located between bearings 7 and 8. The four-speed gearbox was operated on a ball instead of through the conventional Austin quadrant; final drive ratio in top was 4.6:1, well suited to the power and flexibility of the new engine. All other features were common to both Austin 20 models.

Construction of the spacious saloon body was based upon the metal system which was adopted by Austins on the 12 and 20 cars in 1926. Of the three styles of coachwork — timber-clad with steel panels, fabric on timber, or pressed all-steel construction — the last had the greatest potential. It was cheaper to produce, and more robust; the metal could be formed to give a less square outline, and it was felt by Austin that 'rag' or fabric bodies were a passing fancy for, although they were very light, they rotted and rattled to pieces very quickly. Austin's metal body was designed with a steel side-frame base piece consisting of two parts and the components — steel flitch plates, angle pieces, centre-channel pieces, steel door pillars, seat supports, wheel arches, and stiffening brackets and plates — were all spot-welded or riveted. Three steel-channel cross-members were riveted to the frame, and the whole made a foundation framing of exceptional strength. Seat supports were bound securely to the side panels carrying the wheel arches and the lower portion of the rear panel. The side panels in their turn were riveted to plates and the rear pillar. Door pillars were of angle and T section rolled

The 1926 Twenty Carlton

steel, and on the saloon models these uprights supported the roof and carried the doors and door struts. By enabling a reduction to be made in the size of the pillars, the scope of vision of driver and passenger was increased. Since the large shaped panels of metal were either riveted, bolted or welded, the whole treatment gave maximum strength to withstand the strains of hard driving over rough roads.

To remain competitive, a new engine was designed for the Austin 12. Known as the long-stroke engine it increased bhp at 2,000rpm to 27 by increasing the stroke from 102mm to 114.5mm and the capacity from 1,661 to 1,861cc, without raising the RAC hp rating on which the tax rate was calculated. Surprisingly, no mention of this increase in capacity was made at the time or commented on by the press although, in conjunction with the price reduction, getting more car for less money should have been a feature in Austin advertising. When the *Autocar* did review it in March 1927 they stated, incorrectly, that the stroke had been increased from 114.5 to 120mm, giving the engine a capacity of 1,954cc.

One or two other changes were made at this time, when the car number prefix was changed to 4T. A 12V electrical system replaced the previous inadequate 6V single battery, an additional battery being housed beneath the floor of the rear section. There was a longer radiator to deal with the increased cooling needed by the larger engine and the bottom of the windscreen was curved, which took from the car some of its old charm in appearance, although the attractive curved-edge doors with their loop handles remained for a little longer.

Austin introduced one other novel feature into the motor trade in 1926 — lists of standard repair charges. He considered that a motorist was entitled to know exactly how he stood in the matter of what constituted fair and reasonable labour charges for any car repairs or adjustments. Austin dealers welcomed the move, as the majority of owners were more likely to have repair work and regular services carried out if they knew exactly what the cost would be. The most expensive job listed at the time was for the removal and complete overhaul of an Austin 20 engine at £17 10s!

Sir Herbert expected a good year in 1927. As he said: 'Still I believe we shall find 1927 better than 1926 for industry and commerce, principally because the various trade unions have dissipated their funds and have no money left to enter upon vexatious disputes or propaganda.'

Full accounts for the year ending 30 September 1926 were not published until January 1927, showing a gross profit of £648,415 — £100,000 less than in the previous year — leaving a net profit of £330,508 which reduced the company's debit balance to £1,386,938.

In 1927, the steady increase in cars registered in Britain continued; over 100,000 more were added to bring the total to 800,112. As many as 164,553 cars were produced; 61,632 were made by Morris and Austin produced about 37,500. Of these, the 7 accounted for the very respectable total of 22,500, 14,000 were 12s and 1,000 were 20s. Car and chassis exports rose slightly to 27,500, and imports jumped from 16,000 in the previous year to 25,000.

Britain found it difficult to develop her motor export trade in the 1920s; her products were too expensive, and discounts offered to dealers could not meet that offered by competitors. Even in the Colonies, where one would have expected preference, the situation was unsatisfactory. Only about 20 per cent of the cars imported into Australia were made in Britain, and in Ceylon in 1926 only a quarter of cars registered were British. In both these areas the Americans predominated. There is no doubt that we were not particularly good at selling cars abroad, but other countries had import restrictions — just as we still maintained our McKenna duties — and here at home there were high delivery charges and a need to give discounts in excess of the 20 per cent normally given to the motor trade. In some countries, dealers were offered 50 per cent of the sale price, and with such high margins some absurd trading took place amongst which were very high trade-in prices for old cars. British methods could not adjust easily to such trading, but there was an alternative. Ford had overcome the problem by setting up a manufacturing plant in Britain. No British motor manufacturer could afford to do this in another country, but it was possible to induce foreign firms to build British cars themselves under licence. Citroën had already tried with some success in Germany, the result being the Opel, built at Cologne on the lines of the well-known French car.

In February 1927 an agreement was concluded with Gotha Waggonfabrik of Eisenach to make and sell the Austin 7 under licence in Germany and eastern Europe as the Dixi. Herr Chiraupo, a German financier, was involved in a merger of a number of German companies, and one of the firms owned a large derelict munitions factory which it was decided to use for the production of motor cycles. Later, it was felt that there would be scope for a small car in Germany, so Chiraupo came to an agreement with Sir Herbert to manufacture the 7 under licence for a royalty of 2 per cent. German materials and labour were to be used, and the cars would be sold only in Germany and eastern Europe at a price to be determined by the manufacturers. By 1928, the 3/15 Dixi was being produced at the rate of 50 a day, at a selling price of just under £130, and the old Dixi Werke company was absorbed into Bayerische Motorenwerke (BMW), by which time 6,000 Dixis had been sold. Austin received his 2 per cent fee, which was divided equally between himself and the company — nearly £4,000 each, but a great deal less than could have been made from aggressive export selling of British-built Austin 7s.

At home, over 2,000 Austin 7 chassis were being sold each year to the small coach and body-builders offering a wide variety of special 7s. The Swallow Sidecar & Coach Building Company, later to become better known as Jaguar, offered an attractive saloon coupé for £175. There were a host of others, some attractive, some ugly, and they continued to bring added variety to motoring throughout the 1920s.

Austin 7 racing successes continued in 1927 when, on 5 August, F.H.Boyd-Carpenter and C.K.Chase took a modified 'Cup' model called *Mr JoJo* to Brooklands to capture the 750cc long-distance records held by Camuzet's Peugeot. They took them all except the 24 hour, with speeds varying from 62.53mph for the 12 hour to 63.50mph for the 3 hour. During the 12 hour, the car returned an astonishing average fuel consumption of 42.4mpg.

There had been no rush to produce the six-cylinder 20 after it was announced and first displayed at the 1926 Olympia Show. Only 10 were made in 1927. One of the reasons for this slow progress was that these first cars, which were designed to obtain the smoothness attributed to the use of six cylinders, proved to be very rough when running at speed in spite of the fact that they had an exceptionally rigid crankcase and a stiff crankshaft running in eight main bearings. Late in 1927, a vibration damper had to be fitted to the front of the crankshaft to reduce torsional vibrations. This damper consisted of three main parts, a central disc with a tapered boss fitting on the crankshaft and two metal rings which were clamped to the disc, which they gripped by friction. Inertia meant the metal rings tended always to run at a steady speed so that when the rate of vibration of the crank-front end fluctuated, a rubbing action was set up between the disc and the rings, which had a damping effect. It was highly successful, and the subsequent 20/6 and the superbly sweet-running 16/6 which followed it kept Austin in the forefront of six-cylinder quality until the feeble 12/6 was produced in the 1930s.

One or two minor price variations were made in the Austin range in June 1927, but the major revision took place on 28 August, in preparation for the Motor Show. The 7 tourer was reduced by £10 to £135 and the saloon by £15 to £150. Three Austin vans were produced at Longbridge in 1927, a 16cwt with a box-van body on the 20 chassis at £445, a 10cwt box-van on the 12 chassis at £325, and a 2.5cwt on the 7 for £155. All 12s came down in price, the Open Road tourer from £325 to £295 and the Windsor saloon by £25 to £325. A cheaper 'special' two/four seater was introduced at £295, and there was also an even cheaper Mulliner two/four seater at £255. All the 20s were cheaper, and the six-cylinder car, although not yet established, fell by £100 for the original Ranelagh limousine on the 11ft 4in chassis at £675; besides which there were three other models available for 1928, the Open Road tourer at £525, the Carlton saloon at £595 and the Ascot saloon at £615. As already mentioned only 10 20/6s were made in 1927, but the six-cylinder principle was established and a new light six — the 16/6 — was announced, although it was not going to be available until March 1928. It was to cost £255 for the chassis, £355 for the tourer and special two/four seater, and £395 for the saloon — only £70 more than the Austin 12 Windsor. As with the larger six-cylinder car only 10 were produced in 1927.

The Austin 12 was not really doing as well as it should. About 80,000 British cars were made in this the most popular size, representing 51.5 per cent of the total output, dominated by the Morris Cowley. The Austin accounted for only 14,000, but it cost around £300, and the average price for a 12hp car was £222. The 7, however, dominated the section of 10hp and less in which there was most potential growth, with 22,500 of the 40,000 cars made in that group, and it was below the average price. Maybe the 16hp six-cylinder car was going to become popular; Sir Herbert had his ready, but he could not sell the Austin 12 in quantity against the Cowley, and Morris was not going to stay out of the growing light-car market for much longer. The latter had not overlooked the six-cylinder vogue.

Austin finances improved in 1927. For the year ending September 1927 the gross trading profit was increased to £962,477, with a net profit of £406,469 after profit and loss charges.

CONSTABLE: "THIS WON'T DO, SIR. I MUST HAVE YOUR NAME FOR CAUSING AN OBSTRUCTION."
MOTORIST: "OBSTRUCTION! WHAT AM I OBSTRUCTING—THE ROAD OR THE DRAIN?"

9 The Motor War and Industrial Peace: 1928 and 1929

*Some people seem to think that my idea is to crush the Austin 7 off the market —
which is absurd.*

W.R. Morris, May 1928

There is ample room for both of us in the market.

Sir Herbert Austin, May 1928

Sir Herbert was never slow to express his views, and he covered a wide
range of subjects. Some of his ideas were unorthodox; in March 1928 he
suggested that Britain should have a stabilised year of 13 months of 28 days,
the extra month being called Sol, to promote the greater efficiency and
convenience of business life. He did not expand on the benefits that he
thought would accrue, and the idea was abandoned after being met by
everybody with stony silence.

At about the same time he gave his opinions on the future of the motor
car. When asked what he thought cars would be like in 1978 he said he
wished he knew, and if someone would tell him he would pay them a
proportion of the fortune that he could make. He did not think there could
be very much difference as the industry was too dedicated to the fuels
available and the methods of production then current, although he had
some perceptive thoughts on other aspects of future travel. As most growth
would be in urban areas, he foresaw a situation in which congestion would
become so bad that the ownership of a car would be pointless, and all
movement would be by high-quality rapid public transport. Time has
proved him partly correct. We have the congestion, but as yet little desire to
provide or to use public transport in cities. For long journeys, he felt that
pollution would become so serious that movement would be by rail with
overhead electric power, which has happened; but he did not forecast

motorways, or multi-storey car parks and off-street parking, simply despair for the future of motoring with increased urban populations and a corresponding growth in private car ownership. Perhaps he had a point.

Sir Herbert's views on what was right for the industry of his own day were, however, absolutely relevant. He had forecast the demand for a light cheap car six years before Morris and more than ten years before Henry Ford, he had come out with six-cylinder cars at the right time, expanded his factory just as demand was rising, sought a merger which would have put Austin-Morris in an unassailable position for all time in Britain, brought out standard repair charges before any other major car producer, and could even out-smart William Morris when he tried.

At the 1927 Motor Show, the first General Motors Vauxhall had been shown. Much to the relief of the British motor industry, it was a fairly conventional six-cylinder 20hp car selling at £475 to £735. Armstrong Siddeley brought out a cheaper 15hp six-cylinder at £360 and Morris's new 2.5 litre Morris Oxford six was priced at £350 for the saloon and £320 for the tourer. Austin had to bridge the gap between his 20hp and 12hp car; the six-cylinder market seemed to be the point at which he should aim. He had learnt from the mistakes of the 20/6 and Morris had set the price level for him at around £350. The 16/6 had not been ready for the 1927 Motor Show because the plan was to use the same chassis for the 12 and the 16, and the new engine was too big for the frame. The track of the 12 was therefore increased from 4ft 4in to 4ft 8in and the bonnet raised and lengthened giving ample space for the new engine. As expected, it was a superb monobloc engine, with an eight-bearing crankshaft, of 2,246cc (15.9hp) with a bore and stroke of 65.5mm x 111mm, and it led the Austin range away from the magneto by using a coil-ignition system. It developed 40bhp at 2,400rpm and with a slightly modified Austin 12 gearbox was capable of speeds in excess of 60mph giving 24mpg at normal speeds, and 20mpg when driven hard.

Although it was announced in October 1927, delivery did not commence until the following March, and in its first full year 6,401 were produced. Prices were £255 for the chassis, £355 for the two-seater or Open Road tourer, £395 for the fabric saloon and £435 for a special de luxe saloon. Being built into the 12 chassis, the first 16s were hard to distinguish from the four-cylinder cars, so after a time smart wire wheels were used on the 16/6 in place of the heavy, ugly steel artillery wheels that had been used since 1924. By August 1928, the new 16/6 Burnham saloon was ready, with an increased interior width and length, a curved roof, single-panel adjustable screen, doors extending below the frame, six opening side windows, three window blinds, and a multi-louvred bonnet. Other refinements included an extension to the fuel filler which enabled the tank to be filled without removing the driver's seat. Sir Herbert allowed this improvement, but it was some time before he would let his designers move the tank to the rear of the chassis, as it was still his firm opinion that all weight should be contained within the two axles. Now there was no mistaking a 16/6 for a 12, and the day of the real saloon car had arrived. No more draughts through the doors or wind or rain seeping through the old divided window; the open touring car was on the decline, replaced by the airtight saloon, shortly to be given an optional sliding roof, which in many cases let in just as much water and draughts when it was closed as had the old tourer.

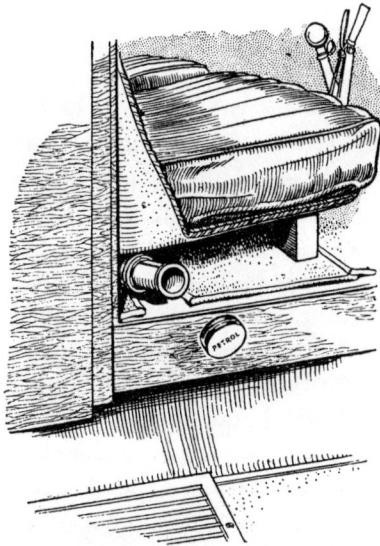

The improved filler, October 1928

Early in 1926, more than 55 per cent of the cars registered in the UK in the 12hp range had been tourers; by the end of 1927 4,000 of the 7,400 cars were saloons. Of the Austin 12 production, there were about 8,000 tourers in 1927 against 5,000 saloons, and the fashion was changing rapidly. One of the reasons given at the time was the increase in the number of cars being used for business purposes — a saloon was preferable to an open tourer for at least eight months of the average year in Britain, and people were beginning to expect more comfort. In the Austin 12 range in 1928, saloons outnumbered tourers by 6,500 to 3,700. The fabric body was at the height of its fashion; 54 different fabric-bodied cars were on the market in 1927, and this rose to no less than 132 in 1928. It was not only a question of fashion; originally it was a cheap way to make a saloon body when the demand for saloons was comparatively small but apart from its poor durability, and in spite of the fact that it was fashionable, it had to die once saloons became more popular than open cars. Metal bodies were then cheaper to produce than hand-built fabric ones because of the increase in quantity demanded and, like all bad things in the development of the motor car, the nasty 'rag' body faded into history. Sir Herbert was pleased, because he had never liked them.

William Morris may have had a six-cylinder car first in 1927, but he did not have anything to compete with the Austin 7. Although Austin and Morris dominated the British motor industry at the beginning of 1928, Morris having produced 61,632 and Austin 37,520 in the previous year, together they accounted for only two-thirds of UK production. Singer came a poor third with 11,000, Clyno followed closely with 9,000, Rover produced 6,000, and Standard, Humber and Daimler about 3,000 each. After taking the output of these top eight firms, the 30,500 left — no doubt a good proportion of which were UK-produced Fords — were made by small companies making from a few hundred to less than 3,000 cars a year. Using as an example a manufacturer turning out 1,000 cars a year at a retail price of £350, giving a net figure — after agent's commission and allowing for production cost and profit — of £280 on each car, his turnover was £280,000 a year. A profit margin of 10 per cent would have given a poor reward, and there would have been little to plough back into research and development of new models out of a scanty £28,000. What hope was there of reducing the price by 5 per cent to combat competition in a period of price cutting? A big firm could increase its output and benefit from mass-production, but with a small output there was no hope of reducing production costs and a 5 per cent drop in the price to an agent could mean a 50 per cent reduction in profits. Reductions of 5 per cent were commonplace in 1928, and the days of the small firms, and even some of the comparatively larger ones like Clyno, were numbered. In November 1928, Humber, Hillman and Commer were amalgamated, and the resultant increased production meant that these famous names were able to survive through the 1930s and World War II.

Although pathetic attempts had been made to break the magic barrier in

1926, the £100 car was still a dream of the future. The Austin 7 was still the cheapest practical car, and Morris had no smaller car than one with an 11.9hp engine competing also with the Singer Junior, the Triumph, Rover, Clyno and Standard. The price-cutting war had begun in September 1927. Morris followed Austin's reductions; the 7 tourer fell by £10 to £135, the 12 tourer by £20, and the various Cowley and Oxford models were reduced by around 5 per cent. The four/five seater Cowley tourer sold for as little as £170, and the Oxford saloon for £250; this made Austin's Clifton at £255 and Windsor at £325 look expensive, but as far as quality and finish were concerned, they were not really comparable. Standard joined in and reduced their 14/28hp car from £275 to £260. The new Standard 9 at £190, the Triumph Super 7 at £149 10s, the Clyno 11 at £190, and the new Clyno 9 at £145 for a tourer and £160 for a saloon, were following Austin's lead in the light-car market.

The new Morris Minor, Morris's answer to the Austin 7 and his attempt to enter the most rapidly growing sector of the market, was first reported in May 1928, although it was not planned to be available until August. A leak in the well-kept secret caused a sensation in the motor trade; a four-seater saloon was predicted as being the standard model at a price in the region of £120 which, with four-wheel brakes and an overhead cam engine, was not going to do Austin 7 sales much good. Morris said that the new car would be two-thirds the size of the Cowley:

> It has been apparent to me for some time that there is a growing demand for the miniature type of car, and the new model has been designed to meet this demand. Some people think that my idea is to try to crush the Austin 7 off the market — which is absurd. But I can say this — the price will not be higher than that of the Austin 7.

It was in trying to dodge observers that the secret leaked out before Morris was ready. They smuggled the test car out in a lorry, camouflaged with a freak radiator and tried it out on lonely country roads at the dead of night. An enterprising journalist must have seen it on one of these trials.

Sir Herbert was quite glad to have these extra few months to decide on his tactics. He said:

> Personally, and as firms, we are on the best of terms with the Morris Company. The public will decide whose car they like best. At present I am content to know that so far as the small car is concerned the English manufacturers have the world market to themselves. Mr Henry Ford, whom I met in America, does not make a car that competes with ours. Mr Morris's decision is no surprise to me. I knew what was going on weeks ago.

Not to be outdone Frank Smith, managing director of Clyno, rapidly announced the Wolverhampton firm's intention to introduce the Clyno 9hp Century at £115. He, too, had sworn his staff to secrecy and carried out disguised tests; the plant was ready to start production at 300 cars a week and he said, 'This cannot be described as a reply to the Morris Minor, as we have been preparing for it for two years. It is larger than either the Morris or the Austin.'

The scene was now set. Winston Churchill, the Chancellor of the Exchequer, took account of Sir Herbert's view on a tax on fuel in his budget in April 1928, when he reintroduced the petrol tax which had been abolished in 1921-2. It was to be 4d a gallon, and it increased road-fund revenue by 17.8 per cent raising the price of petrol to 1/6d a gallon and providing £13 million more revenue in the first full year. However, since there was not to be any corresponding reduction in the hp tax, all it did was to give Churchill more to misappropriate for his annual raids on the road fund for 'general purposes'.

Car prices were getting too low. A number of firms announced increases before the 1928 Motor Show, the new Clyno was not as cheap as forecast, even the price of the Cowley rose by £5. While rumours of further increases abounded, Austin brought down his prices again. The 7 tourer was now £125 and the saloon £135, and there were also considerable reductions over the rest of the Austin range, with the 16/6 tourer slashed by £30 to £315, the Burnham saloon by the same amount to £365 and the 20/4 Carlton from £495 to £455 and a week later to £425. By September, Morris had his Minor fabric saloon selling for £135 and the tourer for £125 — the same as the Austin 7 prices. Morris had set the pace in the area which Austin had dominated for six years.

1928 was a very successful year for the motor trade if not for some motor manufacturers. The customary 100,000 extra cars were registered, bringing the total to 900,557; it had taken six years to treble the number of cars on the road, and it was going to take nine more to double the figure, so the success of the motor car in bringing about a major change in travelling habits was most marked in the years from 1922 to 1928. UK production in 1928 was 165,352 cars, of which only 26,180 were exported. Imports fell slightly to about 23,000. Morris's share of total production fell by almost 6,000 cars to 55,480 and Austin's share rose dramatically from 37,520 to 44,654. The Austin breakdown for 1928 was:

Model	No produced
7	22,709
12	13,714
16/6	6,401
20/4	927
20/6	903

The increase in production in the year was due almost entirely to the two six-cylinder cars; Austin was there to meet the fashionable demand in time. Morris was to concentrate his efforts on the Minor, and this accounted for the marked increase in Morris production in the following year.

This same year, 1928, saw another Austin connection with the continent when M Lucien Rosengart resigned from the Peugeot company in March and with M.E. Salomon as his chief engineer decided to produce the Austin 7 under licence in France as the 5hp Rosengart. The French edition of the chassis was very similar to the English car, but the body was a three-seater cabriolet with two separate front seats and a third seat crosswise at the back. Construction was a metal and fabric combination with steel panels up to the waist-line. Rosengart hoped to build 60,000 cars a year and had already made a few by June; in fact he drove one himself for some months and found that he could attain a speed of 45mph and average more than 30 over some of the better French roads. By October a saloon had been developed and this, priced at £137, together with the three-seater coupé which sold for only £120, was shown at the Paris salon. The French factory had been erected during the war, taken over by Peugeot in 1919 and later bought by Rosengart. The company was registered in Paris as the Société des Automobiles L. Rosengart with Sir Herbert as a director.

In the British 7, the introduction of the Morris Minor led to a number of design changes which were introduced between July and September. Most noticeable was the higher radiator with the new nickel-plated shell; there was also a change to coil ignition, a new dashboard and a flat steering wheel. The Austin 7 Super-sports model — the first supercharged Austin — came out in July 1928 at £225. Only a few modifications to the standard sports model were necessary and the engine ran at speeds of up to 7,000rpm with an output of 27bhp at 4,500. Two prototypes were run in the summer, reaching a top speed of 84mph, but it was Chase in his 1927 200 miles race car who had the greatest success in 1928 when he covered 1,584.32 miles in 24 hours at Montlhéry, giving an average speed with stops of 65.98mph. In all, he gained five more world class speed records for the Austin 7.

Early in 1928 C.R.F. Englebach presented a brilliant paper on the reorganisation at Longbridge to the Institute of Automobile Engineers. One interesting point he made referred to the increase in the number of cars made in relation to the number of people employed, which had risen to 11,000. In 1922 he used 55 employees per car per week; that figure was reduced throughout the 1920s as production rose, falling to 10 people in 1927, and the ratio of overheads to productive labour fell from 241 per cent to 96.4 per cent over the same period. Englebach was not worried about the UK market nearing saturation point; at that time there was 1 car to every 25 of the population. In America it was 1 in 6, and he saw no reason why it should not climb to at least 1 in 12, putting UK car ownership up to 3.75 million, with a 2 million a year industry to cater for it. In reality there was a slump and another war to come before that could happen, and even then it would not be possible with foreign imports, but he could only plan for what he saw likely to happen.

The autumn of 1928 produced an interesting innovation. At the customary banquet for Austin agents and the press at the Connaught rooms during the Motor Show in October Sir Herbert had a screen erected in the great dining hall, and the speeches after the dinner were projected onto a screen in silence. Not a word was heard from the top table throughout the meal. He had sailed for America on the *Aquitania* on 28 December of the previous year, visited the New York Motor Show, met Henry Ford and gone on to Detroit. Morris had gone out on the same ship, going on to Canada, New Zealand and Australia and was fortunate enough to have missed being impressed by the use being made in the States of the silent screen for advertising. Austin however had picked up the idea of using the medium to project speeches. It is a pity that he had not waited a little longer for the introduction of talking-pictures — this might have impressed his guests as a novelty more than a silent screen covered with words. One can imagine the reactions of hundreds of happy, rather tipsy, motor traders being subjected to this revolutionary form of public speaking. Throughout the performance there were cries of 'Speech, speech' and, according to one journalist: 'The guests began to sing a parody of the Austin song' — 'The Austin Unity Song', which had been sung to the gathering, and of which HMV had produced 800 single-sided 10in 78rpm records. All the guests were given one and most were either sat on or smashed outside the Connaught Rooms. The tune was simple and quite catchy, typical popular music of the twenties, but the words were puerile. Little wonder that a record of the song was not taken home by many when it contained such lines as:

Unity of purpose is our watchword day by day, in all we do and say, marching on our way/ We stand united, with Austin as our aim, Our path is lighted with progress for the flame/ No shirkers, all workers, all playing the game for the good will and fame.

Austin agents may not have been impressed by the events that evening, but they must have been very much amused.

Finances of the company during the fifteen months ending 31 December 1928 were disappointing. For this longer period, the gross profit was down to only £861,299, against a figure for the previous twelve months of just under £1 million. Of the £861,939, which included the balance brought forward, debenture interest took £115,800, the sinking fund and reserve £52,950, and £50,000 was transferred to the tax account. Six months' 1st mortgage debenture interest and dividend on the 7 per cent preference shares, and a year's arrears on the 6 per cent preference, were paid on 1 July 1929 bringing payments up to 30 June 1924, and cost £128,220 — £59,664 was carried forward. A further year's arrears on the 6 per cent preference shares were paid in September so that during the fifteen months covered by the accounts nearly £520,000 cash was paid in dividends, interest and income tax. The poor record resulted partly from the fact that production had been less than expected, but even more directly, as a result of the price-cutting policy. Shareholders were criticial of the failure to pay off more dividend arrears, but cash had been spent on the expansion of the plant. Edsel Ford had turned the first sod in the virgin soil at Dagenham, and this was the first blow in the American counter-offensive against the protected British motor industry dominated by Austin and Morris. Soon they were to face a 14.9hp four-cylinder Ford saloon which sold for only £225, to say nothing of the Ford 8 which was to follow it — the first £100 saloon car.

1929 was a good year for the motor industry, not to be equalled again until 1933. Another 100,000 cars were added to the total registrations which reached 998,489. The industry produced 182,347 cars, of which no less than 33,808 were exported, an appreciable rise in numbers over the previous 26,180 of 1928. Imports fell a little to 21,520 and the gap between imports and exports was widening in Britain's favour, due largely to the price reductions of 1927-8. Morris's total production rose to the highest figure yet — 63,522, and it was not until 1935 that he reached that figure again. Austin also did well with 45,849, made up as follows:

Model	No produced
7	26,447
16/6	9,136
12	8,759
20/6	1,129
20/4	378

The 100,000th Austin 7 left the works in July 1929, including French and German production in the total, and the four-cylinder Austin 20 passed away unsung. The last complete car, a Marlborough landaulet, was built in the week ending 31 August; one final chassis was supplied to Startin, the body-builder, in the week ending 7 September — and this excellent car was no more. It had never been a car for the masses, but it was a product of typical Austin reliability, neglected by later vintage car enthusiasts perhaps because it was so much ahead of some other cars of the 1920s with its central gear and handbrake levers, and because those which survived into the next decade were still in use throughout World War II and after. Even when they had ceased to be anything like fashionable, they still continued to survive, often as breakdown trucks used by country garages. Alas, not many of them remain, but they were the father of the Austin 12, and we can remember them for that. It was in October 1929 that the Austin 12 taxi was introduced at £325. This vehicle dominated the London scene for more than twenty years, and even under city conditions gave 80,000 miles before a major overhaul was needed. This reliability was bred from the Austin 20.

Towards the end of 1929, Austin patented his new three-speed gearbox. At the front end of the gearbox a shaft was driven from the clutch which carried top-gear dogs and operated a pair of constant-mesh gears in the normal way. In addition, a second gear was formed at the rear end of the shaft which was used, in conjunction with the internal teeth cut in a drum, to provide a silent indirect drive. This drum was also provided with external teeth, and was joined to the mainshaft which, in turn, was supported in a carrier which was pivoted to a fixed spindle at the bottom of the box. The spindle was also used to provide support to a sleeve carrying a constant-mesh gear which became, in effect, a layshaft. To engage top gear the mainshaft slid forward in the carrier, bringing the dogs into mesh, taking the drive to it direct from the shaft. The silent second gear was the unusual feature, as the carrier was rocked sideways around the fixed spindle, moving the internal gear into an eccentric relationship with the shaft. The mainshaft was then moved forward in order to engage the rearmost gear on the shaft. Second gear was obtained in the simplest

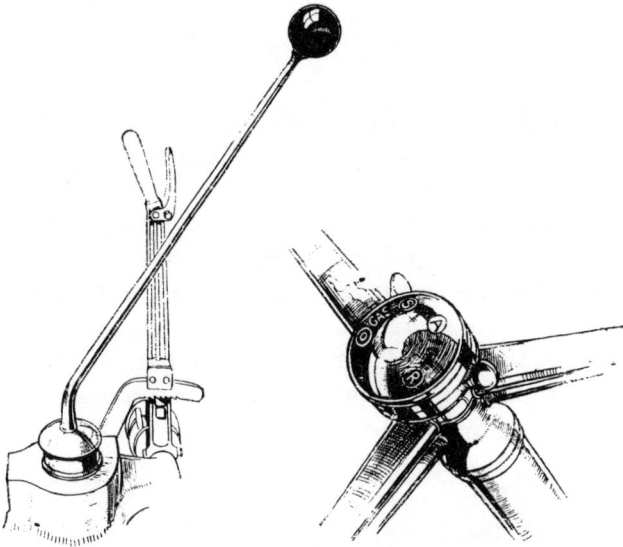

New Sixteen controls and ball-change lever, July 1929

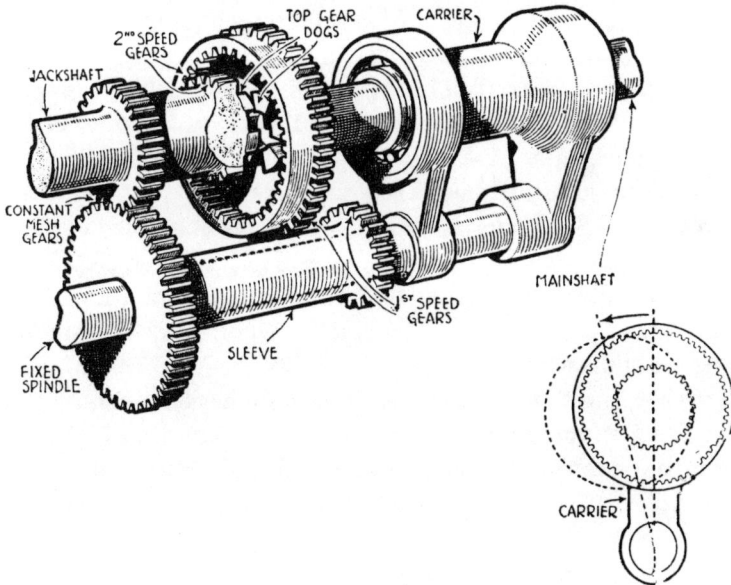

The 1929 rocking gear box

possible manner, using only one pair of gears, the teeth being engaged endwise, as opposed to bringing them into mesh radially, simply by swinging the carrier. For the lowest ratio the mainshaft was brought back, the dogs and internal gear being disengaged, then slid rearwards with the result that the external teeth on the drum were meshed with a pinion on the sleeve, or layshaft. Power was then fed through constant-mesh gears to the sleeve and back again to the mainshaft in the normal way.

Quite a few changes were made in some of the four Austin models that were to form the 1930 programme, the most significant of which was the introduction of the new ball-change gearbox on the 12 and 16, which became standard on the 12 from April 1929 production, although five prototypes had been produced in the previous month. The old square gate had been quaint and provided quite a pleasant gear change, but the travel between gears was excessive, and unless the driver had a fairly long left arm, it was necessary to lean forward to engage first and third speeds. This gate was replaced by a ball, and the lever was both lightened and lengthened, with the movement between each speed reduced to a minimum. Reverse was obtained by lifting up the lever, as opposed to moving a catch under the knob in the old gate change.

From October, all external fittings were chromium plated, this new durable finish replacing the earlier nickel plating, which discoloured very quickly; when it became dull, it had to be polished and lasted no longer than three or four years. On most cars which have survived, the original chromium plate is intact, after nearly fifty years.

Triplex safety glass had been used on windscreens for some time, but from October 1929 all windows in Austin cars had Triplex as standard. Wing shapes were altered to provide better protection for the bodywork, and what was called a 'smart Bakelite fitting' replaced the attractive metal quadrant controls in the centre of the steering wheel to control ignition and gas. The use of the word 'gas' was derived from the American influence on the 20 of 1919, and should not be confused with the choke control for cold starting; it was simply a tick-over or slow-running control which could be used as a hand-controlled accelerator. Both 12s and 16s were built on a new low frame and, at long last, the fuel tank was moved to the back of the chassis.

From January 1929, Sir Herbert had realised that prices would again have to be increased. Rover and Wolseley had to increase their prices, and there was a general upward trend during the year. At least, with the Austins, quality of upholstery was improved and Triplex glass, which had been an optional extra was, as already mentioned, standard in all windscreens. The increases were small at £5 on the 7 tourer, £25 on the Clifton and £10 on the 16s, but they were much more drastic on the 20/6 at a further £35 on all models. From the Motor Show, the sunshine roof was available on all models except the 20 — at £10 on the 16 and 12, and £5 on the 7. This sudden introduction was made necessary by the fall in the popularity of the tourer. For some time sunshine roofs had been sold at £30 to £50; some of them were good, but many were quite useless, and an optional sliding roof at £10, with a manufacturer's guarantee, put most of the converters out of business.

In March 1929, the War Office decided to replace 100 motorcycles with special Austin 7 saloons. These had lower ratio back axles, stronger springs and front-axle towing hooks, and proved to be a great success. Eleven were issued to each cavalry regiment for scouting, and they remained in use with the army for a number of years. At the other end of the scale, Austin 7 racing successes continued. Austin made clear his attitude towards record breaking when asked for his opinion after Sir Henry Segrave broke the world speed record in *Golden Arrow* in March 1929:

Such attempts have value as regards international propaganda, and also in obtaining knowledge of design of vehicles running on the roads at very high speeds. Whether any of this knowledge can be made use of at the present moment is a matter of doubt. I consider these record-breaking attempts are going to extremes beyond our requirements at the present time. They give knowledge in certain directions, but certainly not for our needs now. I do not think, however, that attempts should be stopped, if only for their international value.

Record breaking and competitive racing with production cars were different things. It was a waste of money, but if the propaganda was good it was worthwhile, particularly when it was other people who were spending their own money to publicise the Austin 7! At the Ulster Tourist Trophy, however, Gordon England was asked to return to competitive motor racing to lead the Austin team of four supercharged cars. Thirty laps of the 14 mile circuit had to be covered, and cars in the 750cc class were given a five-lap start over the 410 mile course. Lapping at an average of 63mph on some laps, the Austins finished third at 59.60mph, fourth at 59.49, and sixteenth and nineteenth.

10 The Slump: 1930 and 1931

There are 2,000,000 people in Britain earning less than £7 a week who can afford to run one of the medium powered cars.

Sir Herbert Austin, January 1930

In 1930 and 1931, total UK car production fell from the high point of 1929, 182,347, to 169,669 and 158,997 respectively. Morris's output was affected in 1930, but more seriously in the following year; from the 1929 peak of 63,522, it fell to 58,436 in 1930 and 43,582 in 1931. Although Austin production dropped from 46,029 in 1929 to 39,251 in 1930, it rose slightly to 39,676 in 1931 due entirely to the introduction of the light 12/6. The customary 100,000 increase in total car registrations did not occur in 1930; it rose by only 76,592. In 1931, it climbed by even less — 28,634. To a large extent, the motor industry — Austins in particular — were protected from the worst effects of the 1930s; new car sales fell 9.2 per cent in 1930, another 7.8 per cent in 1931, but began to rise in 1932. Unemployment rose to nearly 3 million in 1933 (23 per cent of insured persons), then declined steadily until it reached 1.67 million in 1938. Total UK car production only fell in the two years mentioned; after 1931 it continued to increase steadily until the war reduced private car production to a dribble in 1940.

World trade dropped by over a quarter of its previous volume between 1929 and 1932. Car imports almost ceased, from over 21,000 in 1929 to 9,751 in 1930, were under 3,000 in 1931 and 1932, rising only to 3,619 in 1933, then began to recover again in 1934. But even then the level was only half that of 1929, and imports never again reached the volume of the twenties. UK exports overall fell 32 per cent in volume and 50 per cent in value between 1929 and 1932, but the motor industry was not quite so badly affected with its increasing sales to the Empire. Car exports fell by some 25 per cent in 1930 to 26,132, and to 18,682 in 1931, but recovered by 1932 to their 1920s proportion of production.

The breakdown of the 39,251 cars built by Austins in 1930 is as follows:

THE SLUMP: 1930 AND 1931

Model	No produced
7	23,826
12	6,889
16/6	7,560
20/6	976

By June 1930, the Clifton tourer was removed from the Austin 12 range and the new 7 two-seater was introduced at £130. The 12 two-seater was removed for a few months and a new Sportsman's saloon was available with either a 12 or a 16 engine at £320 and £375 respectively. Some slight price reductions were announced in September 1930; the 7 tourer and two-seater went from £130 to £122 10s, and the saloons were reduced by £10 to £130. Most of the other models which did not have them already were given names. The new two-seater 12 was called the Eton, the 16 the Harrow, and the other new names were: 12 four-light fabric, Marlow; 12 six-light fabric, Wycombe; 16 four-light fabric, Beaconsfield; and 16 six-light fabric, Salisbury.

The fabric 12 saloon died in 1931. Nearly 1,000 were sold in 1930, about 1 in 7 of total 12 production, but only 63 in 1931, of 2,602 cars made. In April 1930, a final attempt was made to produce a cheap fabric 12 saloon, the Watford; it was £45 less than the other fabric models and sold for only £275. It was a four-light saloon with sliding side windows, a sloping windscreen, and doors hinged along their rear edges, with the forward edges of the front doors sloping forward to the bottom to provide extra room for getting in and out. It had cloth upholstery and the roof was well curved back and domed, and the body sides continued downwards nearly to the running boards. For a fabric saloon it was quite attractive, with a slightly longer bonnet and a shorter scuttle, but only 719 were made, most of them in 1930. Fabric 12 open tourers also suffered; in 1930 they accounted for about 1 in 7 of total 12s produced, but only 162 out of 2,602 the following year.

One factor which helped the motor industry to weather the slump was that the 1930 Budget did not repeal protective duties as had been feared. All motor shares rose again to new heights, including Austin's. Talks of a merger between Austin and Humber-Hillman-Commer, in which there was some substance, also had an effect on share values, as did the issue of a further 6 months' dividend in July on all except the ordinary shares. It was decided to alter the financial year again, this time to end on 31 July to enable stock-taking to be done when the factory was closed for the annual holiday, so accounts for 7 months were produced which showed an excellent gross profit for the period of £858,137, a net profit of £384,342 and £279,820 carried forward. A month's dividend was paid on all shares except the 20 per cent preferred ordinary, which were paid for 7 months, and the fortunate ordinary shareholders were given the huge bonus of a 60 per cent dividend for the 7 months, pushing the shares up to 37s.

All this success, good demand from the home market, a reasonable export record and licence fees from France and Germany, was shortly to be supplemented by a little more money from America. No small cars were made in the States; the Americans seemed so set against them that none were being built even in their own overseas factories. Both Ford and General Motors had manufacturing plants all over the world, in many places where the greatest demand was for small cars, but it was not until well into the 1930s that even in these potential markets they accepted the fact that there was sufficient demand to enter the field themselves. There was not then, as there has not been since, any real desire in the States for a light economy car.

Foreign cars first appeared in a major American exhibition at the 1929 National Automobile Show in New York, Britain being represented by Vauxhall, Daimler and Austin. Sir Herbert and Lady Austin arrived on the *Berengaria* on 3 January accompanied by four 7s, one of which was a little coupé similar to the one which had been shown for the first time at Olympia three months before. Austin was there for two reasons, firstly to represent the Society of Motor Manufacturers and Traders at a motoring conference, and secondly to follow up a previously unsuccessful visit to Detriot in 1928 to see what could be done to market the Austin 7 in America. His object was to discover an American concern prepared to produce the car under licence which he would grant, together with the necessary designs and a team of experts to assist with the preparations for production, in exchange for a directorship and the customary 2 per cent. He set up his headquarters in the Commodore Hotel, ready to meet applicants for the franchise, and advertised in all the major newspapers that 'The Austin Motor Company desires to get in touch with either an individual or group of individuals who are willing to undertake the manufacture and sale of the Austin 7 in America and Canada.'

Austin left America at the beginning of February with a proposal from Mayor E.Moreau of Manchester, New Hampshire, and another from a group of businessmen. Manchester could not find the $1 million required to set up a car factory and on 28 February arrangements were concluded with the other group which resulted in the formation of the American

Austin Car Company Inc in Wilmington to acquire an exclusive licence to manufacture and sell the Austin 7 in the States for the next ten years, terminable if they failed to produce a minimum number of cars. Stock was offered on the London Stock Exchange in August, by which time the new company had made a contract with the Standard Steel Company of Pennsylvania for the purchase of a factory in Butler. One million shares were issued, of which 100,000 were deposited with the Guarantee Trust Company and reserved for the London market. The American issue was over-subscribed at $12.50 a share. Sir Herbert and the Austin Motor Company Ltd had a joint option to purchase 50,000 at $9 each, extending to 15 September 1932, and Sir Herbert was given a seat on the board.

Arthur J.Brandt, who was chosen to direct the company, could not find the technical staff in Butler, so he went to Detroit and gave Count Alexis de Sakhnoffsky the task of designing a miniature interpretation of the current American popular car, and the Hayes Body Corporation tooled-up to produce a body-style then quite unknown on the American market. Two types of body were made, a two-seater coupé and a two-seater saloon. The triangular frame of the Austin 7 chassis was extended to support the body, and from the point of attachment of the rear springs the frame side-channel was extended up to continue to the body rear. Cross-bracing was provided by the one-piece welded floor of the body, which meant that it was necessary to reposition the shock absorbers. The body became an integral part of the chassis by being welded to it; the car used left-hand drive and there were front and rear bumpers, and all thread sizes were changed from the British Whitworth to SAE American pattern.

Sir Herbert had estimated that the Butler factory would be capable of producing 100,000 cars during its first year. Rumours circulated at home that no less than 167,000 Bantams — as the new car was called — had been sold, which was of course nonsense, particularly as Austin had to tell the shareholders in October that, up to that time, neither he nor the company had received any royalty payments from America. He was still confident, and said that production had started in May and that by December over 50,000 Austin Bantams would have been sold; a definite statement was obtained from the American company to the effect that they had orders for 184,117 cars at 30 June. This precise figure and the promise of 50,000 by the end of the year were both wildly optimistic; the actual sales figure was a paltry 8,558. Production fell to 1,179 in 1931 and climbed to 3,846 in 1932.

On the continent the Rosengart, which now bore very little resemblance to the 7, had become very popular; by the middle of 1930, 11,000 had been sold. The first 100 cars had been assembled from imported Austin parts, but after that everything was made at Rosengart's Bellanger factory at Neuilly, which was used later to produce a six-cylinder engine based on the Austin 7 design. Between 350 and 400 Dixis a month were being made in Germany, and altogether about 14,000 had been sold by the end of 1930. The coupés and saloons were priced at £125 and the three/four seater and the attractive little sports two-seater were £110. Sir Herbert was the first person in the Midlands to speak to Australia on the new radio telephone on 30 April. The call cost £6 for 3 minutes plus £2 for each additional minute. He spoke to Caldwell, an Austin distributor in Melbourne, for ten minutes and said that he was discussing seriously with Holden of Adelaide the possibility of their building Austin chassis in Australia. Henry Ford had the same idea, so Austin had to be content with his outlets for production in the States, Germany and France, and with the 20 per cent of his UK production that was exported — most of it to the Empire.

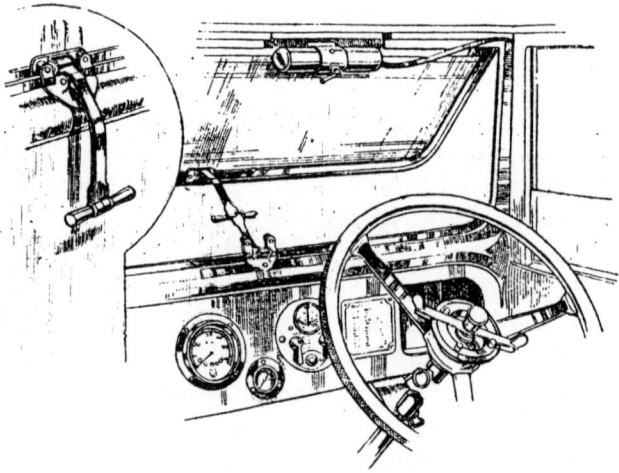

The Seven lay-out, July 1930

At home, the baby Austin 7 began to grow up. Sir Herbert was forced to develop the 7 into a true four-seater because the Morris Minor was able to carry four passengers in reasonable comfort without becoming overloaded. In preparation for the 1931 season, the new saloon was altered by raising the top of the radiator slightly and extending the bonnet back to within about 4in of the windscreen, which was tilted back a few degrees to reduce glare and dazzle. An extra gallon was added to the capacity of the old 4 gallon fuel

132

tank, which could be held in reserve by using a two-way tap. A stronger, thicker gauge under-portion in the three-part metal floor of the fabric saloons allowed for the recommended carrying capacity to be increased from 32 to 36 stones. Domed rear quarters and other alterations increased the body length by 3in, and there was more leg room in both front and rear compartments. The new metal and fabric saloons cost £140, with sunshine roofs at an extra £5, but when Morris reduced Minor prices in August, the 7 open cars were also reduced to £122 10s and the saloons to £130. Some reductions were made in other prices from 1 September: from £30 to £55 on the 20/6 models, £20 to £25 on the 12, and £30 to £40 on the 16 saloons. The blue Austin 12 taxis, 8in lower than any other cab in London at the time, were approved by Scotland Yard in May 1930, and the first one was authorised to ply for hire on 12 June. The price was reduced from £380 to £377 10s in October, and they could be bought for £465 on hire purchase at £50 deposit with weekly payments of as little as £2 10s.

At the end of 1929, Sammy Holbrook, who had been a most popular sales manager for much of the 1920s, and his deputy, both left the Austin company, and until the appointment of a new head of sales Sir Herbert took over selling on his own. Shortly after, the distributors' territories were modified: the Rootes Brothers lost London and the Home Counties to Car Mart and the Austin Oxford Street showrooms; and George Heath was removed from Birmingham which was to be handled direct from Longbridge. Rootes kept the Maidstone area, and the number of retail agents in the Midlands was increased. Austin spent much of 1930 and 1931, at the age of 65, travelling around the country meeting distributors and agents, spreading optimism for both the future of Britain and of the motor industry. He gained the confidence of all his agents, fully restored their faith in the company, and gained loyalties which continued until he died. Everywhere he went he was followed by a gang of local and national journalists eager to hear his latest pronouncements on topics which ranged from Pelmanism and education to trade protection, and the major motoring topic since the early 1920s — when was there going to be a £100 car. This subject was always good for a few paragraphs, and Sir Herbert continually denied any rumours that his company was going to either lose money or to reduce quality by doing anything so silly as to try to sell a car for £100. He had a jolly good car at £122 10s and that was as low as he could go. William Morris had other ideas. In December, he announced the two-seater side-valve Minor, the first £100 car. Austin was surprised at the news and said 'While admitting that there is some strange fascination about the round figure of

£100, we have not yet seen our way clear — or the necessity — to produce a car at that figure without risking to some extent a reduction in the standard of Austin quality'.

Sir Miles Thomas was with Morris at the time, and in his book *Out on a wing* (Michael Joseph, 1964) he tells of how by paring everything down to a minimum, even to the extent of fitting a single windscreen wiper and a gearbox that gave three speeds only, and by cutting the profits to ribbons, the £100 two-seater car became a possibility:

> To our great delight, orders began to pour in for the new Morris Minor but not, thank heavens, for the £100 car on which the profit margin was so slender. We had the foresight to catalogue an alternative two-seater. It had a four-speed gearbox, a two-bladed wiper, and a choice of colour ... It was an interesting exercise in consumer preference that although attention was undoubtedly attracted to the Morris Minor by the fact that one could be purchased for as little as £100, the actual buyers wanted something that showed that they had not bought the cheapest product offered.

This proved Austin's contention that the market did not want a cheap, basic open two-seater. Fortunately for Morris, whose trading profit was to fall from £1.6 million in 1930 to £663,000 in 1931, and after only a small recovery in 1932 to fall below £350,000 in 1933, people did not want his cheapest car either. A good saloon for £100 would have sold, but that was not possible yet. The market in the 8hp class for 1930 and 1931 was at about 28 per cent of total sales and was to hover between 23 per cent and 30 per cent until the war. This gave a potential market of about 40,000 cars in 1930; Austin produced nearly 24,000 of them and only 425 were two-seaters, and only another 3,187 tourers. As Sir Miles discovered and Sir Herbert had predicted, the demand simply did not exist in the class in which a £100 car was a possibility.

Growth must come in another area. The light six-cylinder car in the 14-16hp class seemed to be the direction to take. In 1930, sales in that class were 26.3 per cent of the total, so there was a good potential market, which Morris had entered with the Morris Major and the new Wolseley Hornet at £175. In 1930, 22 per cent of sales were in the 11-13hp group and, of some 38,000 cars, Austin's impact with the rather expensive and dated 12 at only some 7,000 sales was small. Sales in that class fell to 16 per cent in 1931, but in the 14-16hp range they rose to 27.4 per cent. Austin had only the 16, but this was the market to tackle. Morris production fell from 58,436 in 1930 to only 43,582 in 1931, but Austin's rose slightly to 39,676 of the 158,997 cars produced in Britain. Imports in 1931 were down to an insignificant 2,118,

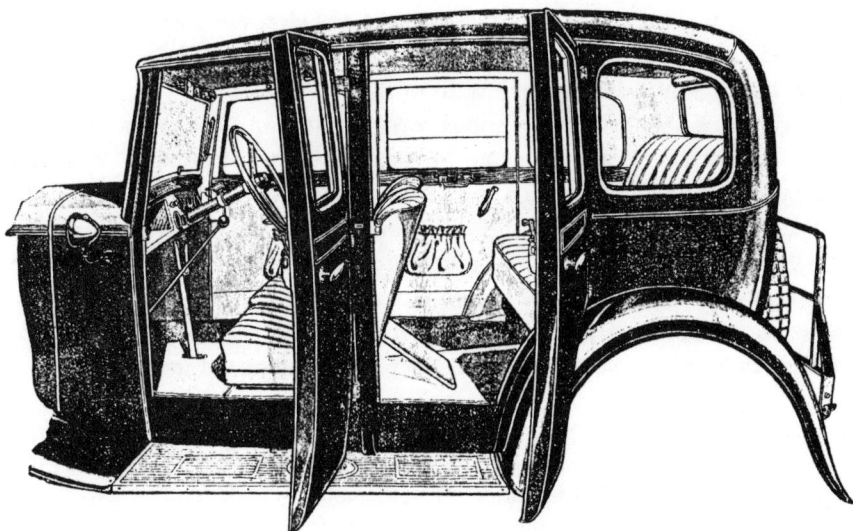
The 12/6 saloon, 1931

the lowest figure in the history of the industry, and although exports were at the lowest level since 1924 at 18,682, even this figure represented about the same proportion of total production as in the 1920s. That Austin did choose the right car at the right time is shown by his production figures for 1931:

Model	No produced
7	21,282
16	5,558
12/6	9,529
12	2,602
20	705

Thus the new 12/6 had reduced the 12's sales from 7,000 in the previous year, but they would probably have fallen anyway in 1931 to below 6,000, so the 12/6 must have resulted in capturing about 5,000 to 6,000 additional sales for the company.

The 12/6 was a very different car from the 12 and the 16. To start with it was not a 12 at all but, rated at 13.9hp, it should really have been called a 14. But to have called it a 14 would have made it look like a replacement for the 16, and this was not the intention. Austin saw a much longer life for the 16

135

than for the old 12, and in 1930 it looked as if all cars over 10hp were going to have six-cylinder engines. As we know now, this was not to be the case and the light sixes had only a limited life. They were not cheap to run, and after the 1931 Budget put petrol tax up by 2d to 6d a gallon the greatest growth area was to be in the 7-10hp range.

Two cars with fabric saloon bodies were finished on 19 January 1931, and these were used by the press and for dealers' demonstrations to coincide with the announcement of this new saloon that was going to be put onto the market for the very low price of £198. The new all-steel body to be made by the Pressed Steel Company was not ready in time, but its design was such that it would weigh no more than a fabric saloon. In fact, only 644 fabric 12/6s were sold in 1931, so the demonstration vehicles were not representative of the styles which were to appear. Sir Herbert admitted that:

> We shall probably find that the car has a few minor faults, but however eager we may be to supply the demand, which we anticipate will be very large, we are not going to let any cars out which do not come up to our standard.

The fabric car took on the old 12 title of Clifton, and the metal body was called the Harley — another 12 name. During 1931, other models appeared and the breakdown of production shows that the metal saloon was by far the most popular:

Metal saloon	7,439 ⎤
De Luxe saloon	1,103 ⎬ Production began 5 Sept
Fabric saloon	644 ⎦
Four-speed saloon	211 Production began w/e 5 Dec
Tourer	64 ⎤ Production began w/e 17 Oct
Two seater	55 ⎦
Van	1
Chassis	12

Peak production was reached in the week ending 23 May, with 463 cars.

The new engine had six cylinders with a bore and stroke of 61.25mm x 84.63mm (1,496cc) and an RAC rating of 13.9hp. The cylinder bore being relatively large compared with the stroke, enabled the weight to be reduced, making for high crankshaft speeds and allowing a very stiff crankshaft without waste of weight or an uneconomical distribution of metal. Two other points in the design of the engine differed from normal Austin practice — the block and much of the crankcase formed a single casting,

136

and there were only four main bearings. Stiff monobloc construction, a short stroke and a very rigid crankshaft were supposed to eliminate vibration, but the 12/6 engine was somewhat 'rough' and was in no way as reliable as the 16. One advantage over all other Austins was the method of mounting the combined engine and gearbox unit in the chassis; it was hung in the chassis and could be dropped out at the bottom as a unit by removing only four bolts, instead of being hoisted out from above.

As well as having only four main bearings in the engine, the gearbox had only three forward speeds with ratios of 20.15, 9.35 and 5.5 to 1, giving a very wide gap between first and second. It was an unpleasant gearbox to handle, and this was not helped by the long, slender lever which made the gears feel loose and difficult to select. A dynamo was mounted on top of the cylinder head, with the fan blade attached to its spindle — an idea borrowed from the Singer 6 — and the old Autovac was at last replaced by a mechanical pump which drew the fuel direct from the 8 gallon tank at the rear to the carburetter. Despite the rather fussy characteristics of the engine and the inadequacy of the three-speed gearbox, the car could cruise at a little more than 55mph and was at its happiest at 40-45; brakes were quite good and it was an easy car to maintain. Apart from the sump, only four places required oil, and there were only six points that needed to be greased, and all of them were forward of the driver's seat. Previous criticisms of the lack of modern appearance in Austin cars had been overcome and the style and shape of the body found no critics. A major advance was made in comfort by the design of the chassis. The frame side-members were very wide at the rear, coming to within 2in of the wheels, which gave the widest possible support to the new all-steel body which was bolted directly on to the frame. This allowed for the springs to be mounted directly under the frame, which was shaped to become very narrow as it approached the engine allowing for a very good steering lock. Whatever else it was, the 12/6, with its new pressed-steel body, four-stud wire wheels, acceptable appearance, six cylinders and a host of real improvements, took Austin into the 1930s with a car directed to a growing sector of the market at the very cheap price of £198, and was the first full-sized British car with a six-cylinder engine to sell for less than £200.

An attempt was made in 1931 to increase sales of the 20 by introducing two new owner-driver models, on 10ft wheelbase chassis — the Mayfair and the Whitehall at £530. In the Whitehall, the body was panelled up to the waist-line, but the top and quarters were covered with fabric. At the rear there was a permanent container for luggage, to which the spare wheel was attached. With a top speed of 69mph, and a high standard of luxury, the car suffered from a fuel consumption of only 16mpg and very few were made. The first was produced in the week ending 17 October and only one other was made that year; production in 1932 was 43; in 1933 it was 40, and in 1934 it was 14, the last being produced on 27 October.

To return to Austin cars in general, bumpers, those ugly features of the 1930s, were introduced in April on all models except the 7 at £3 3s to £5 5s extra. Prices remained constant throughout 1931, until the announcement of the 1932 programme on 2 September. In this the Austin 7s were all reduced to £118, but a new de luxe saloon was introduced at £128. An attempt was made to reduce the number of Austin 12 models to two saloons

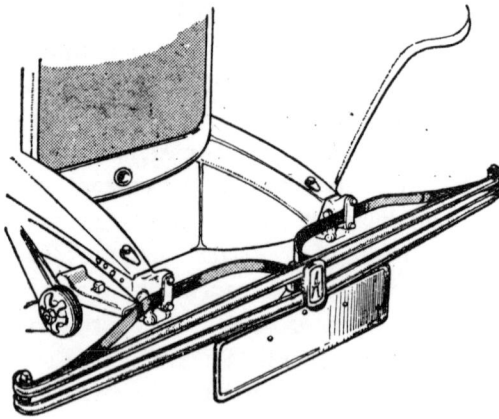

The 12/6 bumpers, October 1931

— the Burnham at £288 and the New Windsor at £268 — but production of many of the other varieties continued, albeit in very small numbers. In the 16 range, the tourer and the Harrow were reduced by £20 to £290, the Burnham by £10, the fabric models were dropped and the Westminster was brought in at £350 and the New Windsor at £298, only £30 more than the 12. The 20 range was reduced to the Ranelagh limousine or landaulet at £575, the Mayfair at £550, and the two 10ft cars — the new Whitehall and the new Carlton — were £525 and £498.

The new 7 de luxe saloon, only £10 more than the basic model, was built on a chassis 6in longer than on the standard car giving a wheelbase of 6ft 9in. It was fitted with leather upholstery, a sliding roof and bumpers, and accounted for 2,970 of total production of the Austin 7 for the three months of 1931 in which it was available. It dominated the scene thereafter, only about 1 in 4 of the saloons during the rest of the 1930s being of the standard type proving, as Morris had discovered earlier, that buyers were not willing to sacrifice quality in order to save a few pounds. Had it not been for the growing fleet market, one which has always favoured basic cars, it is likely that the cheaper versions of the small cars would have been withdrawn. The habit of buying basic cars for fleet use lingered on until quite recently, when the policy has tended to change because of the difficulty in disposing of them on the second-hand market.

Pricing had to be very accurate. There was a point at which the extra price charged could reverse the effect of consumer desire for quality. A de luxe 12/6 at £225 did not oust the standard Harley saloon which could be bought for £198. In the 16 range, the Burnham was sold as a drop-head saloon, but was still available in de luxe form with a fixed head at the same price of £325; and the new Westminster four-light with luggage locker and the Windsor six-light had the new pressed-steel bodies with the belt-moulding pressed in, a lower top section and 12/6 rounded rear-panels. The 12/4 engine was also available in the Burnhams and Windsors. The 20/6 Whitehall on the 10ft chassis, a slightly more refined car than the Mayfair on the same chassis, was the only model to break away from Austin convention by having horizontal rather than vertical flutes on the bonnet sides, which gave it a distinctive, attractive transatlantic appearance. It was a fine car with exceptional performance, using the same engine as in the 10ft 10in and 11ft 4in chassis, but with lighter new front and rear axles and an aluminium body.

Financially, the year ending 31 July 1931 was surprisingly successful with a gross trading profit of £1,376,244, the highest yet recorded, and representing a profit of about £30 on each car sold leaving £489,232 net after deducting debenture service, tax, maintenance, etc. Apart from the fixed interest due on the preferred and preference stock, no less than a 100 per cent dividend was paid on the ordinary shares, and a balance of £270,489 was carried forward. Ordinary shares had stood at 41s 3d in October 1930 but had fluctuated widely until the end of the year and into 1931, dropping to below 30s in November; but they reached 40s again after the dividend was announced. Sir Herbert and Lady Austin were said to have held a high proportion of the 600,000 issued, but the former had always said that he was prepared to buy his own shares whenever he could get them cheaply, and as he was over 65 he may have been considering his future retirement. Licence fees to the company during the year for the manufacture of the Austin 7 abroad came to only £5,658, and as he received half of the total he must have obtained a similar sum for himself, and not much of this could have come from the American Austin Car Co which had just shown a loss of over $793,000 for 1930.

Six Austin 7s were entered for the Irish Grand Prix in July 1930. The works' team consisted of Frazer Nash and Gunnar Poppe on supercharged cars, and Waite, who decided to obtain the additional handicap advantage by using a car with an unblown engine. Generous handicapping gave Waite a good chance, and it is likely that he would have come in second had not he been given the finishing signal when he had still another lap to complete the race. He was placed fifth with an average speed of 58.89mph. Frazer Nash came third on a supercharged car, at 65.94mph. In the following month, three supercharged 7s were entered for the Ulster TT, driven by the same trio. Sir Herbert was persuaded to go out as a spectator, and was there when Waite's car crashed on the wet road. Alf Depper, his co-driver, was thrown over a hedge and escaped with a severe shaking, but Waite was concussed after the car had turned over three times. Frazer Nash's car retired with engine trouble, and everything depended upon the last car in the team, but Poppe could only finish in fifth place at an average of 61.46mph.

Waite's jaw was broken, so he could not compete in any more races in 1930, and for the British Racing Drivers Club 500 miles race at Brooklands on 4 October six 7s were entered, five of them with supercharged engines. The works entered three cars in their team, one driven by Sammy Davis and the Earl of March, another by Poppe and Charlie Goodacre, and the third by Crabtree and Barnes. Two cars dropped out, but Davis and the Earl of March made this the greatest Austin 7 win of all time when they came in first at the remarkable average speed of 83.41mph. Thirteen international class H records were broken later that month by Davis and Goodacre, from 12 hours at 81.71mph, to 200km at 85.076mph; then Davis took the flying-start kilometre at 89mph. And now George Eyston began to perform in the new unsupercharged MG Midget, which began the struggle which was to continue between the MGs and the Austins for the next few years.

Sir Malcolm Campbell took his world speed record car *Bluebird* to Daytona, Florida, in January 1931, and also the Austin 7 single-seat racer. The fight was on between Austin and MG to be the first to reach 100mph in a 750cc car. Campbell managed to get the Austin up to 94.069mph, but Eyston broke the barrier on an MG when he took class H records at between 101 and 103.13mph, becoming the first man to cover a measured distance at more than 100mph in a 750cc car. Sammy Davis drove one of the new generation of Austin 7 racers, which Waite had built to beat the MGs, but the tuned-up Morris Minors were supreme. At the Junior Car Club Double-Twelve race, MGs took the first five places, showing that unsupercharged Austins had more than met their match and that the heavily penalised supercharged cars were unable to beat their new rivals. After other great successes at the 1931 Irish Grand Prix, Cecil Kimber of MG decided that it was time to supercharge the MG. No less than 22 teams of Austin 7s and MGs drove in the Light Car Club's 90 lap relay race for which a special trophy was awarded by the confident MG company. The Austin 7s had their revenge, and the works' team won at an average speed of 81.77mph, taking the new MG cup as their reward.

Austin's great day came on 8 August 1931 — a wet and windy day at Brooklands — when Leon Cushman became the first man in the world to exceed 100mph in a class H record attempt in this country, and the first to better the magic figure over the shorter distances. His speeds were 102.28mph for the flying kilometre and 100.67mph for the flying mile. After Mrs Gwenda Stewart, a well known Brooklands driver of the time, pushed the speeds up again, the MG finished on top in 1931 with a 5km run at Montlhéry at 111.28mph.

11 The 10 and the Light 12/4: 1932 and 1933

It is gratifying to see one more convert to the small car movement.

Sir Herbert Austin on seeing the first Ford 8, 19 February 1932

Sir Herbert welcomed 1932 with his usual confidence and optimism:

> No better resolution can be made for the New Year than the determination to erase from the thought and speech of the nation the word 'depression'. The persistent use of the term has undermined our faith in the future and impaired our initiative. 1932 holds promise of great opportunities. Let us revitalise our enthusiasm by turning these opportunities to our advantage.

He worked hard to achieve this, and with the help of a general improvement in the state of the motor industry, and a slow start by Ford at the new Dagenham factory, he succeeded. New car sales rose by only 1.2 per cent that year but this was enough to make the falls in the previous two years little more than a bad memory; what was to become the great growth in production had begun, and was to continue until the war. Production of cars in the UK in 1932 rose to 171,244, and the total number of registrations rose by about 45,000, but exports rose to 26,701, back to the 1930 total. Morris production continued to be depressed at 50,337, and Austin approached them with a total for the year of 43,802, broken down as follows:

Model	No produced
7	20,121
12/6	6,309
16/6	3,839
12/4	2,452
20/6	605
10/4	8,609
Light 12/4	1,867

The 7 was still supreme in the 8hp range, accounting for over half the cars sold in that category, but there was a reduction in the proportion of total sales in 1932 from 27.9 per cent in the previous year to 23.5 per cent. Demand for large cars was falling, and the growth area of the market was moving towards cars with 9 and 10hp engines. In 1931, only 11.1 per cent of the cars sold were rated at 10hp, but in 1932 the 9-10hp cars took 23.9 per cent of the market. With Ford coming in at the bottom with an 8 to compete with the Austin 7 and the Morris Minor, there was going to be scope for a good, cheap 10hp four-door car.

Ford's held a special exhibition of their own at the Albert Hall from 19-27 February 1932, charging the public 1s 3d to see the new Ford 8. The new light car had been designed to meet the requirements of the hp tax with an engine of 56.6mm bore and a long stroke of 92.5mm, giving it 950cc, nearly 200cc more than the Austin 7; it had to compete with the 7, the Morris Minor, Singer, Standard and Triumph. Twelve cars were made in Detroit, because Dagenham was not yet ready with the English version, and these cars were remarkably similar in design to the Austin, but with a sloping, vee-shaped radiator. Competitors breathed a sigh of relief when they saw its conventional lines, heard that delivery would not be until May, and that the price would be about £125. Ford had been doing badly in America, US exports had declined, and it did not look as if the £7 million investment at Dagenham would have much success in the short term. Ford shares here were regarded as very speculative, dropping to 20s, but rising to 35s in eight weeks when the 8 and the V8 were announced.

In August, after experimental tests under British conditions, a car with a completely different and larger body with a very marked slope to the radiator and windscreen appeared. The fuel tank was moved from the dash to the rear, the engine was more accessible, the distributor was placed on the cylinder head and, following the Austin 12/6 design, the dynamo was repositioned to avoid a triangular vee-belt to drive a separate dynamo and fan. According to a contemporary reviewer: 'The new car was clever in many respects, but it was possible to find fault with it.' Most of those faults were removed in the production cars. Transverse front and rear suspension and synchromesh gearbox, long before it was introduced on any other small car, were strong features, but the car had a three-speed gearbox, soon to be beaten by the Austin 7; the car cost £120 as the Tudor two-door saloon and £135 as a four-door. Speeds obtained on road tests were 58mph on top gear, and 48mph on second. Sir Herbert's 7 was safe, and he was to ensure its supremacy when he modified it later in the year.

Both Rover and Standard had 10hp cars, Morris was to follow, and the Austin came out in good time to begin to fill the gap in what was going to be a very popular class. If the Ford 8 was going to take some sales away from the 7, competition in the growing 10hp section did not look like being so strong. On 18 April, Chris Buckley, Austin's new sales manager attended his first Austin major announcement at Longbridge. Five hundred agents filled the hall when Sir Herbert, who had been in poor health, was wheeled to his chair, helped to his feet for the ordeal of his opening speech, and immediately after it wheeled out again. Reports of his ailment were varied, some said sciatica, some rheumatism, and others gout. In fact, it is likely that he was suffering from that last unpleasant complaint, but it was certainly not caused by taking too much port because he did not drink. In his speech he said that he had been urged on many occasions to transform the 7 into a larger car, and he had always refused because he knew that it would continue pre-eminent in its own class, and that it would not benefit from its promotion.

> The demand for motor vehicles has been scaled down to lower price levels and, in particular, had focussed on cars of 10hp or less. Consequently, I realised that the Austin range only needed the addition of this model to include every size of car in normal request by the general public.

Fourteen fixed-head saloons were built during the week ending 16 April, and these were used for the announcement and as demonstration cars. Later examples with a sunshine roof began in the following week, but were replaced when production of the de luxe saloon began in July. In April only the saloon was introduced, and it was priced at £168. The four-cylinder engine, suspended on rubber bushes at three points, had a bore and stroke of 63.5mm x 89mm (1,125cc), with an RAC rating of 10hp. The crankcase and cylinder block were cast in one piece and the crankshaft and camshaft rotated in three large bearings; 21bhp was available. All that had been

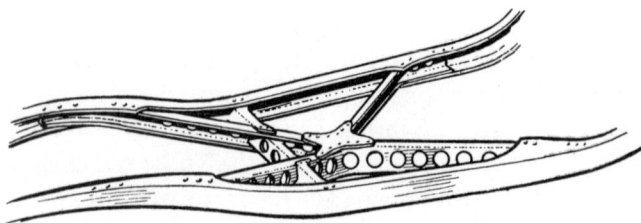

The Ten cross-braced frame, August 1933

Herbert Austin at the wheel of one of his horizontal Wolseleys

The factory entrance, 1906

The first Austin on test: Herbert at the wheel, J. H. Barnett and Vernon Austin standing in the doorway

Disappearing in clouds of smoke: the first Austin on the move

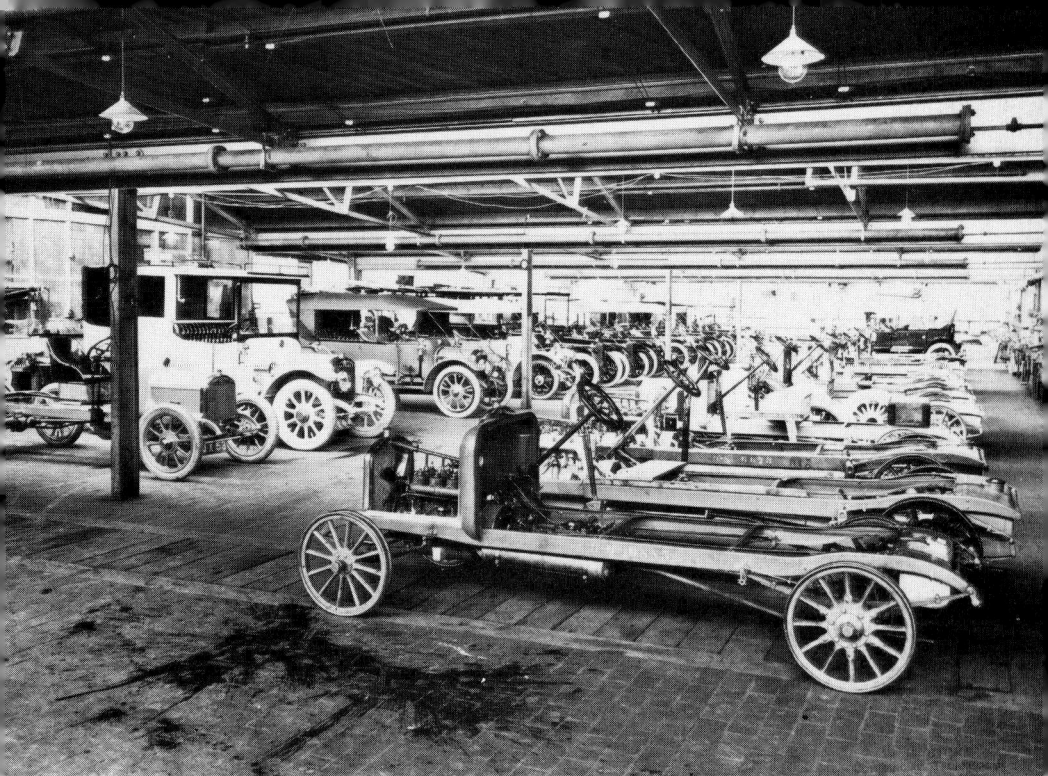

Cars and chassis ready for despatch, November 1913

A 25/30 Phaeton, 1906

Herbert Austin at the wheel of an early car

10HP Courier, fully equipped

Percy Lambert after winning the May handicap at Brooklands

Pearly 3

15HP Town Carriage

The 15HP light van version

Single-cylinder Seven

The Seven engine

15HP Lancaster 3/4 landaulet, January 1913

30HP Vitesse Phaeton, 1914

A late landaulet with detachable wheels and removable seats

1913: 40HP Defiance, curved screen and flush-sided body

The 1913 10HP coupé

1914–18: Austin armoured car

2–3 ton lorry: one of the twin propeller shafts

Central gear-change: two prop shafts and rear-mounted radiator

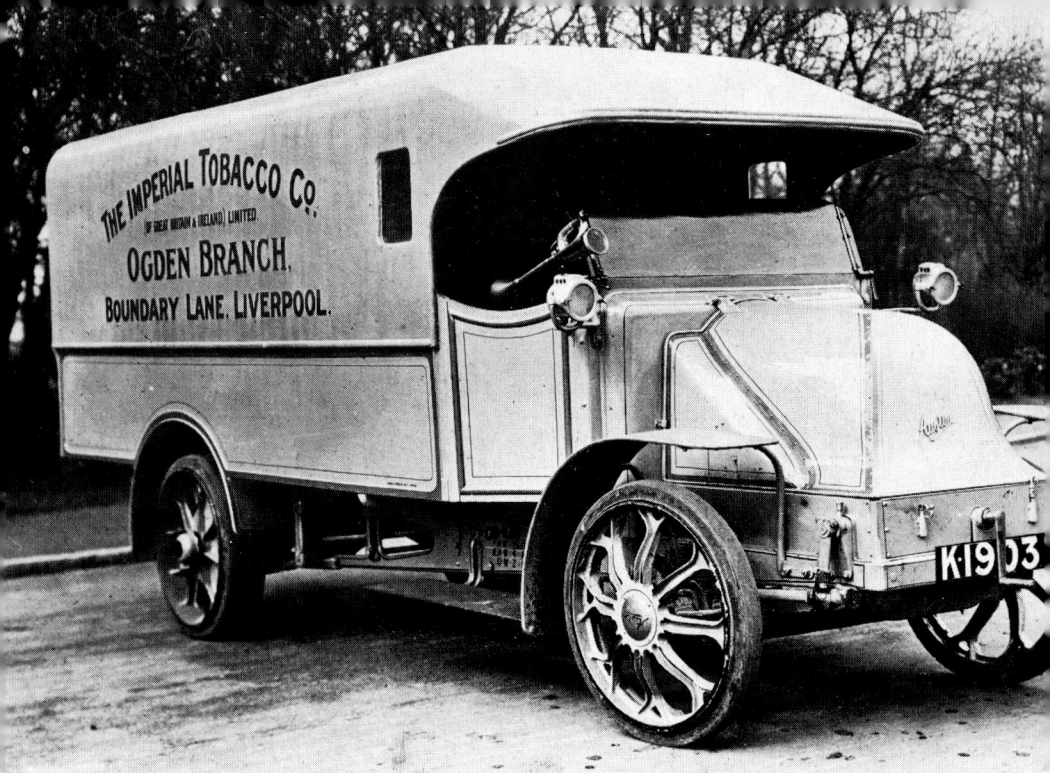

Civilian 2–3 ton lorry

Sergeant Murphy: Felix Scriven after he had just lapped Brooklands at 94.86 mph

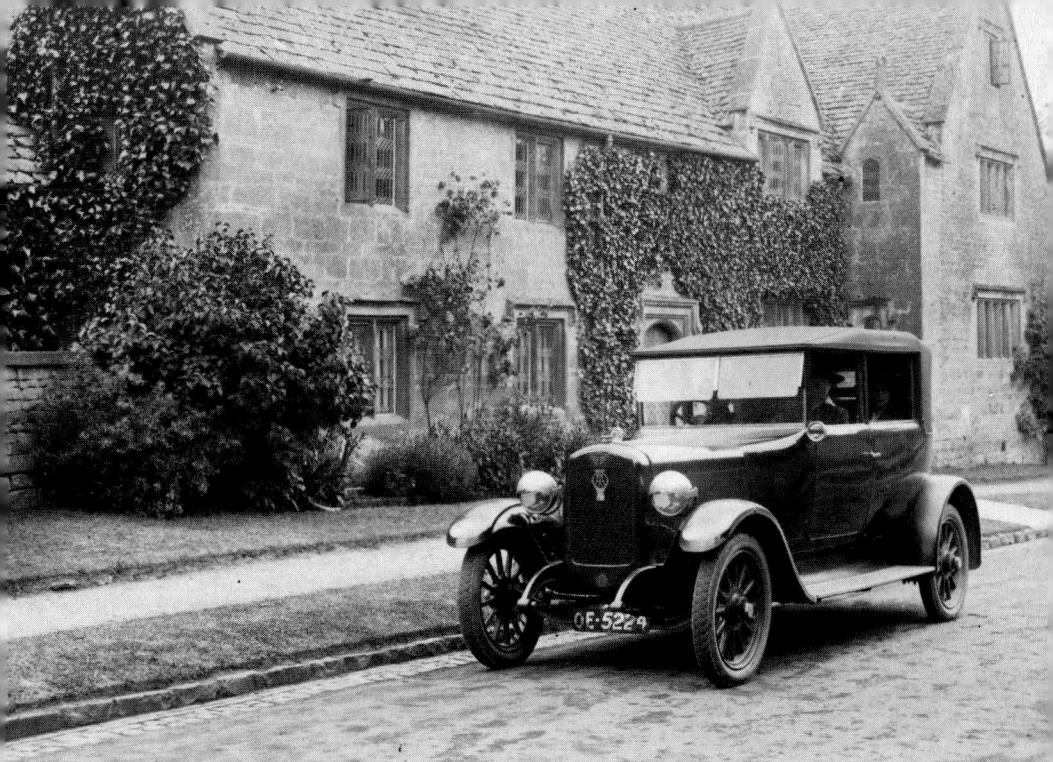

The 1919 Twenty tourer

The 1919 Twenty coupé

A 1922 production Twelve

A Twelve with 4ft track showing the cover over the steering box, 1922

An Austin Twelve in disguise: 13/26 Sizaire-Berwick, November 1923

Twelve Windsor saloon

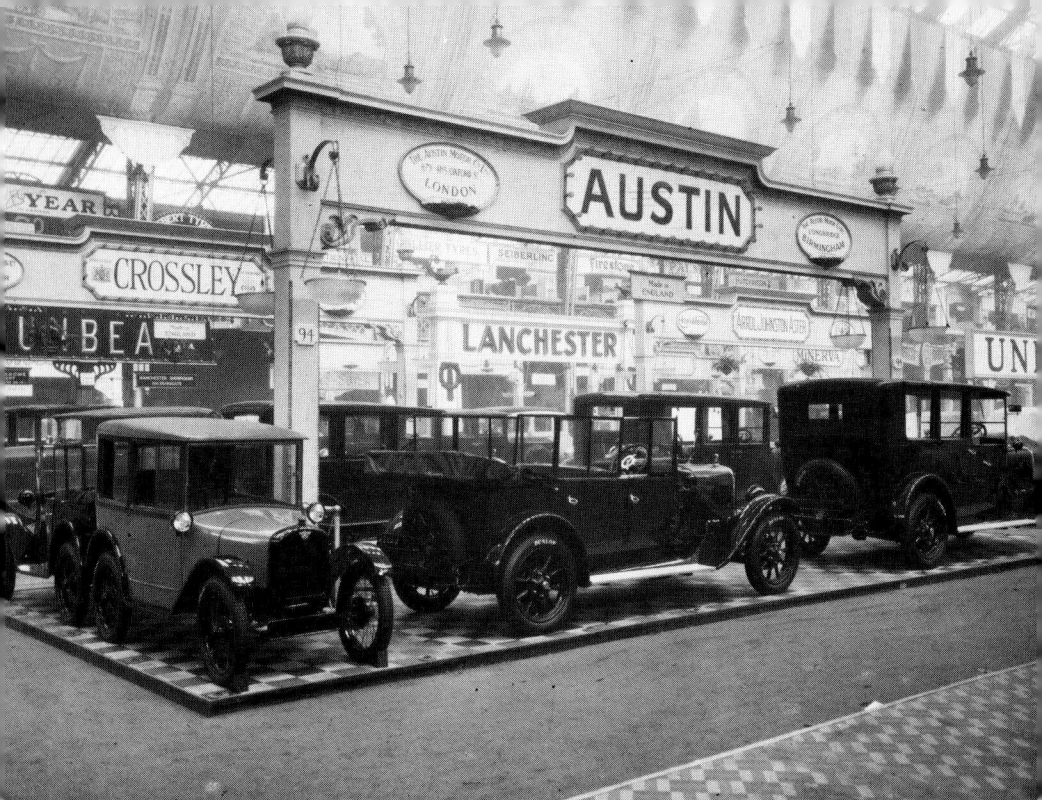

Olympia Motor Show, 1927

Typical Austin taxis

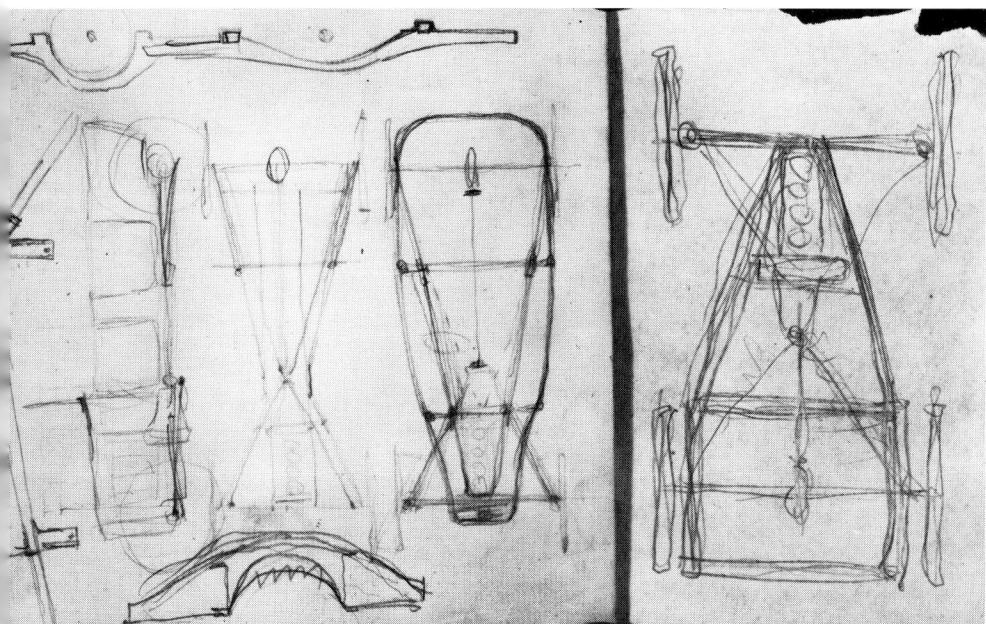

Herbert Austin's sketch for the Seven, showing A-frame and four-wheel brakes

Sir Herbert Austin at the wheel of the first Austin Seven, 1922

An early Chummy with hood up and screens in position

One of the foreign Austin Sevens: a 1928 3-seater Rosengart, rear seat set sideways

The 1931 streamlined Seven single-seater, developed to beat the MGs

Murray Jamieson's Austin Seven racer

1931 16/6 2-seater

1930 16/6 Burnham

Austin stand at the Milan Show, 1931

12/6 Harley saloon

Austin Ten, 1932

A 16/6 Burnham with the new wheel centres

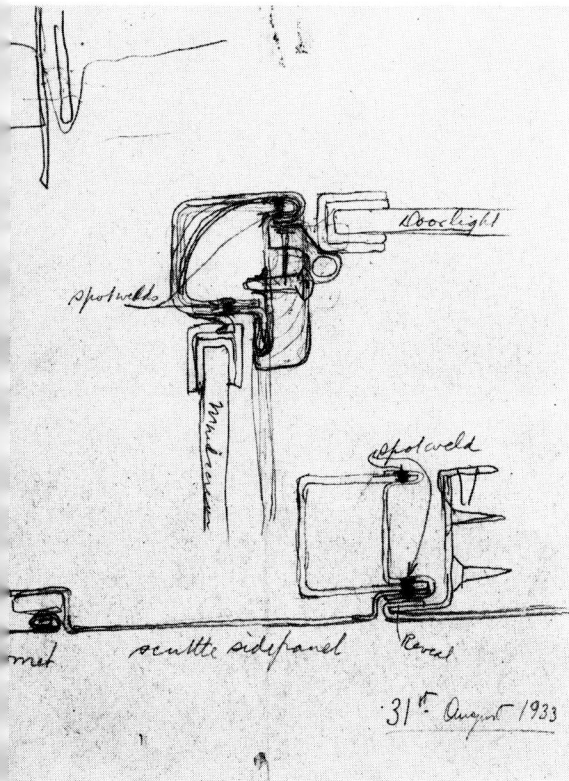

(left) Sketch which Herbert Austin sent (with an explanatory letter) to Dick Burzi. An indication of the extent to which he involved himself in detail . . . *I think we have been going a bit wrong on the front pillar of the new 7HP body – I am showing on other side my idea of the sections across centre of glass screen and about centre of the panel part of the scuttle – of course my sketches are not correct to scale. I've had to make them in a big hurry on the station platform*

(below) The 12/6 sports radiator

The 1936 Ruby

The 1938 Austin Fourteen

The 1938 Big Seven Forlite

The 1938–9 Ranelagh limousine

Leonard Lord's Austin Eight

The attractive lines of the last Twelve

The Twelve bonnet with the detachable sides removed

The 1939 platform chassis

The last Austin Ten

The new 3-ton truck, April 1937

The millionth at the end of the line

The first post-World War II export

Leonard Lord (*right*) with Herbert Austin's brother, Harry, seventy-five and still working at Longbridge in 1946

Post-World War II Austin Sixteen shooting brake

The Atlantic Convertible

Austin's answer to the Jeep

A 1906 advertisement

learnt in the 12/6 had been applied, including the dynamo on the cylinder head, and the mistake — the three-speed gearbox — was removed. As in the 12/6, the new gearbox for the 10, with its well-spaced ratios of 5.25, 8, 12.8 and 20.7 to 1, used the twin-top system with constant-mesh gears of double helical design. This made changing from top to third quite easy, but was not yet up to the standard of the new synchromesh gearbox being used on the Ford 8s. A remarkably sturdy frame was used, very wide with a drop of 2.75in behind the engine, which allowed the body to be mounted directly to the chassis, giving great strength and a low centre of gravity. The floor level was only 14in above the ground, not acceptable on even a bus today, but a distinct improvement at the time. Austin did not make the chassis frame; it was supplied to his design by Projectile & Engineering Co Ltd, but the four-door bodies were built at Longbridge and were not supplied by the Pressed Steel company. Sir Herbert said: 'I have concentrated on road stability. As a consequence of its low weight, 15½cwt, it possesses a power-to-weight ratio that ensures a very satisfactory performance.'

It did perform well, it was pleasant to drive, and was highly reliable. The author had a tourer in the 1950s and even though it was 20 years old and must have done over 50,000 miles — most of that with little or no attention — it ran around London every day with little more being done than to keep the brakes evenly adjusted. A road test by the *Export Trader*, carried out in June 1932, showed a maximum speed in top of 52.3mph and 40mph in third, with a fuel consumption of 35mpg. Acceleration from 10mph to 30mph in third gear took 11⅕ seconds and in top 16⅕ seconds — not sporting characteristics, but with 40ft needed to stop from 30mph, perhaps it was just as well. The tester commented that it was:

> A well made, comfortable, solid vehicle, and if the outline is somewhat square it is due to the fact that practicable considerations such as headroom, body space and passenger comfort were regarded as of more importance than the streamlining contours of a sports car. A sports car the Austin does not pretend to be, but it admirably fills the gap between the 7 and the 12/6.

Production of the 10 for 1932 was as follows:

Fixed saloon	14	commenced w/e 16 April	discontinued
Sunshine saloon	1549	commenced w/e 23 April	w/e 25 June
Saloon de luxe	5960	commenced w/e 2 July	
Standard saloon	338	commenced w/e 10 Sept	
Tourer	114	commenced w/e 1 Oct	
Two-seater	30	commenced w/e 17 Sept	

Van	216	commenced w/e 15 Oct
Gordon	16	commenced w/e 12 Nov
Cabriolet	4	commenced w/e 12 Nov
Chassis	368	commenced w/e 12 Nov

Compared with the 10, the 12/6 was an unfortunate car. It had to have a rear gearbox. In the week ending 5 December 1931, the first new four-speed boxes with twin-top gears were fitted, at first an optional extra at £10, on the Harley. Ratios were 5.5, 8.66, 13.41 and 20.85 to 1, very close to those selected for the Austin 10 gearbox, and the 12/6 three-speed box was soon discarded to the joy of all who had suffered from it. The propeller shaft was also redesigned with Hardy-Spicer universal joints at each end, improved Luvax van-type shock-absorbers were fitted, and the steering column rake was increased to make the driving position more comfortable. A twin-top gear consisted of the direct drive, as formerly, being engaged by a dog, with dog engagement in addition for the third speed. This speed was in constant mesh and the sliding-dog slid one way to engage direct drive on top gear and the other way to engage third speed on the final drive shaft, on which it was free to rotate irrespective of shaft speed. Double helical teeth were used on these gears and on those which drove the layshaft, in place of the noisy straight teeth that would have been essential for sliding gears. These gears eliminated side thrusts and were much quieter in operation. A similar gearbox was available on the 16/6 at £10 extra early in 1932.

One last degradation remained for the 12/6, the nickname of 'the Kensitas car', for which it is perhaps best remembered. Austin believed that advertising was one of the most important features in his general market scheme, and that advertising and keeping a name and quality of a product before the public was even more essential during lean periods than when trade was booming. In 1932 he spent between £3,000 and £5,000 a month on press advertising alone, and engaged Gee Films Limited to make the five-reel 1 hour sound publicity film *This Progress*, the longest advertising film yet made showing a potted history of motoring. There were three reels of factory processes and a final reel of a drive through the countryside in an Austin 10. It was released to be shown by Austin dealers in June 1932. Spending large sums with the press helped to keep the image of the Austin products fresh, and also ensured fair reporting and good editorials, and Sir Herbert seems to have been followed by an almost completely loyal press corps throughout the 1930s. Kensitas were the largest cigarette advertisers in 1932, spending £37,000 on press advertising in May alone, and in January they decided to give away a car a day to winners of a slogan competition. The slogan was to contain twenty words written on the backs of Kensitas packets, and the prizes were to be Austin 12/6 de luxe saloons. In all, 179 cars were given away, and the publicity value to both Kensitas and Austin was enormous. After that expensive venture, they started giving away books in exchange for coupons.

Austin had sold the cars at something less than the retail price, and the Motor Agent's Association forwarded to him a resolution that MAA members did not consider the practice adopted by 'certain manufacturers' of giving cars as competition novelties was in the best interest of the motor trade, but that if these methods were to be adopted the cars should be distributed through the ordinary channels on normal terms. Austin did not like being told how he should sell his cars, and replied that he was not surprised that there had been talk about this scheme as there had been a good deal of misrepresentation. The difficulties were caused mainly, he said, by the local agents themselves, who attempted to buy the prize cars from him at ridiculous prices. Kensitas had paid a very satisfactory price for the cars, and had Austin not accepted the offer then another firm would have jumped at it. Apart from his usual optimistic pronouncements, later in the year Austin and Englebach spoke on the radio for thirty minutes. At the Motor Show banquet, which was held again in October 1932 after being cancelled in 1931, the dealers and many of his competitors presented him with a portrait in oils which had been painted by the artist George Harcourt.

In February, Herbert Parkes who had gone on the Austin board in 1926 resigned his seat on taking up an appointment as a permanent member of the Railway Rates Tribunal. His place was taken by Herbert Pepper of the Birmingham solicitors Pepper, Tangye and Winterton. Pepper was also a director of Guy Motors Limited and of the Star Motor Company of Wolverhampton. Austin ordinary shares had fallen to 23s 9d in January, but rose to 35s just prior to the announcement of the results for the year ending 31 July. Gross trading profit for the year fell by nearly £300,000 to £1,078,145, leaving £390,387 net, with most of the spare cash being added to the credit balance which stood at £319,220. Austins were lucky to have done so well, many firms were having trouble — Rover had just reported a loss of £96,000 and had carried forward a debit balance of £280,000 — and the Austin board decided to keep as much money in the business as they could to allow for any bad years in the future. The ordinary dividend was cut by half, a 25 per cent dividend and a 25 per cent bonus being given, and there was great disappointment which caused the shares to drop again to

27s 6d. The low dividend was felt to be a precautionary rather than a necessary measure, not strictly dictated by financial necessity — the trading profit may have fallen by 22 per cent, but the net profit was still substantial. Everybody knew that the American Austin Car Company had lost $2.75 million in the fifteen-month period to March, but was it not Sir Herbert himself who had said that exports were booming, that in Australia in 1929 12 per cent of the car imports were British, and that by 1931 it had risen to over 52 per cent? The fact was that this substantial increase in the British proportion was excellent, but the other part of the equation had been neglected; total imports into Australia were 93,000 vehicles in 1929, but fell to only 3,000 in 1931. Australia also was in trouble.

There were twenty-six different Austin models at the time of the Motor Show in October 1932. This was rather less complicated than it sounds; the 20/6 was still available, on either the long or the short chassis; the 16/6 and 12/4 engines were both built into a similar chassis; the 7 remained predominant; the new 10 was well in its stride; and the 12/6 chassis was used for an alternative 12hp four-cylinder engine. On the 7, a new four-speed twin-top gearbox was used, improving the car's specification over that of the Ford 8 which still had only three speeds. The starter motor was mounted forward of the flywheel on the off-side, and the oil-filler pipe was inclined. A single casting was used for the combined inlet and exhaust manifold, and there was a new Zenith carburetter and a rear-mounted fuel tank. Prices were reduced, the new two-seater costing 100 guineas, the new tourer £110, and the two saloons £115 and £125.

On the 16/6 a new Berkeley de luxe body, lower than the Burnham which it superseded, cost £318 and was introduced during the week ending 10 September; the Harrow and Open Road continued but at £12 less at £288, and the new Westminster was reduced by £15 to £345. Stocks of the old 12/4 Burnham and Windsor bodies were sold off in October, and after then the bodies for the two engines were the same except that the 12/4 could be bought as a standard Berkeley for £265. The other 12/4 prices were £30 to £33 less than the 16/6.

The 20/6 was now only available as the Ranelagh at the same price of £575, and the Whitehall reduced by £27 to £498. Thermostats were fitted to control the cooling system, and there were new chromium-plated lamps and pressed-steel luggage carriers.

Three new models were added to the 10hp range: a standard saloon for £155, a four-door tourer and a two-seater tourer with dickey seat at £148. Body lines, as they merged from the roof and the sides into the back panel, followed a more graceful curve, and this permitted removal of the beads which had formerly divided the back panelling. Headlamps were increased in size and the tyres were heavier, 4.50in x 18in, but no other modifications were necessary.

On the 12/6, the de luxe body construction was now coach-built and improved to help eliminate drumming and, of course, the four-speed gear box was now standard. A thermostat was fitted and prices were reduced slightly, by £3 on the open cars and £7 on the Harley de luxe saloon. Finally, a new engine, the light 12/4, was available as an alternative in a similar chassis. It had a bore and stroke of 69.3mm x 101.6mm (1,535 cc) an RAC rating of 11.9hp, and it developed 24bhp at 2,400rpm — the same as the 12/6, but with two less cylinders for about the same capacity. There was a three-bearing crank and the crankcase and cylinder block were in one casting, being held in the engine by three-point suspension. In all other respects the car was the same as the 12/6. With a top speed of 51mph and an average fuel consumption of about 29mpg, it was a much better engine than the six-cylinder version, and altogether less fussy and troublesome.

It was not cheap, the de luxe saloon being the same price as the 12/6 Harley, but the standard saloon was £178 and the two tourers were £168. Production details for the model for the remainder of 1932 were as follows:

De luxe saloon	1,328	commenced w/e 10 Sept
Standard saloon	329	
Tourer	51	commenced w/e 16 Oct
Two-seater	22	
Van	97	commenced w/e 26 Nov
Gordon	19	
Chassis	21	

The contention about quality and price held good for a comparatively expensive car as it did for the cheaper ones. Customers were willing to pay £20 more to get a de luxe model.

Five major extensions to the Longbridge buildings had been made since 1927 covering ½ million square feet at a cost of over £250,000. The South works remained the administrative centre with drawing offices, tool room and experimental and research blocks. A new area of floor space, known as Trentham Buildings, after the contractor, was added to the south side of South works just below the flying ground. This permitted considerable reorganisation at West works which was rearranged for complete body production, assembly, painting, trimming and wiring. North works was re-equipped with machines for engine production, including the machining of cylinder blocks from the adjacent foundry, and the production of nuts and bolts and other small components. The revised layout provided four engine-assembly racks which were fed with components from nearby machinery lines. Engine blocks were all roller-conveyed, with lifts or 'lowerators' to raise the blocks to the head of new roller conveyors, or to bring them from roof-storage levels down to the assembly tracks.

Flow production was used in the West works and conveyor lines zig-zagged or looped to make the fullest use of the floor space available in carrying bodies through all stages of preparation for painting. Throughout the whole of Longbridge by the early 1930s the production of cars was dovetailed to fit the conveyor system. Engines were brought ¾ mile from the North works to No 2 machine shop where the gearboxes were added. From there the units were taken by conveyor to the erecting shop where, on arrival, they were switched automatically to the appropriate assembly track. In a similar way, axles were carried forward from their assembly shop to the chassis-erecting shop and bodies, brought from West works by road, were lowered by crane onto the completed chassis. The car was then moved forward on its track into the body-mounting shop for finish assembly.

New extensions were built facing the Bristol road from the old entrance gate to Lowhill Lane early in 1932 to accommodate the Austin Service organisation. They were used for servicing and repair work, and to house and despatch spare parts, and had a very wide unobstructed single-floor span with a glass roof covering 150,000sq ft. A new timber store and sawmill were built to release space to extend the press and panel shops and, in mid-1932, an extensive scheme of mechanisation was applied to the paint process on the 7, 10, 12/6 and 16 bodies. Bodies were slung on a continuous chain in one of the lines, driven by an electric motor. Each bare steel body passed through cleaning and de-oxidising operations; it was then carried through a glass-panelled spray booth and on through an oven. Rubbing down and polishing was done by hand and spraying and beating operations were repeated. In all, nineteen coats of spray were applied, and the finish was excellent. Unfortunately fashion demanded a preponderance of dark-blue and maroon in the 1930s, and the pigments in these colours at the time were not fast. The result was that there was a good deal of trouble with fading, but on the black and green finishes the paint was of high durability and, if the coachwork was kept clean and abrasive polishes were avoided, fifteen to twenty years life could be expected from a Longbridge paint job. At the end of the process, a pneumatic hoist removed the bodies, and the chain continued to take up another bare body at the start of the track. A further 128,000sq ft of floor space was completed in the summer of 1933 to cater for the new models being introduced, costing over £30,000. The 10 and the light 12/4 were eating into the cash that had been put aside for them but, as will be seen, they were going to earn their keep.

In January 1933, after the Treasury lifted the ban on optional conversion schemes, the opportunity was taken to convert the 6½ per cent first mortgage debenture stock, of which £1,078,820 was redeemable at any time on three months notice at 103 per cent common, to an issue of £1.1 million 5 per cent first mortgage stock to be issued at par. Those who decided to change were to receive a cash payment of £3 per cent, plus interest at 6½ per cent to May. The stock was covered over three and a half times in capital and over nine times in interest and sinking-fund requirements by the profits of the year ended 1 August 1932. Interest rates on loans had fallen, and 6½ per cent was out of step with the market, but a reduction in the rate to 5 per cent saved £18,000, equivalent to a 12 per cent dividend on the ordinary shares. The issue was a great attraction and it was over-subscribed eight times. As 850,000 of the existing debenture holders accepted, there was very little left to be given to other investors, and when trading began the stock sold for £103.

1933 was another excellent year for the motor industry and car registrations increased by more than 70,000. Over 1.3 million cars were produced in America, making it by far the biggest motor manufacturer in the world, but Britain came second with 220,779; France was a fairly close third at 175,000. Imports into this country remained at a very low level, 3,619, owing to continued protection from the McKenna duties, but exports nearly doubled over the previous year to 41,334. Morris activity was at a low level with a production of only 44,049, but Austin reached a new record of 57,741, over 13,000 more than in 1932.

The 10 just beat the 7 into first place, and the 12/6 suffered a marked decline with the introduction of the new four-cylinder engine. Full production figures for 1933 were:

Model	No produced
10	20,937
7	20,475
Light 12/4	7,020
12	2,996
12/6	2,896
16	2,788
20	629

Austin had chosen exactly the right time to bring the 10 onto the market. In 1933, cars of 8hp took 25.6 per cent of sales, and the 10hp class reached 26 per cent, a position which it was to hold for a number of years at the expense of the larger cars of 11-16hp. Buyers still wanted an 8hp car at about £120, but the feature for the middle years of the 1930s was the 10hp car costing about £170.

Morris was still earning a profit of over £1 million a year, but some of the other medium-sized firms in the motor industry were much less successful. Rover, having made a loss in the previous year, managed a small profit of £47,000, but still carried forward a debit balance of £271,000, and Singer made a net profit of only £43,000. Ford, which made over £1 million in 1930-1 and £382,000 in 1931-2, made a loss in 1932-3 of £288,000. They had not paid a dividend for two years, their shares had fallen from 50s to 15s 3d, and investors were being advised to sell them before they fell any lower. The company had been a victim of circumstances — the completion of Dagenham had coincided with an unforeseen growth of European tariff walls. They had solved the problem of producing cars, but not of selling them.

Austin ordinary shares, the great speculation of the early 1930s told a different story. They stood at 43s 6d in February 1933 and rose steadily to an all-time high of 70s in September. Trading results for the year ending 31 July 1933 came out in September. The gross trading profit had risen to £1,188,440 leaving £506,798 net, with £357,497 being carried forward. Jubilant ordinary shareholders got their 100 per cent again, this time as a 25 per cent dividend and a 75 per cent cash bonus. No mention was made in the accounts of royalty payments from abroad. The motor industry in America, France and Germany was not doing well; the American Austin Car Company lost over $402,000 in the year to 31 March 1933, and Austin's real success was in direct exports to Europe and the Empire.

A cabriolet version of the 10 was introduced in March 1933 at £168. Four bodies were made in the previous year for exhibition in Paris, as it was thought this style would appeal to the French market. Another 1,018 were made in 1933, so it had only a limited demand, whether in France or at home. A large luggage compartment, merging with the rear body-lines, created a distinctive appearance, but the important feature was the well-designed roof which could be opened halfway to give the advantages of a sunshine roof, or dropped completely to the rear.

The year 1933 saw an increase in the demand for sports versions of standard production cars. The MG, which was really only a tuned-up

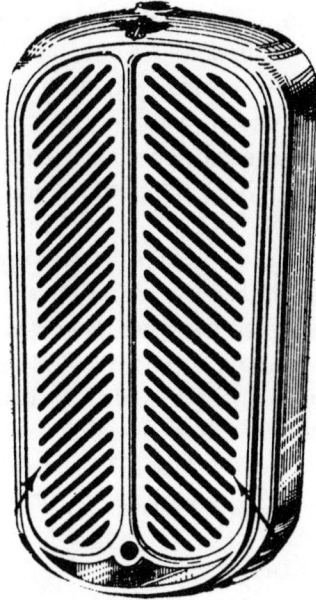

The 12/6 radiator grille

Morris Minor, and to a lesser extent earlier sports variations of the Austin 7 had led the way, but Austin began to enter the field seriously in May rather surprisingly, with the 12/6 sports tourer. It cost £268, £73 more than the Open Road tourer, but it was a vastly different car. The new four-door body had low, rakish lines, a wildly sloping windscreen, cut-away body sides, and certainly looked like a sports car, bearing no resemblance to any other Austin. To ensure greater stability, the chassis frame was dropped in the centre, and three of the rigid cross-members passed beneath the propeller shaft; special rear springs were used with the forward anchorages being lower than the rear shackles, allowing the seats to be placed 4in lower than on the standard model. Propeller-shaft diameter was increased, batteries were housed under the bonnet and, in place of bonnet louvres for cooling, the separately adjustable doors on the bonnet sides which were to become a familiar feature on all Austin models later on, were first used. There were no running-boards and the radiator was placed behind a distinctive pressed-steel stone-guard cowl which had two sets of sloping slots through which air could pass. The steering column was raked to a low angle and there was a new close-ratio four-speed gearbox of 18.26, 11.7, 7.58 and 5.5 to 1 ratios. Extra performance was given to the engine by using redesigned manifolds and a new Zenith down-draught carburetter, the compression ratio was increased to 7:1 and there was a special high-lift camshaft and stronger valve springs which, with a balanced crank, all helped to produce 40bhp and to give the car a maximum speed of over 75mph. The author has neither driven nor even seen one of these sports tourers, and it is difficult to judge the performance with only a few press reports as a guide. Production began during the week ending 29 April and only 86 were made that year so perhaps we will never know. In 1934, the tourer was named the Newbury. A very attractive saloon version called the Greyhound, the bodies of which were imported from Ambi-Budd in Germany, was added in August, costing £305. Only 59 of them were made in 1933, and the name had to be dropped — becoming the Kempton — because it was already used by another manufacturer.

Next came a real sports car, the Austin 7 Sports 65 at £148, and in the six months of 1933 during which it was available 234 were sold. The car was a low-slung two-seater, the driver's seat being only 14in from the ground; the radiator was lower and squarer than on the standard cars and was protected by a chromium-plated stone-guard. Alterations were made to the front axle and suspension, and there was a new inlet manifold and down-draught Zenith carburetter which produced 23 bhp at 4,800rpm from the engine, which was modified in much the same way as on the 12/6 sports model.

One more sports car completed the trio, the 10/4. It was given a smaller version of the 12/6 Sports tourer body, and the first car was produced in the week ending 19 August. It cost £215 and only four were made in 1933, 76 in 1934, and 48 in 1935. Similar modifications were made to the engine, and it was provided with a close-ratio gearbox.

Replying to a question in an interview during the early summer of 1933, Sir Herbert forecast an increase in car prices:

> I am constantly being asked this question, my answer is, 'Yes, most likely'. Naturally too many considerations affect the price question for me to make any more definite assertion at the moment, but undoubtedly there is a general tendency for commodity prices to harden.

The 1934 programme was announced on 14 August, some weeks before those of the other large manufacturers, and the Austin prices were increased by £2 to £3 on the 7 and up to £20 on the 20; but at the same time one or two alterations were made which more than compensated for the small rises. The outstanding innovations for 1934 were semaphore

The Ascot luggage carrier, August 1933

illuminated direction-indicators, the new Ascot and Carlton bodies, the rigid chassis and the synchromesh gearbox.

Manufacturers had been trying to improve the old crash-type gearbox on which it was necessary to double-declutch between gear changes. They developed the twin-top constant-mesh box, and in February the Austin 20 was fitted with the final version with new ratios and constant mesh on three of the forward speeds. Incidentally, the box on the 10ft Whitehall chassis combined with a final drive-ratio of 3.92 against 4.67:1 increased the top speed performance of that car. All that was needed, now that constant-mesh double-helical gears had proved a success, was to take the need for skill out of gear-changing. To make a change even with this latest box, it was necessary to cause the sets of gear wheels to revolve at more or less the same speed. This meant that the speed of the road wheels and the speed of the engine had to be in correct relationship, which required a degree of skill and judgement possessed by few of the new motorists, so a way had to be found to overcome their lack of precision. A synchromesh device eliminated the disparity between the speeds of the gear-coupling and the gear with which it was to mate by using a bronze cone clutch which synchronised the speeds of the two members concerned, acting as a brake on the faster member or a clutch to speed up the slower, until there was no relative movement between the two members to prevent the dogs sliding smoothly into mesh. All Austin gearboxes were provided with synchromesh on third and top gears. Synchromesh on second came later, and was not used on first gears until quite recently, so an Austin gearbox of 1934 was in most respects

187

the same as those still in use today.

In addition to the freewheel, other manufacturers had tried an alternative, the much more complicated and expensive pre-selective gearbox. It had certain advantages, but some form of variable speed transmission without spaced gearing must be the real answer; something better and smoother than the automatic transmission that we have today would solve all the problems of matching the inflexible petrol engine to the variety of speeds and loads demanded by the road wheels. Austin had such a device, as described in the next chapter.

Alternative engines, at no extra cost, were available in the 16 and 12/6 models — an idea already tried by Ford, Vauxhall and Hillman. In the former case, there was a new alternative 18hp engine, with four-bearing crank, monobloc cast-iron crankcase and block of 69.5mm bore and 111mm stroke (2,510cc) giving 17.9hp. The Berkeley and Westminster saloons and the two open models were still available on the 16's 9ft 4in chassis, but a new 10ft chassis was introduced to take a new saloon body, the Carlton. This, and its smaller version on the 12/6, the Ascot, had an enclosed spare-wheel carrier as an extension at the rear which could be lowered for use as a luggage platform. Bonnet side-louvres were replaced by the row of doors that had proved so attractive on the 12/6 sports car. As on the 16, there was an alternative engine, not of a new design but the standard 12/6 bored out by 4.25mm to 65.5mm, to give a capacity of 1,711cc and a hp of 15.9. On the 10, the frame was strengthened by cross-bracing below the propeller shaft and the 6V electrical system was replaced by 12V. All models were given spare-wheel covers and, of course, synchromesh gears.

In 1930 the 12/4, which had been on the market for eight years, was to have been discontinued, the idea being to supersede it by the two new models, the 12/6 and the light 12/4. Although it was kept rather in the background, production was maintained. The design of the car made it more expensive to produce than the later Austin models but, even at the higher price, it continued to sell sufficiently well to be kept in the catalogue. It was given new, lighter front and rear axles for 1934, better brakes and the lower cross-braced chassis.

Austin cars were reaching the peak of their perfection, all the improvements which had been added over the previous two or three years having produced cars which were going to be familiar for more than another ten years. All that remained from the first Austins was the distinctive chromium-plated radiator shell, and even that was not going to last much longer in spite of what Sir Herbert said when asked at a Motor Agents Association

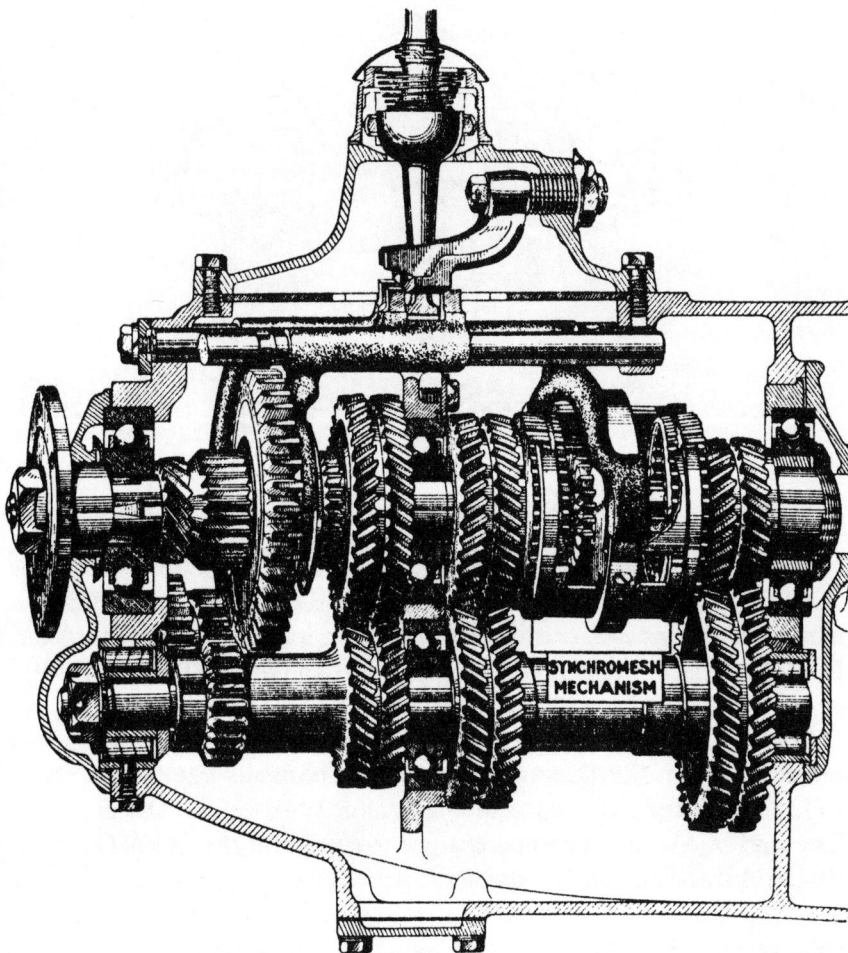

Twin-top gear box

dinner in October 1934 when he was going to bring his radiator shape more into accord with current trends in radiator design: 'When the Rolls-Royce company change their radiator, I will change ours'.

What of the success of the alternative engine sizes on the 12/6 and 16/6? In 1934, 4,339 12/6 cars were made, and 2,331 of them had the larger 15.9hp engine. By 1935, of a total of 4,143, the number of larger engines had increased to 2,830. Given that the 12/6 engine was not much good, perhaps it would be more relevant to look at the 16. It must be remembered that there was no extra charge made for the larger engine yet, in 1934, 2,954

189

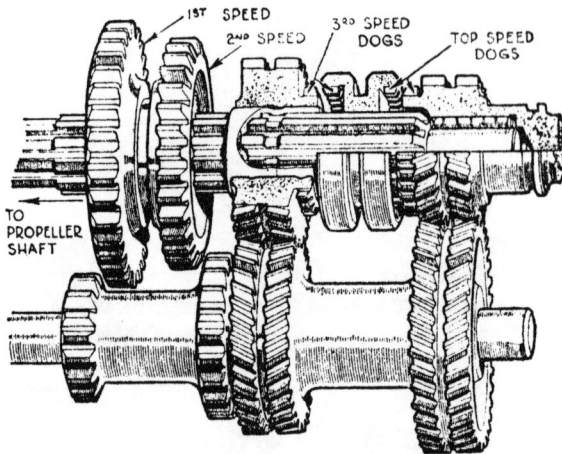

Synchromesh gear box, October 1933

customers chose the 16 against only 2,630 who selected the 18. By 1935, the smaller engine was provided on 2,052 cars, and the larger one on 3,280. A more marked tendency existed with those who wanted the 12/6 sports car. In 1934, 79 chose the small engine against 228 who wanted the 15.9; in 1935 only 14 chose the former against 136 choosing the latter.

1932 was not a year marked by any great Austin 7 successes in racing or in record breaking. L.P.Driscoll set up a new Brooklands 750cc lap record at 103.11mph, but Eyston beat him shortly after by getting his MG up to 112. The Earl of March, in a supercharged Austin, beat the two MGs at the BRDC British Empire Trophy race in April, completing the course at over 92mph. Barnes and Goodacre finished second and fourth at the German International race over a 21 mile course at over 85mph. In spite of an average speed of 91.13mph over 248 miles at the LCC Relay race, the 7 team only managed to come fourth, being beaten by the Wolseley Hornets. An MG beat the three Austin supercharged team cars at the BRDC 500 miles race, and Austin decided not to enter for either the Ulster TT or the new 1,000 miles race which was to replace the old Double-Twelve. This was really an admission of Austin's inability to increase the performance of the side-valve engine to compete against the MG Midgets.

In 1933, an attempt was made to produce a car that would win back some of the international class records from the magic Midget. A very serious young man wearing glasses had impressed Stan Yeal, a member of the competitions department of Austins, by the way in which he handled his

190

car, and in its performance. His name was T.Murray Jamieson, and he was soon working for Austin with a free hand to build a 750cc racer which would win back the records which the MGs had taken. Jamieson took the car which he had built to Montlhéry in October, and although he was unable to reach his goal of 120mph, he took three MG records, one up to just under 113, and Jamieson knew that there was nothing more he could do with a supercharged 750cc side-valve engine.

12 The £100 Car and the Enclosed Radiator at Last: 1934 and 1935

Excessive streamlining is a flash in the pan.

Sir Herbert Austin, 1934

Frank Anderson Hayes, an American inventor, had been working on automatic transmission systems for a number of years. During World War I he had met Captain J.L.Cloudsley of the Cloudsley Engineering Company of London and, a chance meeting on a railway station having brought them together again, they worked on Hayes's transmission together for five or six years. Cloudsley introduced Hayes to Austin and the three of them worked on perfecting the idea, which was by then protected by US and British patents, and a prototype was ready by 1932. The Hayes infinitely variable transmission was a remarkable device. I was fortunate enough to own one fitted in a 1935 16 in the 1960s, and if only the minor defects from which it suffered could have been overcome, and if it had been provided with an automatic clutch, I am sure that the subsequent development of automatic transmissions would have taken a different course.

In the Hayes transmission, pressure was self-contained and automatically applied through a friction drive in which spherically edged roller discs made contact with outer and inner cup-shaped pressure surfaces. An infinitely variable gear was provided within chosen limits of 1:1.5 and 3.6:1, the change in ratio being hydraulically operated, automatically effecting a balance between the power being developed by the engine and the tractive resistance of the car at any moment. On the first cars fitted with the transmission in 1934 there were two long levers on the steering wheel. When the lever on the left was at its top position it allowed the ratio to run up to its maximum, but when lowered it reduced the highest ratio to any desired extent. The second lever, on the right, controlled the maximum speed to which the engine could rise when the accelerator pedal was fully depressed. Only a few of these transmissions were fitted to 16hp cars from November 1933 and in 1934, and they were available for an extra charge of £40.

Two levers proved to be too complicated for the average driver to master, for the car still had all the normal controls, including a clutch and a lever to select forward and reverse, so from 1935 a new system with only one lever to control the hydraulics was employed. This was available on the 16 and 18hp saloons in 1935 at £50, but only about fifty were sold in spite of a massive advertising campaign which used as its slogan 'All you have to do is steer', which was not strictly true because the clutch still had to be engaged to take up the drive from starting, and disengaged on coming to a halt. Extreme difficulty was experienced in machining and grinding the discs and rollers which had to be made with great accuracy, but I think that the Hayes self-selector failed to gain the popularity it deserved for a number of other reasons, not least of which was the extra cost. It still required a clutch, so was not really automatic in the accepted sense and although it was infinitely variable and completely smooth in operation, drivers gained the false impression that the engine was running at a higher speed than necessary for conditions of drag and load.

One factor more than any other which led to its being abandoned, however, was the manual control. It was meant to be used, but the transmission was so effortless and efficient that drivers left it in one position, and after about 10,000 miles with the friction wheels running to the limit set by the control a groove was worn in the discs which caused the transmission to stick in one position. It continued to plough a deeper groove and the result was that the roller could not get a free run over the friction surfaces. No agents were allowed to touch the Hayes transmission and it was not an economic proposition to return the car to the factory for repair; the only solution was a replacement box at £50.

Hayes's principle was used later in alternator drives in aircraft but it was never developed for use in automobile transmissions; there was an unfounded rumour at the time that General Motors paid Hayes and Austin a large sum to cease their experiments, but for whatever reason, the Hayes transmission deserved a better fate and I see no reason why it could not still have a future. General Motors, through Knudsen, the director, did pay the company £20,000 for three years for the manufacturing rights in the US, but did not take up the option. Had it not been for the introduction of synchromesh in the early 1930s, and had there been a real desire for automatic transmission in Britain, Austin might have persisted.

For the year ending 31 July 1934, the company's gross trading profit increased by over £300,933 to £1,502,212, leaving a net figure of £661,280 and £362,933 to be carried forward. Ordinary shares stood at £3 3s in

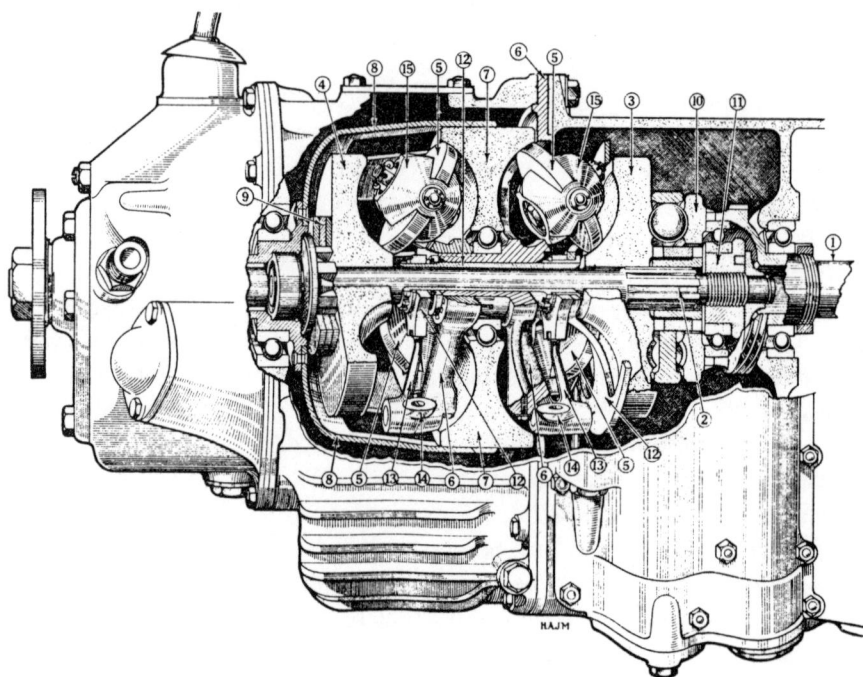

The Hayes transmission, November 1933: the driving shaft (2) on which the two outer races (3 and 4) float, takes its drive from the clutch shaft (1). The two sets of three rollers (5) held in the fixed assembly (6) transmit the drive to the centre race (7) from which it is taken by a drum (8) to the propeller shaft. The rollers (5) in their carriers (15) can rock to different positions between the driving and driven races to provide the variations in ratio, this rocking being initiated by the control sleeve (12) which moves the levers (13) and the rockers (14). The control mechanism being sensitive to variations in engine speed and tractive resistance, provides automatic functioning. The pressure on the assembly to ensure a positive drive is derived from the spring washers (9) and the balls which in transmitting the drive between the torque ring (10) and the outer race (3), have a wedging action in their inclined grooves.

November 1933 and increased steadily to reach £5 in March 1934 after the successful appeal in the Courts against an action for infringement brought by the makers of the Pytchley sliding roof. The Court of Appeal reversed a previous decision in which the Mechanical & General Inventions Company and Edouard Lehwess were awarded £98,550 against Austins for an alleged breach of agreement in connection with the design of the sunshine roof. A

194

nominal sum of £2 without costs was awarded to the plaintiffs on a lesser claim. The case lingered on until Austin won it finally in July 1936. Shares reached £6 by September, and this valued the £150,000 of issue share capital at nearly £4 million. The announcement on the dividend came on 19 September, and it proved that the market was justified in placing such a high value on the stock. When trading began again they rose to £7 each. Shareholders were given a 25 per cent dividend and the same 75 per cent cash bonus that they had received a year before, but in addition this time there was to be a three for one scrip issue of Ordinary A shares without voting rights. To do this it was necessary to capitalise £450,000 of the reserves, and it brought the stock back to its pre-1927 value. An additional 100,000 5s A ordinary shares was created, to be issued at 10s each, a half to be available to the present directors, and the balance to senior employees of the company on the condition that they were not sold within the following twelve months. In April 1933 the company started the Austin pension scheme, one of the first major private funds to be formed. It was contributory with free insurance, and for a minimum of 6d a week a pension could be obtained at 65. Funded by a contribution from the firm of £80,000, it was available first to administrative and office staff, and later extended to cover 14,000 manual workers.

Trade was booming in 1934. Again Morris was not as successful as Austin; his production reached only just over 55,000 cars and the company's net profit was halved. Real success and domination for him were to come in 1935. At the 1934 Budget, the government announced a reduction of a quarter in the hp motor tax to take effect from 1 January 1935. British motor car output compared with 1933 increased by over 35,000 to 256,866 and the total private car registrations were lifted by over 100,000 to 1,333,590. Although British exports rose a little, by some 4,000 cars to 45,327, imports climbed to 10,851, a rise of over 7,000. Austin production was 68,291, made up as follows:

Model	No produced
7	22,542
10	24,149
12/4	2,934
12/6 ⎫	2,008 ⎫
15.9 ⎭	2,331 ⎭
Light 12	8,252
16/6 ⎫	2,954 ⎫
18 ⎭	2,630 ⎭
20	491

It will be seen that the 7 and the 10 were equal partners, and between them they represented 60 per cent of the Austin output. Only a half of the total new UK car sales were in these groups, so these were by far the most popular cars in their respective ranges. The light 12 did quite well at over 8,000, as did the 16/6 and the new 15.9hp variant of the 12/6. The other models were less significant, although they made a useful contribution to total production. One sad note was recorded at the shareholders' meeting that year, the death of Arthur Beck in July 1933 at the age of 69. He was a prominent figure in the industrial life of the Midlands, and as well as having been a director of Austin's since 1925 was also an active member of the National Union of Manufacturers, a director of the Metallic Seamless Tube Company, owner of the Royal Potteries, Weston-super-Mare, and a director of James Parsons, Gloucestershire Brick and a number of other companies.

In July there was a strike at the Pressed Steel Company's factory at Cowley, and 1,000 bodies a week were lost to the industry just four weeks before show stocking of the new models. Workers there wanted payments for time working instead of a piece-work deal, and a union closed shop. Skilled men at Pressed Steel were getting the equivalent of 1s 6d an hour, which was the normal union rate. Management refused to change their system and the strike failed within a few weeks in time for Austin, who was the first manufacturer to announce a programme for 1935, to get some new cars ready for display. Within a few months he decided to begin work on a new press shop at Longbridge which was to contain fifty power presses. An agreement had been made between all car makers to delay the introduction of new models until just before the Motor Show. In order to be first, the cars for the following year had previously been brought out to beat competitors at a very early date.

Although there were no new Austin chassis, some prices were reduced and there were some new features. Public demand was far more for new body-lines rather than any radical mechanical changes. Raked windscreens were popular, but Austin considered he had sloped them far enough; in fact his were left almost upright because he considered that a greater degree of slope 'caused eyestrain amongst drivers'. So the August 1934 changes concentrated on simplifying various controls, increasing the comfort and convenience of the coachwork and generally securing a more attractive appearance.

A new 7 was produced embodying a new radiator design in which the familiar core was shielded behind a deep cowling with rounded lines and vertical slats cellulosed in the same colour as the body. At its base the cowling merged into the front wings, and the radiator filler was beneath the bonnet. The bonnet was lengthened and there was a new dropped chassis, a four-speed gearbox with synchromesh on the three high gears, a cleaned up tail to the body with a spare-wheel cover and luggage grid, smaller wheels and a Hardy-Spicer propeller shaft. The changes transformed the old Austin 7 into the new Ruby saloon, but there was a twinge of regret when the old familiar radiator shell departed, as it had been associated with the Austin name since the firm was founded. At £120, £8 less than the old saloon, the Ruby was excellent value and there was an even cheaper model without a sliding roof at £112. Continuing the jewel theme, the Pearl cabriolet cost £128, but the cheapest and perhaps least precious of the stones was the short-lived two-seater Opal. It was an extension of the 1933-4 car, retaining the old radiator, and it was sold at the magic £100. Only 1,015 were sold in 1934 and 735 in the following year, although by then the price had been increased by £2 10s; Austin was discovering, as Morris had done before, that there was no real demand for a cheap low-quality version of a popular car. Of the 22,542 7s sold in 1934, 13,638 were £120 Rubies, and only 2,901 customers saved themselves £8 by giving up the sunshine roof.

Synchromesh was extended from two speeds to three by adding it to the second gear on all models in the range. Automatic ignition control was applied to all engines, and every car was given recessed direction signals operated from a self-cancelling switch on the steering column. All the cars took on a much longer, leaner appearance, basing body designs on the earlier Ascot saloon with rounded wings; the Harley and the 10ft 20/6 chassis were discontinued, and there was an attractive new York saloon on the 16/18 chassis.

Morris had dropped the Minor and replaced it with the 8, he also had a 10/4 and a 10/6. For the fourth year Ford held a private show at the Albert Hall; they were rather surprised that Austin and Morris still placed so much emphasis on the 8hp models and felt that the public was going to want the 10 in 1935. Ford's intention was to continue with the 8 or Popular, but to concentrate on its 10hp version, the de luxe; and to make Ford cars even more attractive they brought out the first reconditioned engine exchange plan. Austin and Morris were both right, the Austin 7 reached its peak of production in 1935 and Morris, largely as a result of the success of the new Morris 8, made more cars in that year than at any other time prior to the formation of BMC in 1952.

For the 1935 Austins, Sir Herbert claimed that:

> Our aim throughout has been for clean and flowing body lines in keeping with modern taste; unification of equipment and simplification of control — a consideration in these days when safety features mean so much.

He reacted to the pessimism from some quarters that the industry was reaching saturation point with his typical optimism, and said that he was definitely of the opinion that we had not yet touched the fringe of the possible market for cars in this country, and that he would not be surprised to see 9 million in use by 1944. There was only about 1 car to every 35 people here against 1 to every 5 in America; the figure here simply had to increase. It did not happen; only 2 million cars on the road was reached by the time war stopped production and it did not get beyond 2.5 million until 1952. He still believed, as he had in 1928, that sooner or later all private cars would be banned from main roads in central London during daytime, and that car owners would have to leave their cars on the outskirts. That was going to be the result of having 9 million cars in use; they would be better and safer cars, the roads would have to be improved and there would also have to be 9 million better drivers.

Since 1930, there had been three major Acts and 70 Orders and Regulations containing over 455 individual regulations relating to motoring. On the one hand, Austin said: 'That the industry had been able to survive and progress is one of the wonders of the age', while on the other he was concerned about the number of road accidents, and the need to make roads safer and to improve driving standards. He bemoaned the fact of more and more legislation damaging the direct employment he gave to 17,000 workers at Longbridge, yet he became a member of the Ministry of Transport's Road Safety Committee that helped to frame the 1934 Road Traffic Act with its Highway Code, pedestrian crossings, halts at major roads, the 30mph speed limit and the dreaded driving test. He had strong views on the last two, maintaining that driving tests were a useless restriction, except in the case of public conveyances, for 99 per cent of motorists involved in accidents would pass any reasonable test. The same applied to what he called the 'panic legislation' of the 30mph limit in built-up areas. He did not regard that as necessarily a safe speed; in some cases it would be too fast, in others unnecessarily slow. It would merely add to the serious traffic congestion already existing in some districts. He made the usual plea that one would expect from a car manufacturer about making the poor motorist, already paying far more than his just share of taxation, the scapegoat for the rising tide of road accidents. All road users, not just motorists, would have to co-operate and they would all have to be made aware of their responsibilities.

Hore-Belisha, the Minister of Transport, agreed with some of Austin's views. His name is remembered still for his Belisha beacon pedestrian crossings and his 1934 Road Traffic Act which gave us the driving test, the Highway Code, the 30mph speed limit and a standard system of road signs, many of which are still with us today. There is no doubt that his Act made the roads safer both for motorists and pedestrians, but like a later Minister of Transport, Ernest Marples, who gave us the first motorways but suffered from the 'Marples must go' campaign, he was not popular with the motorists of his day. Because he brought in perfectly good legislation to stop car horns being sounded after dark, Hore-Belisha was advised that he would be far better employed if he devoted his attention to preventing church clocks from chiming all night long. In some ways, there were similarities between Marples and Hore-Belisha. They were both showmen to a certain degree, and in spite of the excellent legislation which they introduced they became the butt of the motorists' frustrations.

Sir Herbert had always been a generous donor. He continued with his benefactions in 1934 by donating £4,000 for a deep X-ray cancer machine for the Birmingham General Hospital, and in October he gave £10,000 to the Prince of Wales in memory of his son Vernon to establish a new TocH building in Birmingham. In that same month, he became a grandfather when his daughter Zeta, who had married Lambert of Carey & Lambert, the Southampton Austin dealers, presented him with a grandson named Austin Gerald.

Shortly after he was elected President of the Society of Motor Manufacturers and Traders in May, Sir Herbert, assisted by Miles Thomas from Morris's, set himself the task of controlling price-cutting amongst dealers by introducing a scheme for price protection. Dealers in popular cars took about 22½ per cent of retail prices, including rebates, and in some cases even obtained 27 or 28 per cent. Austin's discount structure gave a dealer with an annual net cash turnover of £750,000 in Austin cars a 20 per cent discount plus a 5 per cent rebate, though only about half a dozen firms qualified for terms at this high level, the majority obtaining a similar discount of 20 per cent but 2½ per cent rebate. Morris dealers were allowed 25 per cent if they sold more than 1,000 cars a year, otherwise 22½ per cent. Dealers gave 10 per cent to the 'casual trader' who could only obtain his cars through them, and they kept the balance of 12½ per cent or more for themselves for stocking the car, preparing an invoice and cashing the cheque. The 'casual' — or non-stocking — trader could however overcome the disadvantages to himself by becoming a dealer, thus qualifying for a better discount, by the simple expedient of registering a new car for his own use, or as a demonstrator.

As there was no set price for a second-hand car, the stocking dealers with their greater discounts could manipulate trade-in prices, and thereby secure a disproportionate share of the new car market. It gave them a double advantage over the 'casual trader', and led to their offering unrealistic trade-in values for scrap cars. In some cases, dealers were prepared to secure a sale for a profit of as little as £5. Faced with this unfair competition, no wonder that there were wholesale transfers from the 'casual trader' to the stockist class. In effect, the retail trade could not sell new cars at less than the manufacturers' retail list price, but the trade-in allowance led to the same result in the end. Sir Herbert suggested to the Motor Trade Association that manufacturers should control price protection, and this was accepted. The MTA was reconstituted and separated from the Motor Agents' Association leaving itself, under the presidency of Miles Thomas, with the sole function of policing the motor trade. They introduced a *National Used Car Price Book* to set levels for second-hand car prices.

The MAA produced its *Used Car Market Report*, the 'Little Book', each month, and William Glass published his *Guide to Used Car Values*. In the MAA report, values were based upon averages reported to them by the trade and then modified after taking into consideration such imponderables as 'market tendency'. This resulted in a somewhat biased guide which relied upon returns from the very firms whose activities the report was designed to control. Only 350 models were covered. Glass dealt with 4,244 models in a much fairer way, using as his basis prices asked in all 'for sale' advertisements. He calculated a basic retail value, and by removing 10 per cent arrived at an allowance value for a trade-in. His system proved to be the most acceptable and, even today, no motor trader makes a decision without a glance at *Glass's Guide*.

Car manufacturers and concessionaires undertook to insert clauses in their 1935-6 agreements insisting that all their agents must be MTA members and the association, with manufacturers and concessionaires on its council, had the power to expel members who broke the agreements.

In connection with selling cars, Austin was quite content to spend comparatively large sums on advertising, and the second Austin film *Wheels Onward* was made in 1934. It was a rather dull five-reel talkie and was available for dealers to show in conjunction with their own sales campaigns; other similar films followed each year until the war. Unlike Stenson Cooke of the AA who was giving regular motoring talks on the radio as early as 1926, Austin was slow to come to the microphone. He was always happy to make speeches and to give interviews to journalists, and he wrote dozens of articles for newspapers and magazines, but he did not broadcast until January 1933 when he and Englebach gave a thirty-minute verbal guide to Longbridge. He spoke again in February of the following year, this time with half an hour of his own views on 'Industry and National Character'. We now come to 1935. Austin production in this year reached a new peak of 73,562, but this was more than 20,000 behind Morris who now accounted for nearly a third of total UK production. The breakdown of the Austin total is as follows:

Model	No produced
7	27,280
10	27,377
12/4	1,960
Light 12	6,915
12/6	1,313
15.9	2,830
16	2,052
18	3,280
20/6	555

Total car registrations reached 1½ million in 1935 and UK production rose by over 70,000 to 325,192, with exports fairly steady at 51,209 and no really worrying increase in imports which reached 13,563, mainly due to the importation of the Ford V8 before it was produced at Dagenham. Looking at the industry as a whole, Austin and Morris were still dominant; of the 325,000 cars produced in the UK Austin and Morris between them made about 170,000. Other manufacturers were as follows:

Ford	48,000 (15,000 being 10hp)
Vauxhall	23,000
Humber	23,000
Standard	23,000
Wolseley	11,000
All others	27,000

Ford produced about 25,000 commercial vehicles, and with Vauxhall had the major share of that market, but they could only manage a 5 per cent dividend again on the ordinary shares on profits of under £½ million. They had brought out the first £100 saloon but were well behind Austin and Morris in making profits. With the reduction in car tax taking effect in 1935, even Ford had expected that the 10 would dominate, but by the winter of 1935-6 the 8hp class still accounted for over 30 per cent of new car sales, putting the 10s into second place. Morris, Austin and Ford had good 10s and good 7s, although Austin's baby was dated, and Ford had the £100 8hp saloon, for 1936. Austin's capital on issue for the year ending 31 July 1935 stood at £2,622,459, and the gross profit was only slightly down on the previous year at £1,469,144, leaving a net figure of £623,923 with a substantial £370,842 carried forward. The reorganised ordinary shares stood at 35s in May and rose to 58s in August, but fell sharply to 43s when the dividend was announced. Once again, it was decided to keep as much cash as possible for new plant and machinery, so the ordinary dividend proposed was a modest 25 per cent plus a 25 per cent bonus.

In May 1935, Sir Herbert and E.L.Payton formed a new unlimited Company, A & P Trust, with a nominal capital of £12,575 in 500 £25 ordinary shares and 1,500 cumulative preference shares of 1s each. Its purpose was to carry on business as a general investment trust company. Earlier that year, Payton had extended his already large business interests by purchasing a site in Knightsbridge to the west of the Hyde Park Hotel for about £400,000, which he developed after demolishing an attractive row of eighteenth-century houses. Payton was motivated by money and profits; his policy was to rebuild on a site every thirty years and he believed that London could remain prosperous only if this was done. Much of his site was demolished again after the war when other speculators followed his example. Austin does not appear to have been involved with him in his property deals, but the two men registered another private company in August — Kastamonia (No 2) Limited — to acquire the Kastamonia Copper Syndicate Limited to prospect and explore mines. Austin was its chairman, and Payton the sole director. Shortly afterwards, Kastamonia (No 3) was registered to carry on the business of a general investment trust company, followed by Kastamonias Nos 4 to 8. Kastamonia featured in Sir Herbert's will, and it is likely that at least one of the companies was used as a trust fund to avoid death duties.

A steel concern, formed by Austin and Payton in September 1935, must have appealed to Sir Herbert far more than did a mere trust company. Longbridge could not operate without steel, but the latter was subject to uncertain deliveries and to prices set by suppliers operating a price ring. Imported steel was subject to severe duties but Sir Herbert, who had been protected from foreign competition for more than fifteen years by the McKenna duties, could not complain about that. Since the severe depression of 1931, the British steel industry had been rehabilitated largely as a result of the boom in the construction industry and in 1935 it produced nearly 10 million tons of steel, 9 million tons of which went to meet UK demand. British motor manufacturers took 850,000 tons of steel a year, but only Dagenham had the facility to produce its own, in the blast furnace which was opened in June 1934. In September, however, Tunstall Steel Limited was formed with a nominal capital of £100 to manufacture steel sheets, forgings and stampings for the Austin company. An increase in nominal capital to £517,500, Sir Herbert and Payton subscribing £84,000 for B £1 ordinary shares, was rapidly followed by the purchase of a 60 acre site at Aldersley, near Wolverhampton. Sheffield steel makers were furious, and arranged a hurried meeting with Austin as they saw a huge loss to their trade if car manufacturers decided to produce their own steel. Obviously Austin and Payton were serious, and it was also rumoured that they were interested in making a bid for the Ebbw Vale steelworks and colliery, which had been idle for a number of years. Richard Thomas however bought Ebbw Vale, introducing the latest American methods, and the Tunstall Steel scheme was suspended for two years. Austin had shown the steel trade that there was a way of overcoming price fixing, he had a potential steel supplier in Richard Thomas, and he owned half of a 60 acre site at Wolverhampton for which his contribution was £42,000.

Sir Herbert visited Germany again in January 1935 with the range of Austin exhibits, which seemed rather pointless in view of the fact that import restrictions made it impossible to sell more than a handful of cars there a year. Hitler always made him very welcome, but the Germans were building up their own industry to cater for the rapidly increasing demand. Only two firms controlled outside Germany managed to make any impact: Ford and General Motors with the Opel. These, as was customary with the US giants, bought control of existing firms or set up their own factories in the countries that imposed restrictions. Austin had more success in Eire. In 1935 the Free State banned the importation of complete cars and chassis without licence, so an arrangement was made with Lincoln & Nolan, Austin's largest Irish agent, to assemble Austins in a new purpose-built factory. Morris and Ford both followed suit, overcoming the restrictions and at the same time increasing employment prospects in Eire.

In August, Austin decided to make a bold stand against the fetish of change for change's sake and, except for minor improvements, his models remained virtually the same. Changes that did not bring any solid advantages in comfort or safety entailed only expenditure of money which was not then available for increasing quality or reducing price. Some interesting price revisions were made to help the dealers in the highly competitive climate of 1935-6; the 7 saloon went up from £120 to £125, and there were small increases in all the 7 range except the cabriolet and the Nippy. The cars remained unchanged except for improved braking, but there was a new Open Road tourer mounted on the dropped chassis, with the disappearing luggage grid and spare-wheel compartment. This increase in price was

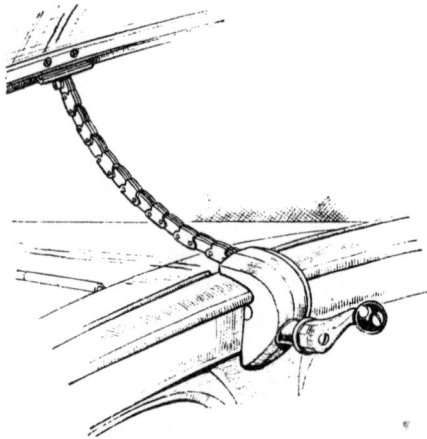

1935 front screen mechanism

surprising in view of the reduction in the price of the Ford 8 from £120 to £100, but as the £125 7 saloon accounted for the bulk of 7 sales, the small rise did little to affect the volume of production, and allowed for a little extra profit on each sale. In the Austin 10 range the Lichfield, with Luvax hydraulic shock-absorbers replacing the earlier friction type, went up slightly to £175 for the sliding-roof version but the fixed-head saloon, which was not the most popular, was kept at its old price, while the touring versions were increased by £6 to £158. As with the 7, the sports and cabriolet versions were unaffected. In appearance, the Lichfield and the Colwyn cabriolet were improved by the adoption of a swept roof line in conjunction with a new design of windscreen.

To meet increasing competition in the popular 12hp range, the light 12 Ascots were reduced by £10 and the open cars, selling only in very small quantity, went up to £188. Thus there were now only two prices — £208 for the Ascot and £188 for the fixed-head version, the Open Road and the Eton two-seater. In the same car 15hp and 13.9hp six-cylinder engines were retained as alternatives, but instead of being offered at equal prices the 15.9 engine cost £10 more on each of the five models — the fifth being the Kempton sports saloon. In each case, the prices of the open cars were increased to correspond with those of the cheapest fixed-head saloons. On all of them there was a new Zenith down-draught carburetter and a new worm and sector steering gear. Exactly the same pricing policy was applied to the 16s and 18s, the latter remaining unchanged with the 16 brought down by £10 and, in the case of the Hertford saloon on the shorter wheelbase, by as much as £20. Perhaps the most important changes were made to the 16 and 18 cars, which were now provided with a new Girling braking system, new steering gear and a Jackall hydraulic jacking system that could be operated from the driver's seat. Only the Mayfair limousine and landaulet were offered on the 20/6 chassis, at the same price of £650; the Ranelagh and the 7 Speedy were both deleted.

13 A Peerage and the Cambridge: 1936-1938

Some modern cars are very bad as regards visibility. After all, a car is to ride in — not to look at.

Lord Austin at the 1936 Motor Show

The year 1936 began with the introduction of the 10 Sherborne in January, which continued in production only until the following August. It was mainly noticeable for the rear body styling — a sustained sweep ran without interruption from the roof to the extreme tail of the body in accord with what was called 'modern conceptions of streamlining'. It was the ugliest Austin body of the 1930s, retaining the upright front that was becoming so outdated, and adding to it a sloping tail which gave the impression of having been added as an afterthought, though it was claimed that the so-called 'sweeping line' enabled an extra window to be added to each side, so that the car was transformed into a six-light saloon. An impression of length was given by the waistline moulding which commenced at the radiator and ran the full length of the car, and there was a good new flush sunshine roof which could be locked at any position from closed to a maximum opening. In fact, the car was 7in longer than the Lichfield, and the extra window on each side could possibly have been provided without the sloping tail, but Austin felt that he really ought to make an attempt at streamlining even if most other manufacturers were already beginning to become bored by it. Interior trim was quite well thought out, the rear seat being flanked by arm rests. The seat was slightly deeper than in the Lichfield and the front seats were larger. Rear headroom was not reduced, but a slight slope at the front reduced the clearance there by ½in, and doors were provided with built-in door locks.

The new car cost £178 in this form and the equivalent Lichfield was reduced to £168. Both models came in a choice of six colour schemes, upholstered in leather, Bedford cord or moquette. A fixed-head Sherborne was available for £162 10s, having leathercloth seats and lacking bumpers and interior visor; the Lichfield version was reduced to £152 10s. Unfortunately details of production of the different 10 models from 1936 are not now available, but sales figures for the 10 as a whole fell slightly in that year. As it was the most popular range — 61 per cent of cars registered were 10hp and below — it would be reassuring to feel that the Sherborne was responsible for the slight decline in the 10s fortune in 1936. When the superb Cambridge, a very advanced product, came out later in the year, it pushed Austin 10 sales up by nearly a third.

Movements in the price of the ordinary shares did not fluctuate much during 1936, ranging between 44s and 54s, and investors were coming to expect the 25 per cent dividend and 25 per cent bonus which had been customary and which was declared again for the year ending 31 July. Gross profits rose very slightly to £1,469,696 with net profits £70,000 less than in the previous year at £553,793; £3,000 more was carried forward. In February, the board authorised the expenditure of £399,000 on new buildings, equipment and modernisation, and with investment of this scale being ploughed back from profits, shareholders could not expect much in the short term. Intensified competition and increases in costs of material and labour made it more and more difficult to show good profits, and it was necessary to retain as much as possible to allow for future setbacks. The capital reserve account stood at £400,000, there was an extra special reserve of £475,000, and an additional £105,000 was invested in subsidiary companies. In 1935, Nuffield nearly doubled Morris production and pushed profits from £½ million to over £1 million, but as he held most of the ordinary capital himself not much of that went to shareholders. He preferred to distribute it himself to the many causes which he supported. Ford's were still unable to give better than 5 per cent to their shareholders. Progress in the industry was maintained with 170,000 more cars on the road than in 1935 and British car production rose by more than 40,000 to 367,237. Imports fell by over 1,000, but exports continued to increase and reached a new record of 64,765. Morris still dominated the scene with an output of about 95,000 cars, but Austin's total fell slightly to 71,855, made up as follows:

Model	No produced
7	23,500
10	27,000
Light 12/4-12	12,000
12/6-14	4,100
16-18	4,000
20	505
412/4 (Taxi)	750

These totals are correct to within 2 or 3 per cent and the most significant figure is that for the light 12/4 (later to become 12) which was transformed in August when the new Ascot body was introduced. This almost doubled the demand for the Austin 12. The 7 and the 10 should have been more successful and, like the 12, the latter was given a new look in August which boosted demand; the poor old 7 was getting too old and nothing much was done which helped it until 1937.

It is interesting to see how the two great companies saw the market. Prices are not strictly comparable, the Austin small cars being cheaper than the Morris ones, the larger Austins considerably more expensive but they both catered for the same hp ratings as is seen in the following table:

Austin hp	Morris hp
7.8	8.06
9.9	9.99
11.9	11.9
15.9	15.9
17.9	17.7
23.5	25.01

Ford policy was quite different; they had only the 8, 10 and V8. In 1935, Morris produced 30 per cent of all cars, Austin 24 per cent, and Ford came a poor third, but in the 8hp range, Morris took half the total sales, Ford came second, and Austin was pushed into third place. The Austin 10 encountered severe competition from Morris, Ford and from the very popular Hillman Minx. How right Austin was proved to be when he built the Cambridge.

While reductions in taxation in January 1935 had encouraged more people to become motorists, and stimulated the sales of small cars, the longer term effect was to cause a proportion of the small car motorists to buy new cars in a higher hp category. In the 11-14hp categories, registrations increased by as much as 33 per cent in 1936, so Austin saw how things were going to develop. They still called the 15.9hp car a 12/6 and something had to be done to get rid of some of the wide range of models that had a smaller potential. How nice it would be to have a range that went 7, 10, 12, 14, 18, 20. This is exactly what happened in August 1936.

In May, Sir Herbert followed the example of that great motoring benefactor Lord Nuffield by presenting a small fortune to an educational establishment. He gave £250,000, which must have represented a high proportion of his own rather meagre personal wealth, to Lord Rutherford's Cavendish Laboratory at Cambridge University for scientific research into radio-activity. With the exception of Payton, whose wealth was derived from his many other interests, Austin directors did not build up vast fortunes. When Sir Francis Pepper died at the age of 73 in November, he left only a little over £80,000. Later Austin followed his major endowment with a gift of £7,000 to the Birmingham United Hospital for radium equipment and £1,000 to the National Hospital in London, and also paid off the debts owed by the Coach Harness Company, one of London's most historic City Guilds. In 1934 William Morris had been honoured and taken the title Lord Nuffield after his £1 million gift to Oxford University, which created Nuffield College. In June 1936 a delighted Sir Herbert, in his seventieth year, was made a baron in King Edward VIII's first and only birthday honours list. Unlike Morris, he decided to retain his name in his title — Lord Austin of Longbridge.

After a careful review of the market trends, the Austin company formed the opinion that it was more important to have a range which conformed closely to the largest potential demand than to have a complex and very varied selection of models. One could not benefit from economies of scale on a model which sold at the rate of only a few thousand a year. When he introduced the new models on 11 August, Lord Austin said that in view of the increased cost of production, it was a considerable achievement to have provided — without any appreciable advance in list prices — the extra value represented by the refinements he enumerated. The company's justification for such a price policy rested in the belief that their dealer organisation would, by intensive effort, achieve the increased volume of sales necessary to finance the huge additional expenditure the new programme represented. They were setting out on a year of unusual promise — a year which bade fair to prove one of the most prosperous the company had experienced for a long time. Like most of his apparently over-confident predictions, and in line with his optimism, he was right; 1937 production was to beat all records.

All models were provided with Girling brakes — not before time. There were new flexibly centred clutches, flexible engine mountings, new frames with cruciform members arranged to extend into liners, pressed-steel wheels and extra low pressure tyres. Bodywork was changed completely, in both style and construction, with the new saloons of a restrained streamline design with luggage trunks at the rear. Steel bulkheads braced the all-steel bodies and isolated the interiors from the power units; new seating, upholstery and trims added comfort and refinement. Gone were the combinations and complications in the alternatives in engines and body styles. Whereas in the previous year there had been 42 models to choose from, for 1937 the number was to be reduced to 24.

Without doubt, the new Goodwood 14 and the Cambridge 10 were to take Austin cars years ahead overnight, this change of August 1936 being as momentous as the change from the 1914 Austin 20 to the 1919 version. The Goodwood used a slightly modified version of the 15.9hp six-cylinder engine in which output had been improved to give almost 39bhp. It was available in de luxe form with the new flush sliding roof at £235 or as a fixed-head at £215. It had a top speed of 68mph, gave 25mpg, could stop from 30mph in 29ft and accelerated from 0-40mph through the gears in just over 17 seconds. The new 10 Cambridge could do almost as well, but gave no less than 34mpg on average. In both cars, the boot was divided into two sections, the lower holding the spare wheel horizontally. In addition the locker lid, simply controlled by a central lockable handle, could be brought down flat to form a strong unrestricted luggage platform as before. Silence had been carefully studied, and the whole of the panelling, floor, doors and roof were lined with a sound-insulating material to guard against any reverberations through the steel body. There was also an air silencer on the carburetter. Rubberised underlays with felts above them were placed beneath the carpets, a telescopically adjustable steering wheel as used earlier on the 16/18 range was added, and the new hour-glass steering box was used. On the Open Road and the Eton — there to pad out the catalogue more than for any other reason — the old body persisted, but only with the 15.9 engine and still, for a reason now obscure, retaining the 12/6 title. On the Kempton sports saloon the body was improved by the application of a new tail. The light 12/4 (now renamed simply 12) engine was available in almost the same chassis, the new body being renamed the New Ascot, at a cost of £210 with a sliding roof and £190 without. It was 6in less in overall length with a slightly shorter wheelbase.

As mentioned earlier, the Cambridge, at £178 for the de luxe and only £160 for the fixed-head, replaced the Sherborne. Wheelbase and track were slightly longer and wider, but most of the interior space was really derived from the setting forward of the engine by about 4in in the chassis, giving that much more space for passengers. This was done by bringing the steering assembly, track rod and drag link in front of the axle, using a reversed drop arm. As on all de luxe versions of the new body styles there were sun visors and they all had new two-dial instrument panels, flanked by a cubby hole supplemented by large door pockets. The Cambridge was much more than a face-lifted Sherborne, and I make only one criticism of the new body, feeling sure that Lord Austin, that great advocate of all-

The improved Ten rear end

round visibility must have made it himself at the time — the small divided rear window was dangerous. There is no reason why its size could not have been greatly increased, and the wide central division removed.

On the 7, the main alteration was the new three-bearing crank introduced in mid-June, the object being to produce a smoother engine by adding a split plain bearing; at the same time a thinner head gasket improved the compression ratio and increased bhp from 13 to 16. There was the new, smooth clutch, Girling-style brakes and as regards bodywork a fully panelled saloon of slightly altered lines, with sliding in place of tilting seats. Open models retained the existing chassis as a basis and the prices were not increased. A more pronounced slope was given to the screen and appearance was improved by full panelling on the doors and the inclusion of a full-depth central pillar. Even the rear quarter-lights were designed to lift with a winder instead of opening at their trailing edge. Bodywork on the open cars and on the cabriolet was not modified to the same extent. The 18 and 20 models remained much as before, pressed-steel wheels were standard, and the only engine on the former chassis was the 17.9hp, only the Hertford, York and Chalfont being available.

Austin put on a night-shift to cope with extra demand, and, by the end of 1936, 25,000 people were on the Longbridge payroll. There was very little serious industrial trouble for such a large number of employees, but in November a group walked out in a dispute over rates for the new Cambridge and Goodwood bodies. Temporary time-fixing for bonus was always applied to any new process, adjusted later as machines and presses settled down, and bonus payments were then reduced. This time, the men

211

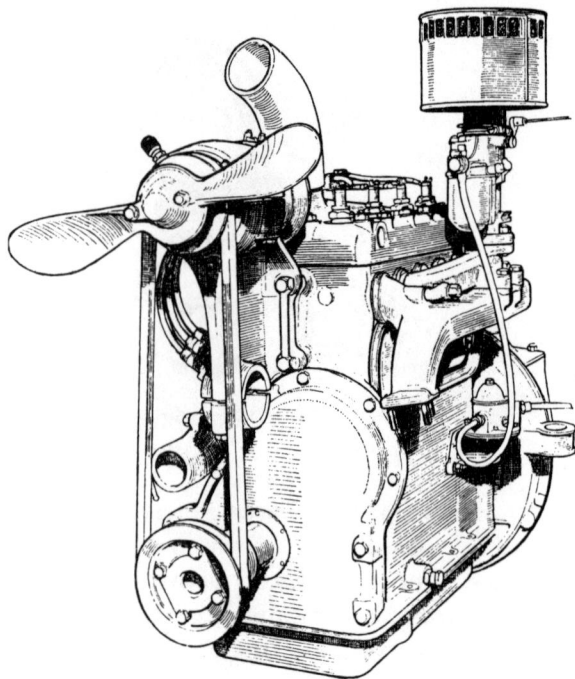

The 1935-6 light 12/4 power unit

were not happy with the result and West works had to be closed, putting 5,000 out of work. Englebach told them to come back and they could talk and settle it, which they did after four days. It was not possible for him to negotiate with them until they returned as there was an agreement with the unions that prevented him from entering into any talks until strikers returned to work. This very satisfactory arrangement only held good with union members and fortunately, as a result of this dispute, many more Austin workers joined either the Transport and General Workers Union or the National Union of General and Municipal Workers.

In January 1937 new cabriolet bodies were introduced for the 7 and the 10, the latter using the name Conway in place of Colwyn, at the slightly increased price of £182 10s and, unlike the earlier models, the space between the cant rails was entirely free of crossbars when the roofs were open. The cars were simply standard saloons with a folding top in place of the metal roof and rear panels. Only limited numbers were sold, and those did not last for very long as the tops soon gave trouble, rotted and fell to pieces. Later, in March, the prices of the fixed-head 7 and 10 saloons were

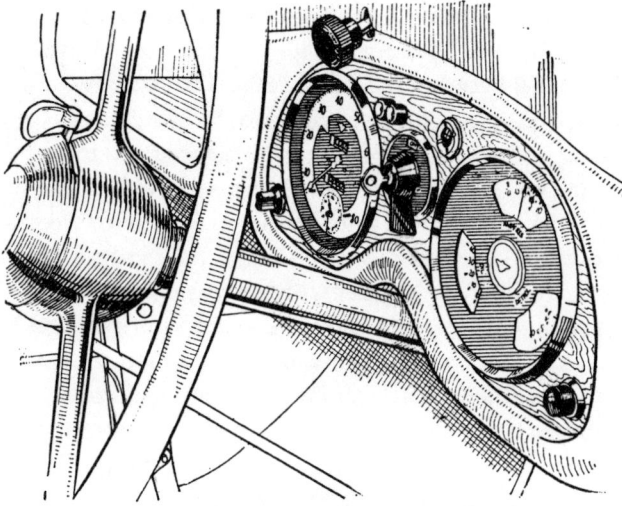
The new dashboard, August 1935

increased by £4 and £8, the 12 New Ascot and the 14 Goodwood fixed-heads by £10. Price rises averaging about 5 per cent, and common to all manufacturers became effective from about July, but there was no noticeably unfavourable effect on sales until November and December. Austins stood off several thousand people just before Christmas, but the effect was short-lived and full working was resumed when, as the optimistic baron once again forecast correctly, sales began to increase. As already mentioned, they reached an all-time high in 1937, not to be exceeded until 1949.

The industry lacked any experience whatsoever of the effect of rising prices either on total demand or on the relative position of the more and the less expensive cars. Given a continuance of national prosperity, the trade hoped that the volume of total purchases would be unaffected, but feared that demand would shift somewhat from the dearer to the cheaper models. Prices were so closely graded that it was feared psychology might influence buyers; rather than pay £265 for a car which cost him £250 last time, many a purchaser might choose a slightly lower model in the same general class, the price of which was formerly £235 and was now £250. This accounts for the small differences between the top and bottom of overlapping ranges — £5 between the 12 and 14, £12 between the 10 and 12. Policies like this were adopted so that production could be switched from one model to another very quickly when the fickle public altered its buying pattern.

The old arbitrary conception that an income of at least £400 a year was

213

indispensable for the potential car owner was discredited by the events of the mid-1930s. In 1937, there were 800,000 incomes of over £500 in the UK, and 1,500,000 between £250 and £500. That summer over 1,825,000 cars were in use; making allowances for two-car families and for cars being used on business the evidence suggested that ownership had penetrated well below the £400 income level. Would a 5 per cent increase in car prices reduce total demand, or would it lead to an increase in the requirement for small, cheap cars? Vauxhall thought so, and for the first time started to tackle the lower end of the market with a very good 10 with independent front suspension, which simply had to be a success in 1938 at £168. Rootes also brought out a new Hillman Minx in the 10hp class, the first small car to have a decent-sized boot. This class was certainly going to be well catered for in 1937-8.

The Fourteen Goodwood, August 1936

The average hp of cars sold in 1936-7 was 12.2, compared with 12.0 in the preceding season and 11.9 in 1934-5, due mainly to the popularity of the new 14s whose share of the total market rose from 8.7 to 11.2 per cent. Who could tell what would occur in 1937-8, and the least a manufacturer could do was to have a wide range available. Amongst the car producers, Morris (including Wolseley and MG), Austin, Ford, Standard, Vauxhall and Rootes (Hillman, Humber, Sunbeam, etc) — the mass producers — still supplied the largest part of the market accounting for no less than 86 per cent of the home sales and 95.5 per cent of exports in 1936. It is interesting that Ford and Vauxhall were already American-dominated, and Rootes's old empire was to fall to Chrysler after the war. The others remained British and it is sad to see how their position as market leaders has been eroded in recent years.

Competition in 1937 was just as fierce as it is today, and success in any one season turned on the extent to which the appearance of a new model fitted in with changing fashions of popular taste. In the first year of the introduction of a new car like the Cambridge success was almost guaranteed unless, of course, a new Minx or a new Vauxhall 10 caught the public's imagination to its detriment. Fortunately, this was not the case. Small firms like Rover, Riley, Triumph, Armstrong, Alvis, SS, Singer and Jowett suffered from the possibility of wide annual fluctuations in sales affecting their profitability in a single year, and amongst them only Singer was active in the export field, the remainder concentrating on home sales. They could not afford to bring out new models and they were doomed to failure in a period of inflation because they could never hope to benefit from economies of scale.

In the luxury market, where Rolls-Bentley and Daimler-Lanchester accounted for only 1.3 per cent of the UK sales, there was a little more stability. There was always a demand for a small number of hand-built expensive cars and they were not in competition with any other British producers.

Exports still continued to increase, by nearly 14,000, from under 65,000 in 1936 to 78,113 in 1937, far below the US total of 208,000, but creditable and better than the figures for Germany (38,000) and Canada (35,000). In spite of the McKenna duties, imports at 18,560 rose almost to their 1929 level. The 11.3hp GM Opel and the 6.7hp Fiat at £125 accounted for much of the increase, and there was a fear that, with the devaluation of the franc, French mass-producers like Renault, Citroën and Peugeot would follow suit. As it happened, none of them was going to produce very many more private cars for the next ten years.

Total UK production rose by only some 10,000 to 379,310. Austin, a very close second now to Morris, had another record year making 89,175 cars, as follows:

Model	No produced
7	23,000
Big 7	5,500
10	35,000
12	15,500
12/6-14	5,950
18	3,400
20	380
12 (Taxi)	445

Surprisingly, the 7 was holding its own, the 12 was a great success and the 14 and 18 hardly worth the trouble. The real earner was the Cambridge 10, and if the Big 7, later to become the 8, could revitalise the 7, Austin was going to continue in the top two.

Accounts for the year ending 31 July 1937 followed the 25 per cent dividend plus 25 per cent bonus on the ordinary shares for the third year running. But on the Stock Market all motor shares were depressed and this result did nothing to revive the Austin stock, which had fallen from nearly 50s to 30s during the year. Results were quite good, the gross profit had risen by over £150,000 to £1,665,125 but the net figure was only £2,000 more than in 1936 at £555,577 with a reduction of £70,000 carried forward. The new National Defence Contribution, a tax on company profits to help pay for rearmament, took the tax bill up by £85,000, and a further £100,000 was spent on an extension to the foundry and on new engine machine shops.

Austin price increases, in addition to the small adjustments announced earlier in the year because of the soaring price of steel resulting from increased demand from the growing armament industry, came on 12 July. On the 7 range they were increased by about 8 per cent, on the 10 by as much as £17 and all the old models were scrapped leaving only the Cambridge with its two variants, the fixed-head and cabriolet. The remaining 12/6 open cars and the Kempton went, leaving the Ascot 12 in the same three variants of body style as in the 10, and the 14 Goodwoods. Prices were increased by £20 to £25. On the larger models, the old 20 Mayfair limousine and landaulet were still there at £650, but on their last legs; the 18 was transformed and its introduction, with that of the new Big 7, was brought forward to coincide with the new price increases rather than delayed until August. The old York 18, with the 20 the last models to retain the 1936 body style, was criticised gently by one motoring correspondent as being like a bishop's wife — generously proportioned, full of good works, a little old-fashioned as to dress and a trifle dull. Two new models replaced it, the Norfolk with five seats on a short chassis and the Windsor with seven seats on a chassis nearly a foot longer at 10ft 3in. It was an excellent roomy car, but quite expensive at £375 and it was far from being a success — in 1938 less than 2,000 were made, dwindling to a few hundred in the following year.

The Big 7, announced at the same time, but not publicised much until the first Motor Show at the new Earls Court building in October 1937 when the SMMT moved their annual event from Olympia, was supposed to fill the gap between the 7 and the 10. It did not take much guessing to see that it was going to be a replacement for the old 7, although that old faithful had a little more to earn for the company before it was dropped. With four doors and an A frame chassis 6.5in longer than the 7, there was much more room inside. The transverse front spring and quarter-elliptic rears were retained, but the engine was entirely new, and with a single-cast block and three main bearings, its 56.77mm x 88.9mm = 900cc (7.99hp) gave 25bhp at 4,000rpm. The two saloons cost £160 and £155, nearly £30 more than the 7, but were reduced in November to £149 10s and £145. Would buyers want a two-door 7 at £131 or a four-door Big 7 at £149 10s?

From December, the engine on the 14 was given an aluminium cylinder head in which the compression ratio was raised from 6.5:1 to 6:1; with a new carburetter the power was raised to 46bhp at 4,000rpm and the top speed to over 70mph. Like the 18, it was a good car, but demand for it fell away in the two difficult years before the war.

Lord Austin, now over 70, was getting old and tired. He was invited to become president of the MTA in May in the hope that his still considerable influence would combat the rising feeling amongst agents against the national price-protection policy, and in this he was successful. Much of his time and energy was devoted to work with the new shadow aircraft factories, and he continued with his generosity to the Birmingham hospital. In May, he gave them another £1,000, bringing his total gifts to that cause alone to £22,000. He celebrated his golden wedding anniversary in December, and 18,000 staff subscribed towards a large gold salver which was presented to the old couple at Longbridge. In his speech which followed he said he thought that 21 was the best age for marriage. He and his wife were the same age and he believed it was fatal for two people to marry if one was very much older than the other; they were bound to drift apart because they could not grow up together and maintain similar interests. When Lady Austin spoke, she said that he was a very obstinate man, but happy if he got his own way! Even his usual optimism, which he never lost, led him to a very wrong conclusion when he said: 'Neither think nor use the words "depression" and "slump". I personally do not see why the good times should not carry on indefinitely.'

In April 1938, an aluminium cylinder head became standard on the 10, the valves were altered and the power output of the engine was increased, helped by stronger valve springs and new exhaust and inlet manifold. Just before that, in March, a new two-door Big 7 called the Forlite was added to the range at £139, the four-door being then named the Sixlite. The Forlite had much larger doors and tip-up seats. Prosperity declined in 1938, income tax was increased by 6d in the £ and a 1d increase in the petrol tax was made at the April Budget. Rearmament was costing a great deal, and although Austin exhibited at the Berlin Motor Show again, there was sufficient fear of a war with Germany for a 150yd air-raid shelter tunnel to be built at Longbridge. During the war it was used as both shelter and underground factory. The motor industry was always a sensitive index of changes in the general level of prosperity, and it was not surprising that the slight recession at the end of 1937 and the beginning of 1938 was reflected in a decline in the number of new vehicle registrations. During 1938 as a whole, however, total registration increased by 150,000 to just under 2,000,000, representing something of a revival towards the end of the year, but total UK production fell by 38,000 to 341,028, back almost to the level of 1935, and UK car exports declined by nearly 10,000.

The US and Canada recorded much steeper declines, and Germany was to follow them. The recession was felt in varying degrees by different manufacturers and, of the big three, Austin seems to have suffered the most due to the lack of a competitive 8hp car and the decline in the sales of the 10. Morris production was steady at about 95,000, but Austin's fell by nearly a third to 60,224 made up as follows:

Model	No produced
7	8,500
Big 7	16,414
10	18,238
12	11,000
14	2,750
18	2,583
20	156
28	138
12/4 Taxi	445

Unwarranted fears of German imports worried all car makers in Britain. They were concerned about 'dumping', especially with rumours that the new Volkswagen was going to cost only £60. The GM Opel sold for £135, and competed with the Austin 12 at £220 and the Morris 12 at £205. It sold in Germany for RM2,010, which was about £170 and was billed to GM, the British importer, at only £65. In the first three months of 1938, 2,974 German cars were imported against 295 in the same period a year before. Their imports accounted for about half of the total imports of foreign cars in this period, against only 6 per cent of the total for January to March 1937. As it turned out, total imports for the whole of 1938 dropped by half to 9,180 but, during the early part of the year, the effect of short-term impact of German importations, together with the recession, worried not only Austin, Morris, Ford and Standard, but it also worried the shareholders. It was reflected in the low share values and comparatively high gross yields of £5 9s 6d per cent on Ford's ordinary on a share price of 18s 3d, to no less than £10 8s 3d per cent on Austin's at 24s to which the shares had fallen in May from the 57s high of 1937. Morris and Standard shares both yielded over £8, so the market — except in the case of Ford — was expecting quite substantially lower dividends and profits. It got them. Morris's profits fell and Austin's fared no better.

For the year ending 31 July 1938 the gross trading profit fell by over £380,000 to £1,282,828. This was not much better than the 1933 figure and, on top of that, the net profit declined to £362,158, not much more than half of what it had been in 1934, when total production was not all that much greater than in 1938. The only consolation was that £303,447, almost exactly the same as in the previous year, was carried forward. Total dividend on the ordinary shares fell from 50 per cent to 30 per cent, still made up in two parts in the traditional Austin manner, of a 25 per cent dividend and a 5 per cent bonus. Shares went up a few points on the announcement; the market had expected less because there had been suspensions and short-time working at Longbridge that spring, brought about partly by the transfer of essential skilled men to the shadow factory, but mainly because sales were falling.

Some manufacturers announced the de-control of the prices of their products in mid-1938 in an attempt to dispose of the large stocks held prior to the production of new models to be brought out for 1939. At Earls Court in October, the first Motor Show to be televised, there was to be a new Standard 8, an improved Hillman Minx, Morris 8s and 10s and the Bantam 9. There would also be many old models for disposal for of course the MTA price book of second-hand values for trade-ins would not apply, but despite their efforts dealers were left holding stocks of second-hand cars at inflated prices which could only be sold — if at all — at a considerable loss. Sir Albert Atkey, one of the major Austin distributors, told a story which, although humorous, contained the essence of truth on the acceptance of second-hand cars at 'book' price whenever he sold a new Austin. If, for example, he sold an Austin in 1938 for £225 out of which he made x profit (where, he added, x was the unknown quantity!), he had to take in a 1937 model at 'book' price for which he had to allow £175. He saw this as a profit of x− y, y representing the loss he would make on selling the old car. Being anxious to dispose of it, he would take in exchange another maker's 12hp six-cylinder car, which according to book, was worth £130. Now his profit was x− y− z! Being anxious to dispose of this £130 car, he took a 1936 model of another make worth £84. His profit was $x - y - z - a$. The last stage of this imaginary transaction was to take in an Austin 7 worth £72. In selling the original £225 worth of goods he had turned over £686, out of which he had got £72 worth of profit locked up in an old car. The last straw to break his imaginary camel's back was when a motorist with a large American car, wanting to reduce his running costs, offered to take the 7 as a swap on level terms. The sale of a new £225 Austin left Atkey now with whatever he could get for an unwanted second-hand American monster. Atkey was a shrewd business man and his company remained viable, but others were less fortunate. Pass & Joyce, after making a loss of £17,000 in 1937, were offered a plan to save them from liquidation by a temporary personal loan from Payton and Car Mart. The latter both withdrew their offer when Henly's took an interest, but another bad trading year would have forced others to go the way of Pass & Joyce.

Austin followed Ford in 1938 by introducing a replacement exchange engine scheme for 10s, 12s and 14s at prices ranging from £14 to £18 10s. New engines had to be purchased at the full price and, provided that the old ones were returned in reasonable condition, the appropriate difference was credited back to the dealer. In this respect the scheme was not on a par with that operated by Ford, but it did bring extra work to Longbridge at a time when business was slack. Ford, Morris and Standard all reduced the prices of their 8hp cars that summer and Austin followed suit even more by taking what he called the bold step of lowering prices in the belief that costs of material would fall; costs for glass had certainly fallen as a result of the Langegaye deal (see p236).

Detail improvements giving better performance and greater comfort, and the replacement of the 20 by the 28, were the main features of the Austin programme for 1939 announced on 27 July. Greatest concentration was on the 10, 12 and 14, which also bore the greatest reductions, the 10 coming down by £10 to £185 for the Cambridge sliding-head, the 12 Ascot was now £225 and the 14 Goodwood sliding-head sold for £245, a reduction of £15. An important change on the 12/14 was the new bodywork with higher and wider doors, although the general outline of the bodies remained as before. Aluminium cylinder heads were standard on all models except the 7 and Big 7, inlet valves were larger on the 10 and 12 and compression ratios were raised generally, increasing the power output at 4,000rpm to 32 and 42bhp respectively. The 14 had been altered in November 1937. On the 7 range, the Ruby saloon came down by £6 to £125.

Bonnets were given concealed hinges, and sturdier rear axles with full

Girling brakes having cone instead of cam expanders for the shoes were applied to all the larger models. Suspension on the Big 7 was improved, but no changes were made to the engine. Externally, the most notable feature was the addition of running boards to meet the chief criticism of the new model that the body was 'splashed severely in dirty weather'. On the 10, 12 and 14, new piston-type shock absorbers improved the suspension, and they were all given the new pistol-grip handbrake coming out of the dashboard — a nasty thing which has been coming and going over the years to the dictates of fashion, particularly when attempts have been made to sit three people across a bench front seat. On the same three models, the sides of the boot interior which restricted the boot to the width of the lid were removed, making the full width of the car available for luggage. On the 10, entry to the rear was improved by the use of hinged front-seat squabs; and on the 12 and 14 the centre door-pillars were moved back, thereby widening the front doors, and the rear doors were increased in width, going further towards the back of the body. A greater height was obtained by taking the doors up further into the roof curve, the window-line being kept in the old position by making the top edge of the door a little deeper. Externally, the 12s had a longer bonnet and the radiator was more nearly vertical, giving additional length to the top. Minor additions, like over-riders on the 14, 18 and 28, and new door handles curved in at the ends towards the body for all models, completed the programme.

The old 20/6 was dropped and replaced by a huge chauffeur-driven luxurious new 28hp car styled on the lines of the 18. The new Ranelagh limousine was to be £700 — £50 more than the 20 — but by November it had been reduced to £595. It was 6ft wide and 17ft 2in long and the six-cylinder engine had a bore and stroke of 86.36mm x 114.3mm (4,016cc), rated at 27.75hp, giving 90bhp at 3,200rpm. Only a small number of these sleek, fast, quality cars were made, 138 in 1938, 152 in 1939 and 10 in 1940.

An unusual Austin named *Daisy* took many records at Montlhéry in May 1934. It was a six-cylinder 20 standard car prepared by Marchand in France for the Yacco Oil Company and it won as many as 10 World and 21 International class records when it covered 25,000 miles in nearly 300 hours at 84.145mph, including all pit stops. Nothing more was heard of this fast 20, but the 7s were to continue to perform well for a few more years. Jamieson persisted with the side-valve racer and in March 1934 Driscoll broke the flying kilometre record at 122.74mph. Burgaller beat MG records for the standing-start mile and kilometre at 83.59 and 73.34mph, but by the end of the year MGs won them back, holding every International class H record. Murray Jamieson's overhead cam racers were ready in 1936, and it was with these cars that Austin hoped to beat the flying mile record of 130.51mph held by an MG. Speeds of over 120mph were reached at Brooklands and in October 1936, 9 records from 5 to 100 miles were taken by C.J.P. Dodson followed by many others, his highest average speed being 121.21mph, but he could not reach the MG's speeds of over 140mph for the short distances.

Lord Austin intended to shelve the racing programme in 1937, except for the French 24 hours' race at Le Mans but Jamieson left to join ERA and Austin relented and allowed the official works' team to compete in a limited number of events. Goodacre won all four events in an ohc 7 at the JCC Coronation meeting at Donington, and the Austin team won the 250km race at Brooklands on 26 June at the extraordinary average speed of 105.63mph. Dodson and Hadley continued to race the two overhead-camshaft cars, winning races and breaking the Shelsley Walsh hill climb record for 750cc cars.

Bert Hadley, who was given his first chance to race Austin cars by Murray Jamieson, and who was loaned a side-valve 7 racer by Pat Driscoll to use on the Mountain circuit, recalled the situation regarding the racing cars after Jamieson joined Austin. First, there was one fully streamlined car, built for record breaking but which Jamieson had been denied the freedom to design the way he wanted, and which he raced at Montlhéry. It was soon eclipsed by the MG Midget and Pat Driscoll drove it afterwards on the Brooklands outer circuit, apparently finding it quite a handful. Two side-valve road racers were built with similar power units to that used in the streamlined car, and were driven by Driscoll and W. Baumer. Baumer was more successful with his because he had access to more reliable fuel in Germany. There were three overhead-camshaft cars driven first by Dodson, Driscoll and Goodacre; a fourth car was partly built; and sufficient components were scheduled, and in most cases completed, for six cars. Hadley drove the side-valve car throughout 1936 and was up-graded in 1937 to the ohc machine, which he found an armchair ride compared with the lighter cars. Kay Petre, the famous lady racing driver still alive today, took over the side-valve car previously driven by Baumer and was able to master the tricky piece of machinery better than most men. All sorts of ideas to improve the ohc cars were shelved when war began, and had the second Shelsley of 1939 not been abandoned, Hadley felt confident that an Austin would have climbed in under 40 seconds.

14 Leonard Lord, Rearmament and War: 1939-1945

Englebach had been works director of Austins since 1922, he was getting old, and his thick-lensed spectacles were becoming less effective in correcting his failing eyesight, which had deteriorated to such an extent by early 1938 that sometimes he had to be guided around the factory. Austin knew that he would soon have to be replaced, so he approached a young man named Leonard Lord. Englebach retired on 1 March 1938 but retained his seat on the board until his death in February 1943.

Leonard Percy Lord, with 'brusque, ruthless exterior' according to Lord Thomas of Wolseley who disliked him sufficiently to reject Payton's invitation to run Austin's jointly with Lord in 1946, and about whom a graffito artist wrote in a Longbridge toilet 'Oh Lord, Give us Engle back', was called a coarse, inhuman man by some, but was remembered by others for his kindness and generosity. A man who disliked salesmen and accountants and whose philosophy was 'make proper bloody products and you don't need to sell 'em', and whose influence on the British motor industry for thirty years — according to Graham Turner — did more harm than good, Lord was only 41 when Lord Austin invited him to succeed Englebach. Son of a superintendent of the local public baths, he was born in Coventry in 1896, educated at Bablake School and apprenticed, some reports say, to the engineering department of Courtaulds; others favour Alfred Herbert machine-tool makers. He worked at Coventry Ordnance, Daimler and various places in London and Peterborough. In 1922 he joined Hotchkiss of Coventry and stayed with them until 1927 when he left to go to Wolseley Motors just before Morris bought them. His work at Wolseley impressed Morris, who appointed him managing director in May 1933 in which capacity he controlled Morris Motors, Wolseley and MG cars. He did it well, revitalising the group, improving the cars, doubling the output and increasing the profits. He resigned in August 1936 after a bitter quarrel — many of his quarrels became bitter — with Morris who refused to increase his share in the profits; he regretted his action almost at once, but

Morris would not have him back in his old capacity. After travelling abroad for some time he returned, and in January 1937 Morris made him manager of a £2 million trust fund which he had set up to give aid to special areas of high unemployment.

Gone were Englebach's charm and his quiet personality. Here was a crude, ruthless newcomer to Longbridge who, with his new-found power and thrusting, calculating inhuman personality was going to take the fullest advantage of something he had never controlled before — a factory in which a complete car could be produced under one roof and where two elderly senior executives were nearing the end of their careers. Austin had chosen him partly for his undoubted organising and engineering ability, but also because he knew that Lord would do everything in his power to beat Nuffield as a car maker. On the one hand Lord, when asked about some sackings could say bluntly that he had not even started — there were some early retirements but no evidence of vindictive dimissals: on the other he could be both generous and thoughtful. One example was his secret subsidisation of the Austin ex-apprentices dinners — why should he give them money? Yet Graham Turner says that he strenuously resisted the idea of an apprentice scheme put to him by a senior executive at Austins. Did he really believe that it was pointless to train for industry — the evidence does not support it. Another example concerned a letter sent to him in 1945 suggesting that two of the post-war Austins should be named Arnhem and Alamein. The writer was sent a charming reply, offering him £10 for his most helpful suggestion. Lord even took the trouble to tell Davidge, the publicity manager, to write to the Society of Motor Manufacturers and Traders, who kept a register of proposed names, to book Arnhem and Alamein for Austin cars and also Taxicar for the new post-war Austin taxi. Lord also fancied Lancaster, but Armstrong-Siddeley beat him to it.

Austin had no time for 'yes men'; he liked those who were prepared to offer him reasoned argument, and who were forceful in manner and who had strong opinions. Lord was certainly in that category. He was not able, suffering undoubtedly as he did from an inferiority complex, to create for himself a large following of colleagues who liked or even respected him, unlike Austin who generated respect bordering on idolatry from almost everyone with whom he was closely associated.

For his first six months at Longbridge, Lord's desk was empty. He spent most of his time in the works planning his reorganisations and getting his first new Austins designed. His initial task, however, was to remove all 'No Smoking' signs from the factory. Austin had disliked smoking and no one was allowed to smoke on the job, consequently every time a man wanted a cigarette he went to the toilets and remained there for ten minutes. Perhaps to avoid this waste of time, or perhaps because he always had a cigarette in his own mouth, Lord swept away the prohibition. From then on, men — strangely enough not women — were allowed to smoke at bench and machine and almost anywhere else apart from the paint shop. He even set up cigarette dispensers. Austin was furious but he could do nothing as he had not been consulted and it was too late to reverse Lord's decision.

Austin's personal involvement in all design decisions persisted until he was well over 70. He decided to take his first long holiday for many years so Dicki Burzi, the designer stylist, decided to redesign the Austin 12 body. One of Dick's first jobs had been the fabric body on the old 12 in the late 1920s just after he had joined Austin from Lancia, so he knew just how adamant Austin was about changing a design without good reason, and the extent to which he never allowed anything to be altered without his approval. Dick spent the weeks on preparing a full-scale coloured drawing and put it out of the way on Austin's return. Shortly after, Austin came into his office and said that he wanted the 12 body restyled and that he was on his way to a meeting and would return later to discuss the details. His designer had the finished drawing — two weeks' work — on the drawing board when he returned, and although it was obvious that he could not have done even an outline sketch in the time, Austin said nothing. He must have liked the design because it became the New Ascot. Austin's influence began to diminish, he was too old to become absorbed in the detail, and once Leonard Lord was installed he never came down to the design department again.

Lord respected Dick's work and entrusted him with the styling in the same way that Austin had done, but allowed him rather more freedom. One day after the war Lord came into Dick's design studio clutching the rust-stained radiator cap from his Bentley, which was modelled with the Bentley flying B trade mark; he put it on the desk and said, 'That's what we want, make something up like that.' Dick made a stylised A from plywood and covered it with silver paper; it was approved and became the flying A Austin emblem which was to be used with the traditional Austin winged wheel and replace the Austin script which Herbert Austin had designed in 1906. The first Austin cars to have the new symbol were the Bentley-type luxury cars, the Princess and the Sheerline.

During the early part of 1938, the board decided to embark on the production of medium-sized commercial vehicles. This was not an entirely new venture for the company; the twin-prop 2-3 ton may have been something of a commercial failure in 1913, but they had been quite successful in the small van market with the 7, 10 and 12. F.T. Henry, who was then employed at Longbridge, remembers seeing the prototype with a Bedford bonnet, cab and radiator cowl, but an Austin emblem in place of the Bedford, and several others who were at Longbridge at the time recall having seen Bedford trucks in the works. The new truck therefore was to owe something to existing competition which had already proved successful. The entry into the commercial vehicle market was announced in October, after 168,000sq ft of new shops and 25,000sq ft for a repair and servicing department facing the Bristol Road were erected at a cost of nearly £½ million, and it surprised some of the Austin agents who regarded the industry as an unregulated, fiercely competitive, order-snatching, uneconomical section of the trade, consisting of the worst of the old horse-traders offering large discounts and even less conventional inducements. There was severe competition but, as the recent results of Leyland, AEC, Albion Motors and others had shown, it was possible to produce profit records that compared favourably with those in the private car industry. Trouble centred principally on the absence of price control, of control over distribution and on the widely differing definitions of carrying capacity. Austin agents, dealing almost exclusively in new and second-hand cars, were not too happy about handling Austin lorries. Resumption of commercial vehicle building by such an important company, with its powerful dealer network, could only add to the competitive conditions and the only hope was that there would be a revival in the home and exports markets.

In 1937, 67 per cent of the commercial market was held by Fordson, Morris Commercial and Bedford, only 14 per cent was in the heavy class, and Austin, Rootes and the smaller firms had only the remaining 19 per cent. In 1938 the production of lorries declined from 118,000 to 105,000, with exports dropping from 20,000 to 14,000. Ford made over 16,000 in each year, and the bulk of the rest of the business to be tackled by Austin was firmly in the hands of Morris, Bedford (owned by GM) and the Rootes empire. It looked as if there might be a revival in trade in 1939, but even if there were, Austin's new lorries would find it hard to make serious inroads into markets dominated by so many experts. In fact, the lorries — the first of which was built in early February 1939 — were not bad vehicles, ranging from 1.5 to 3 tons (later there was a coach chassis and a 5 ton version) with prices from £190 for the 1.5 ton chassis to £272 for the 3 ton long chassis. Well-made Austin-built bodies and metal cabs with sliding sunshine roofs as optional extras gave the new commercials near-car comfort for the driver, but the best feature was a new 3.5 litre six-cylinder engine. It was the first overhead-valve Austin engine to go into production; with a bore and stroke of 85mm x 101.6mm (3,459cc) it developed 70bhp at 2,800rpm, and it survived as a lorry engine until 1948. At the time, considerable work was done on developing a light diesel engine for the new trucks. Two experts in diesel design were brought from Mann and Daimler-Benz, but Austin advised them to return home to Germany in the summer of 1939 just before the war started. Two prototype trucks ran regular trips between Longbridge and Holland Park, one with a Dorman engine to prove the chassis, the other with a prototype diesel. Lord convinced Austin that the middle-range truck market was to be in petrol engines, the result being the new ohv 6. The Bedford-derived prototypes were loaned to Trentham, the local building contractors, for field trials, and they became enthusiastic over them, praising them for their rugged reliability. It is difficult to say how well Austin would have fared in the commercial vehicle market with this K series had it not been for the war. Although they were excellent army lorries, they would probably never have reached the 16,000 a year of the Fordson before the war, much less the 30,000-40,000 which that company produced each year from 1946 to 1949. For the first five months of production only 1,592 Austin lorries were made.

Austin made a substantial contribution to the military demands during the war as the following table shows:

Longbridge Commercial Vehicle Production, 11 March 1939-2 June 1945

	1½ ton	2 ton	2 ton (AMB)	3 ton (4 wheel)	3 ton (6 wheel)	3 ton (fwd)	5 ton	Morris chassis	Bedford and troop carriers
Mar - Jul 1939	453	602	-	537	-	-	-	-	-
Aug 1939 - Jul 1940	2,278	1,136	1,851	3,152	-	-	-	804	-
Aug 1940 - Jul 1941	1,894	687	4,715	3,240	905	-	-	1,465	-
Aug 1941 - Jul 1942	-	4,116	1,818	2,397	2,744	521	2,771	1,787	1,704
Aug 1942 - Jul 1943	-	3,399	1,433	2,786	3,201	3,055	2,472	1,516	836
Aug 1943 - Jul 1944	-	1,774	2,180	3,963	3,650	4,024	1,237	1,114	752
Aug 1944 - Jul 1945	-	2,971	1,105	1,022	2,779	4,680	935	-	81
	4,625	14,685	13,102	17,097	13,279	12,280	7,415	6,686	3,373

Grand total: 92,542

227

Production (Austin only) for each financial year was:

Mar - Jul 1939	1,592
1939 - 1940	8,417
1940 - 1941	11,441
1941 - 1942	14,367
1942 - 1943	16,346
1943 - 1944	16,828
1944 - 1945	13,492
	82,483

By 1938, the British motor industry could produce 385,000 cars and light vans and 85,000 commercial vehicles a year. During rearmament it shifted much of its resources into aircraft and armament production and total vehicle production during the war was quite low:

	1940	1941	1942	1943	1944
Cars and light vans	21,338	20,692	23,183	21,605	19,704
Commercials	112,531	124,738	137,339	127,703	113,251

These totals fell short of the quantity required, no one really appreciating that by 1942 demand from the services would be approaching 400,000 vehicles a year. The result was to import from America and Canada as follows:

	1940	1941	1942	1943	1944
Vehicles imported	24,629	81,632	187,723	252,471	197,740

Throughout the war, Austin's contribution in the commercial field was small at around 10-12 per cent of the UK output, but they produced nearly all the cars used by the services in 1940 and 1941, falling away after that, as will be seen in the table opposite, as they concentrated more upon armaments and aircraft.

Lord wasted no time in bringing his influence to bear on the appearance of Austin cars; in less than a year he had his new 8 ready, and it was introduced in February 1939. There was no time to do much to the Big 7 engine and gearbox, and apart from increasing the crankshaft diameter and using barrel-type tappets little was done to the existing 900cc engine. The new cars had to be sold at approximately Big 7 prices, so there was not much scope for major changes. A pressed-steel rear-axle casing was designed which reduced the unsprung weight, and the Austin 7 suspension was replaced by semi-elliptic springs controlled by Luvax piston-type shock absorbers. The old A-frame chassis went and great lightness and strength were given to the new chassis in the form of a metal platform — an important step in development which led to unitary construction after the war. Side members of the chassis were channel-section pressings facing outwards and, where the body still joined the frame, the sill and the side members formed a box section, the floor becoming an integral part of the frame. At the front end of the chassis there was a box cross-member, with a similar one farther back which provided rear support for the engine. From this second member two channel-section members ran forward and outward to the chassis side giving further stiffening to the forward end. Integral with the chassis floor were two box members to take the seat rails, and the tail end of the chassis was stiffened by another deep box and cross-member.

Longbridge Car Production, 11 March 1939-2 June 1945

	7hp	Big 7	8hp	10hp	12hp	14hp	Taxi	18hp	28hp	Total
Mar - Jul 1939	152	6	15,488	10,085	4,226	845	124	471	64	31,461
Aug 1939 - Jul 1940	-	-	24,912	11,650	1,978	4	464*	1	88	39,097
Aug 1940 - Jul 1941	-	-	5,206	11,780	63	-	49	-	10	17,108
Aug 1941 - Jul 1942	-	-	710	3,775	-	-	-	-	-	4,485
Aug 1942 - Jul 1943	-	-	35	5,918	-	-	-	-	-	5,953
Aug 1943 - Jul 1944	-	-	-	6,885	-	-	-	-	-	6,885
Aug 1944 - Jun 1945	-	-	-	3,549	-	-	-	-	-	3,549
	152	6	46,351	53,642	6,267	849	637	472	162	108,538

* 263 of these were WD utility cars

Externally, the striking appearance of the car was a complete departure from the previous Austin design. The Lord look gave the radiator cowl a rounded nose with a chromium-plated grille of horizontal bars cast in sections of six. Bonnet sides were bolted to the scuttle and the radiator shell formed a solid front, but the sides could be removed for access to the engine. For normal access, the top of the bonnet hinged from the back and lifted forward from the front end, supported by a stay when open. This 'alligator' look, by no means a new idea since Renault had used it before World War I, was novel at the time, and became common to all cars later on. Bodywork was generous in size and smooth in outline, the screen angle really did sweep back, sloping to an even greater angle than the radiator grille. Deeply domed wings and small running boards finished off the car, and six different varieties were available; the saloons were in the GRQ series and the open cars, from May (starting at chassis 177,363) were GQC. Prices were as follows:

Saloon four-door sliding head	£149
Saloon four-door fixed head	£139
Saloon two-door sliding head	£139
Saloon two-door fixed head	£128
Four-seater Tourer	£135
Two-seater Tourer	£132 10s

On 18 May, an overgrown 8 — the new Lord 10 — was introduced at £185 for a four-door sliding-head saloon and £175 for the fixed head, and £175 for a four-seater tourer, at July 1938 prices. The radical platform chassis concept was used again, but the new body was nearly 4in longer and 1.5in wider than the old 10. The engine was unchanged except for a new aluminium cylinder head, enlarged crankshaft and barrel-type tappets. Lord's final car, the new 12, was introduced on 29 August 1939 just a few days before Britain declared war on Germany. It used the old-style chassis frame, but with the new front end and body style. There was a more rigid front cross-member with a torsion anti-roll bar stabiliser front and rear, but there was little change to the mechanical specification. An air-conditioning duct was built into the fascia which also had provision for the radio which, as with a screen de-misting system, could be obtained as an extra. The spare wheel was housed in a compartment behind the rear number plate.

The year 1939 was another bad one for the industry. Car production fell by nearly 40,000 to 305,000 and Austin car production fell by about 2,000 cars to 57,367, made up approximately as follows:

Model	No produced
7	1,000
Big 7	1,600
8	20,000
10	22,000
12	9,100
12 Taxi	445
14	2,649
16/18	370
20/6	51
28	152

On 18 December, £24,898 was capitalised for a bonus share issue of one 5s A non-voting share for every 25 held, which was equal to a 4 per cent

bonus in addition to a 15 per cent dividend. This raised the issued ordinary capital to £622,459

Car production continued for some time after September 1939, and the export trade continued well into 1940 after the purchase of new cars in the UK was banned. Purchase tax was introduced as a temporary measure to obtain extra money by indirect taxation and to limit consumption and, like the income tax brought in temporarily to pay for another war more than a century before, it was never removed, although in the case of cars its name was changed and it now exists as a mixture of car tax and VAT. The new hp tax at £1 5s for each RAC hp took effect from January 1940, but very little motoring was done after that and new cars gave way to war work at Longbridge. Lord concentrated on running the Austin shadow factory and, as well as his work there, Lord Beaverbrook appointed him government controller of Boulton Paul Limited to reorganise and increase the production of the Defiant night-fighter planes.

In addition to the production of aircraft and of the vehicles listed earlier, Longbridge also produced a wide range of other war material:

armour-piercing 2-pound, 6-pound and 17-pound shells	1,350,000
ammunition boxes and magazines	3,350,000
steel helmets	2,500,000
jerrycans	600,000
Churchill tank suspension units	110,000
mine pressings	440,000
Oerliken gun magazines	110,000
lifeboat engines	3,500
Vickers and Hispano machine-gun magazines	300,000
industrial engines	20,000
fire pumps	10,000
Beaufighter and Miles Master wings	4,641
bomber fuel tanks	15,000
Bristol engine exhaust rings	122,000
bomb tails	120,000
Horsa glider fuselages	359

As regards actual aircraft, Austin potential for production on Air Ministry contracts had existed long before World War II. At the outbreak of World War I there had been only some 12 firms in the aircraft industry, most of which had been solely in experimental production for less than three years. During the first year of the war less than 2,000 aircraft were built, a figure which rocketed to more than 30,000 by 1918, much of this expansion being made possible by the use of subcontractors for components in addition to the expansion of existing aircraft firms. This heavy demand

The 1939 Eight

for aircraft fell away rapidly after the war and total requirements by 1924 had dropped to 503, to rise only to 1,456 in 1930; the average annual demand for military aircraft between 1928 and 1933 was 612; 893 were supplied in 1935 and the figure rose to 1,830 in 1936. With such a low annual demand in the early 1930s, the dozen or so firms producing military aircraft could not view their future prospects with much enthusiasm.

For the decade from 1925 to 1935, Air Ministry policy was based on the realisation that the existing aircraft industry was too small and too weak to meet demands for war production. By 1927 it was felt that assistance from outside the industry would be essential, which meant adding a shadow industry to the already established aircraft production capacity, and in 1936 it was decided to plan for war production on this basis. Air Ministry expansion in 1934 involved increased demand, but up to the end of 1935 the existing aircraft industry was able to meet this with production from within its own capacity; thus they could cope with the first phase of re-equipping the air force, which demanded 2,400 machines in two years. The second scheme, in May 1935, put a requirement forward for 2,000 aircraft a year, and some firms extended their factories to meet the demands set by the revised programme. In February 1936, yet another larger programme was worked out, followed by another calling for 8,000 aircraft by March 1939. By May 1936 it was realised that the existing resources were inadequate to meet the programmes and it was at this point that it was decided to form shadow aircraft and aero-engine factories.

The shadow industry was authorised by the *Statement Relating to Defence*, based upon plans which had been formulated as early as 1929. The factories were outside the aircraft industry and the motor industry was

232

chosen as being the most easily adapted to aircraft production; the factories were owned and financed by the government and managed by the various firms on its behalf. On 20 February 1936, Payton stated that the Austin company had been approached about the possibility of large-scale aircraft manufacture being carried out at Longbridge — it was widely conjectured that a small private aircraft with a cruising speed of 100mph costing under £300 was being contemplated. Payton said that the announcement was quite unauthorised, without denying it, so the idea may have been considered; however, no one who was at Longbridge at the time has any recollection of plans being drawn up to produce a modern version of the Whippet. Lord Swinton, Secretary of State for Air, had seen Austin and the Rootes brothers, and had persuaded Austin to become chairman of the motor industry shadow scheme — a position which he held until May 1940 — and had asked them both to establish aircraft factories for the government. Neither of them was keen to enter the aircraft industry, but they both agreed to put their manufacturing experience at the government's disposal. Perhaps the initial payment of up to £50,000 a year plus a management fee of £225 per airframe and £75 per engine was too much of an attraction in a period of declining new car demand.

Lord Nuffield behaved rather differently. Wolseley Motors had an off-shoot called Wolseley Aero Engines Limited, which was engaged in the manufacture of a series of radial aero engines variously known by the signs of the zodiac, of which the best known were the Leo and the Scorpio. The sales of these engines was disappointing because by the time each engine was developed the Air Ministry procurement people always wanted something bigger and more powerful. Nuffield had invested well over £100,000 of his own money in this venture and became very irritated at this constant shifting of specification, but he did not join the shadow factory scheme because he had his own capacity and decided to continue on his own with the Wolseley engines. The government did not buy them but Sir Kingsley Wood, Swinton's successor, prevailed upon Nuffield to go to London where he persuaded him to erect the large Spitfire factory at Castle Bromwich. His aircraft venture was not happy; the Rolls-Royce engine was redeveloped almost monthly to give more power, which meant that the Spitfire airframe had to be altered from time to time. Nuffield who was a distinctly mass-production man objected to all these alterations which meant long-dated and costly adaptations to dies, jigs, tools and fixtures, and he bluntly told Lord Beaverbrook that he could either have modifications or aircraft, but he couldn't have both. Constant friction arose between

Nuffield and Beaverbrook, culminating in Nuffield over the telephone querulously saying something to the effect that maybe the minister would like him to give up control of the Spitfire factory, whereupon Beaverbrook promptly told him that he was very grateful for his offer and accepted it.

Meantime, in the spring of 1936, negotiations were begun at Austin's to acquire 23 acres of adjoining land from local farmers at Grovesley Lane, Cofton Hackett. The Bromsgrove RDC approved the plans in April and the aim was to complete the new factory in six months at a cost of £300,000, employing 5,000-6,000 men. Work began in August on the buildings which measured 1530ft by 410ft, covering 20 acres; the airframe factory erected later covered another 15 acres, with a flight shed adjoining it of 500ft by 190ft, where the completed aircraft were housed prior to test flying from the airfield on top of the hill. The engine selected for shadow production was the Bristol Mercury VIII air-cooled radial which developed 825bhp at 13,000ft. Five firms — Rootes, Austin, Daimler, Standard and Rover — concentrated on different components, Austins dealing with crankshafts, reduction gears and oil supply and control gears for the variable pitch air-screws. In addition to producing parts, the company erected and tested complete engines for half of the parts built in the five factories, the other half being dealt with in Bristol. Austins first set of components was accepted on 15 September 1937, and the first completed engine was tested on 25 October.

Two airframe factories were built, Austins for the Fairey Battle and the Rootes factory at Speke for the Bristol Blenheim, and later the Halifax. The Battle was from its inception an unloved aircraft, but the rapid expansion essential to gain parity with the fast growing Luftwaffe meant concentration on a light single-engined bomber that was easy to produce, and the Battle was chosen of necessity. As early as 1933, one year after it was introduced, the air force considered that the specification was not likely to produce an aircraft fast enough for its future requirements, and although some modifications were made in 1934 it could not be made a serious competitor to the twin-engined machines. It was the only light medium bomber developed from an Air Ministry specification ready to go into production, and both Fairey and Austin could produce such aircraft in reasonable quantities without much delay; 400 were ordered from Austin in May and June 1936, and parts for a further 100. It was decided not to give Austins the order for an additional 386 which had been planned in addition to the 500 to which the Air Ministry was committed, because they wanted Austin to produce the superior Wellington bombers. However, they were not considered capable of making them and in a frenzy of enthusiasm Austins offered to make an additonal 676 more Battles before 31 March 1940. No one at the Air Ministry believed they could do it, and Austin had to be content with an allocation of a further 363.

When Sir Ernest Lemon reviewed the shadow industry's prospects in September 1938 he found that Austins were behind schedule, and that there was likely to be a serious deficiency in deliveries by March 1940. But as it happened, Faireys had capacity to produce any that Austins could not. A further contract was placed with Austins on 27 June 1939 on condition that they increased their labour force by 5 per cent a month over the following few months. By this time the Battle was obsolete as an operational aircraft and was relegated to a training role but 300 more were ordered at the outbreak of war to be used for target towing, and production of them continued at Longbridge until December 1940, their contract having been reduced by 334 on 7 November.

Battles were used operationally in the 1940 spring offensive in France, but their low speed and light armament to repel attack made losses very heavy. Austins had produced 1,031 in the 27 months from September 1938 to December 1940; 1,263 had been ordered, reduced to 929, but just prior to the changeover to production of Stirlings, 100 final Battles were built. About 700 four-engined Stirlings were produced, and from May 1943 the company switched to the Avro Lancaster, making over 300, also turning out some Hurricane Mk IIs. The shadow factory scheme, in spite of all the difficulties in adapting to aircraft production, turned out 12 per cent of the wartime output of aircraft — most of them were bombers representing 45 per cent of all the bomber planes delivered to the RAF.

Lord Austin, approaching his 73rd birthday, went to France in the summer of 1939 to rest, and apart from his chairmanship of the shadow factory scheme, did not involve himself much with the wartime activities at Longbridge. In January 1941, after a bout of influenza, he developed double pneumonia, and although he recovered he was so weakened by his illness that he died on 23 May. He left only £509,712, but this first figure was provisional as his block of ordinary shares were not sold at the then deflated price of 16s. Lickey Grange came up for sale soon afterwards and was bought by the company for £37,200 and was donated to charity to become a home for blind people. Lady Austin moved to Hampstead and died a year and a day after her husband.

In his will, Austin made provision for his wife, two daughters and grandson by cash payments and the income from a trust fund which accounted for less than a half of the Estate. The balance he left to a charitable institution to be chosen by his trustees. Soon after his death, Payton was elected chairman and Lord became technical director, the only other members of the board being R.G. Ash, Waite and Englebach. Payton remained chairman, but in 1942 Lord and he became joint managing directors, Lord also gaining the title of deputy chairman. Lord now had the power he wanted; Hancock, Austin's old chief designer had left in October 1941 and his place had been taken by Haefeli who had been at Longbridge since July 1914. H.N. Charles, an old Morris Motors man, was appointed development engineer.

Payton hung on until November 1945 when he retired on the advice of his doctors, and on 28 November Lord was elected chairman of the company. He was supported by two new directors, A.C. Herring VC, a stockbroker, and J. Gibson Jarvie, founder and chairman of United Dominions Trust, who became deputy chairman.

E.L. Payton died early in 1946. He was a financial genius, chairman of four other companies and a director of seven more. One of his concerns had been the Foundling Estates which made a small fortune in property in the early 1930s; his other interests involved finance and investment, engineering, coal mines, breweries, multiple stores, insurance underwriting, agriculture, and property and estate development. A typical example of his astute business sense occurred when the Triplex glass contract went to Lancegaye in 1938. He obtained an option on 700,000 1s shares with a nominal value of £35,000 to be taken up at par should Lancegaye fail to complete the deal. Triplex could not afford to let Lancegaye steal the Austin contract, so they took them over in June 1939, and Austins took up the Payton option of 700,000 shares for £35,000, which were then converted into Triplex stock valued at £101,298. Small wonder that so many companies sought Payton as a director, and there is no doubt that his influence saved the Austin company in the 1920s. He left a personal fortune of over £2 million.

But, there is also no doubt that Payton and Austin together were becoming too cautious over the Austin company's affairs. Leonard Lord had a more daring and ambitious approach.

Before he retired, Payton had the satisfaction of supervising the reduction of the mortgage debentures, which he had been working at since early 1938; £22,910 of the 5 per cent debenture stock was redeemed at 101 per cent in January 1943, which left £944,280 outstanding. In May the shareholders and the Court approved the plan to free the company's property and assets and the scheme was announced in October. On 1 January 1944 the stock was redeemed at £103, with interest, and a new issue of 4½ per cent cumulative redeemable preference shares at 20s 3d replaced them. They were redeemable at any time before 31 December 1978 at 21s. The £42,493 (against the £71,500) that it cost to service them each year was covered nearly twenty times by the 1941 profits, so they were in no way a speculative risk. Some 76 per cent of the holders of the debentures took up the new stock immediately, and only a small proportion of the balance took cash.

The company's capital structure remained rather involved, consisting of £5 million divided into:

	£
7 per cent cumulative preference stock	250,000
6 per cent cumulative B preference stock	1,000,000
Preferred ordinary	750,000
Ordinary	150,000
A ordinary	497,361
Unissued 5s A ordinary	10,556
Unissued and unclassified £1 shares	2,350,000
Available to become 4½ per cent cumulative redeemable preference shares	1,000,000

Accountants and shareholders must have become very frustrated during the war. Stock-taking, a prerequisite for any set of accounts, could not be completed, and there were long delays in producing figures and in declaring dividends. An AGM was held on 30 December 1939, but no business was conducted, and in March 1940 a modest dividend of 10 per cent was paid on the ordinary shares for the year ending 31 July 1940. Accounts for 1940 and 1941 were not audited and published until March 1942 when a further 10 per cent was declared for ordinary shareholders. For the two years, the gross trading and net profits were low; £69,200 of the profits was allocated for war damage contributions, £850,000 set aside for taxation, with £100,000 being transferred to reserves. The ordinary dividend for 1942, again 10 per cent, was not paid until April 1943; £300,000 was earmarked for reserves, depreciation and repairs, bringing the total held to £2.8 million; over £1 million was kept for tax liabilities with a total of £1.6 million for reserves and to be carried forward.

Accounts for another two years were held over until August 1944. Ordinary dividends were again 10 per cent, but for the year ending 31 July 1944 the old 10 per cent cash bonus was added with a meagre net profit of only £214,149, the lowest recorded since 1924. In January 1945 dealing in Austin shares was suspended for a day on the Stock Exchange because no statement of profits appeared with the announcement of the dividend, a question was asked in the House of Commons and preliminary profit figures were quickly made available. Dealing was resumed on the next day when the ordinary shares rose by 4s to 33s 6d. For the final year of the war, although not announced until 1946, an ordinary dividend of 25 per cent was declared on a gross trading profit of £2,077,400 and a net profit of £257,043.

Austins were lucky enough to be able to continue with the production of a limited number of cars during the war, and this was to help them to be the first in the market when the war ended. As early as September 1941, Lord had said that the post-war Austin cars would be a continuation of the 1939 models, and a production line was kept going to produce the 10hp model for the government. In 1941 experiments were carried out at Longbridge with a 3-cylinder two-stroke 6hp engine under Lord's direction. A prototype was run around the factory fitted into an Austin 8, and later on work was done on a prototype Mini car similar to the Fiat Topolino with this same engine but the demand after the war was for larger cars for export. A Mini came later, and the two-stroke engine was not favoured by Issigonis, its brilliant designer, who preferred a conventional development of the A30 unit.

15 Export or Starve: 1946-1949

I have said publicly on many occasions that I cannot share in the spirit of easy optimism which can see unlimited markets ahead with continually shortening hours of work and greater rewards for less and less productive effort.

Leonard Lord, March 1946

We are told that we must co-operate with the workers. With whom are we going to co-operate — the Shop Stewards? The Shop Stewards are Communists.

Leonard Lord, speech to Midland branch of National Union of Manufacturers, March 1947

As explained in the last chapter, when World War II ended, Austins were able to start car production before any other British manufacturer. Plans were well advanced by November 1944 to carry on with the 1939 models, but to add to the 8, 10 and 12 a 16 with a new four-cylinder ohv engine of 79.3mm bore and 111mm stroke (2,199cc), to be used later in the A70 and A90 in a slightly modified 12 chassis. Cars could however be sold only to priority users who could obtain a purchasing certificate from the Ministry of War Transport. Petrol was of course still rationed, anyone with a vehicle currently licensed being entitled to a basic ration from June 1945 of 7 gallons a month. New cars were not going to be cheap as materials were expensive and in short supply, and in addition the heavy purchase tax added another third to the price. In spite of that, with half the production of cars going for export it was years before there were enough cars to satisfy the home demand; at certain times the waiting list was so long that a three-year delivery was quoted. As early as April 1945, £1,000,000 had been authorised by the Austin board to be spent on new machinery, plant and equipment, and as soon as government contracts slowed down the huge task of rearranging the factory began, the Austin 10 line being the easiest because car production on that track had continued throughout the war. Over 5,000 machines had to be moved before the other lines were ready.

Between May and December 1945, Lord planned to make 2,000 each of 8, 10, 12 and 16hp vehicles and 2,000 1 and 5 ton lorries. The 10s were to be started in June, 8s by 16 July, the new 16s on 4 August and the pre-war 12 on 9 October. All these targets were met and the company made 5,785 cars and about 6,000 car-derived vans and trucks by the end of 1945. Prices were high:

Model	Price	Pre-war Price
8	£255 (+ £71 tax)	£149
10	£310 (+ £87 tax)	£185
12	£415 (+ £116 tax)	£235
16	£445 (+ £124 tax)	

They were all four-door de luxe saloons, available in a choice of three colours; there was no time to build in variety and options, and as many of them were going for export the highest possible specification was selected. On 18 July 1945 an Austin 10, the first British car to be exported to America since the war ended, arrived in New York; it cost the equivalent of £400 and was followed by twenty-one more before the month ended. However, there was no great demand for 1939 British small cars in the States and Austins had to wait until they had cars more suited to American taste.

For 1946 the new Labour government sanctioned the production of 200,000 new cars, of which 100,000 were to be exported; and in so far as possible it intended to provide the motor industry with the two scarce resources of coal and steel. The industry made 291,162 cars, but only managed to export 86,492 of them because in most cases the cars were not sufficiently modern to satisfy the overseas markets. Austins were no more successful than the rest — only about 2,000 cars went overseas in 1945. Material and labour costs increased and Austin prices were revised on 13 May 1946, the basic price of the 8 going up to £270, the 10 to £330, the 12 to £450 and the 16 to £495. Further slight increases had to be made in January 1947.

Austins were much more successful as an exporter in 1946; in March alone 2,069 cars and 634 commercial vehicles were shipped overseas. By 7 December no less than 25,578 cars and car-derived vans and 5,456 commercial vehicles had been sent abroad since the end of the war, many of the cars going to the States. Arthur Waite was appointed managing director of a new subsidiary, the Austin Motor Export Corporation Limited, formed in April 1946 to handle all the export business and to increase sales, particularly to dollar markets. In June 1946 Austins bought Vanden Plas

240

(England) 1923, a famous quality coach-builder, and this gave Waite his first real chance to build up his export business with two new models — the first Austin cars to be designed to appeal to foreign buyers, albeit those wanting cars at the top end of the market.

Lord had planned a big Austin in 1939 to replace the 28. He had made two modified six-cylinder ohv truck engines which were fitted into two maroon prototypes based on the new alligator-bonnet 8 and 10 designs, but the project had to be shelved in September. The new big Austin razor-edge prototypes did not follow the design of the pre-war experimental cars, and although the first rumours about them were circulating as early as March 1946, the first appeared in public on 13 March 1947 at the Geneva Motor Show. These expensive luxury cars were the A110 Sheerline, built at Longbridge, and the A120 Princess, the bodies for which were made at the newly acquired Vanden Plas works. With an engine designed to propel lorries of up to 5 tons capacity there was plenty of scope for heavy bodies, and the new cars weighed a little under 2 tons. Maximum bhp at 3,700rpm with a single Stromberg carburetter on the Sheerline was just under 110, hence the new nomenclature A110, a method to be used on all other Austins for a number of years. As RAC hp was not going to be used again as a basis for taxation, and as it was meaningless for any other purpose, there was no point in calling the new Sheerline an Austin 27. In the A120, two Stromberg carburetters increased the power output by about another 10bhp. A pressed-steel cross-braced chassis frame was used and, for the first time on an Austin, independent front suspension; a hydraulic jacking system, Lockheed hydraulic brakes and the American steering-column gearshift were other features. A110s, which looked rather like some 1939 American cars, cost £1,000 plus £278 10s 6d purchase tax; and the A120, much more modern with its headlamps built into the wings, was priced at £1,500 plus £417 8s 4d tax.

Anders Clausager, archivist of BL Heritage Ltd, has discovered that no more than 12 Sheerlines and 32 Princesses, mainly prototype and pre-production cars, were fitted with the 3,460cc engines before the dimensions were altered to 87mm x 111mm, which increased the capacity to 3,993cc by the end of 1947. Sheerline power output was increased and it was redesignated an A125, giving it a respectable top speed of 80.7mph, acceleration from 10 to 30 mph in 7.3 seconds, an average fuel consumption (driven hard) of 14.2mpg, and it cost much less than half the price of a 4.5 litre Bentley. As with the A110, the Princess was reclassified an A135, using the new 4 litre engine, this time with 3 SU carburetters.

During 1946 the old pre-war models continued, and some 42,500 cars were produced: 8hp, 17,000; 10hp, 19,000; 12hp, 3,000; 16hp, 3,500. Austin production figures, as mentioned elsewhere, were not noted for their accuracy. As an example, if the twenty or so official announcements of production figures issued between 1946 and 1948 are studied, even those issued to shareholders at AGMs, it is not possible to reconcile them. BL Heritage has managed to save a collection of microfilms of post-war factory records which escaped Lord Stokes's purges, but it will be many years before they can be studied and made available for research. J.F.Bramley, as publicity manager, should have fared better in June 1946 when he tried to arrive at precisely the millionth Austin car to be built. He was about 35,000 out in his calculations and advised Lord that the millionth Austin would be built in January 1947, but Lord decided that June was a better month for publicity. Bramley had suggested that a 12 and a 16 should be raffled amongst Austin employees, but on 25 June a 10 was taken from the line representing the 999,999th Austin and this was balloted for and won by a worker in No 2 machine shop; and a white 12, representing the millionth car, covered with the signatures of those who made it, was won by a die tool-room worker. He seems to have tired of it at some stage as it found its way to the underground air-raid shelter where it languished until BL Heritage recovered it quite recently.

For the year ending 31 July 1946, the gross trading profit rose by nearly £200,000 to £2,249,370, the net profit more than doubled to £625,369 and £368,688 was carried forward. Dividend on the ordinary shares was 40 per cent. No doubt much of the profit came from government work; the last Lancaster did not leave Cofton Hackett until February 1946 and the final War Office vehicle contract was not cleared until December 1945, but the 8 and 10, although outdated in some respects, were still earning their keep. Ordinary shares still gave a good return, earning over £5,000 for the executors of Lord Austin's charity trust which held 300,047 ordinary shares, 3,141 A ordinary and 4,193 10s preferred.

The government's decision to replace the RAC hp tax with a duty based on the cubic capacity of the engine — a scheme which Lord Austin had advocated for so many years before the war — was introduced first for goods vehicles and buses from 1 January 1946 at a rate of £1 per 100cc. It was extended to cover all new cars a year later, those first registered prior to 1 January being still assessed on the old basis of £1 5s per unit of RAC hp. The object was to conserve fuel by making it more advantageous to run a small economy car, and resulted in a new 16 costing £2 a year more to tax, and the 8 £1 less. As very few small cars were sold in Britain and the emphasis was on exporting cars with larger engines, the new scheme was irrelevant and was soon replaced by flat-rate taxation. The industry asked for this to be levied at £5 a year for all cars, and economy encouraged by adding an extra 3d duty to each gallon of petrol, as this would have produced an equal revenue. In fact, the government brought in a £10 registration fee for all new cars from 1 January 1948, retaining yet again the old RAC basis for older cars. Purchase tax was retained at a third of the sale price, but to discourage the sale of expensive cars on the home market the tax on cars costing £1,000 and over was doubled. This hit the Sheerline, so the price was reduced by £1 allowing it to sell at £999 plus £275 5s tax; but the Princess at £1,350 could not escape and it attracted purchase tax of £751 10s making it the first Austin to cost more than £2,000.

It was not as easy to sell cars in 1945 as one might imagine. After the initial rush of buyers wanting cars regardless of cost, there was purchase tax and petrol rationing to contend with; of the 8,000 purchase licences granted at one stage, only 1,700 holders had taken up the option to buy. The Ministry of Supply released 23,000 cars onto the secondhand market and by the end of 1945 nearly 120,000 ministry cars and lorries had been sold, and there were fears that the resulting poor home market for new cars would in turn affect the export business — it was argued then, as it has been since, that no export trade can succeed without a strong home demand. However, manufacturers had no need for concern. As more men were released from the services the demand for new cars soon exceeded any number that they could hope to produce for domestic consumption.

Britain was a bleak, dismal country in which to live during those early years after the war. There was a very severe winter in 1946-7, coal and oil rationing, power cuts, staggered working hours, and food and clothes rationing. A reduction by a third in the basic petrol ration was followed in the summer of 1947 by its total abolition, the tea ration was reduced to 2oz a week, and in December the allocation of meat was chopped from 1s 2d to 1s worth a week, and all foreign travel for pleasure was banned. Longbridge closed in February 1947 because there was no coal, steel was in short supply, there were many strikes, factories closed all over the country and domestic consumers were without electricity from 9am to midday and from 2-4pm. All this had a serious effect on the export drive. Lord blamed the growing power of the shop stewards, as well as the Labour government. They had nationalised the coal mines and the railways, and Lord knew that there were Labour MPs who wanted to do the same with the car industry.

Ian Mikardo, the MP for Reading, in a Fabian pamphlet published later called *The Second Five Years*, proposed that the six main vehicle-producing ownership groups should be nationalised so that their energies could be diverted to the production of a cheap people's car. He did not bother about the fact that Ford and Vauxhall were American-owned, or that the last thing wanted to swell the export trade in those early days was a cheap people's car. What Lord said privately is not on record, but publicly he said that he would not co-operate in any form of nationalisation. Nuffield and Lord both concentrated on selling for dollars to the States. At first they were quite successful, but the boom did not last very long. Lord went out there for the second time in the summer of 1947 and formed subsidiary companies in both America and Canada. He came back with orders for millions of dollars as a result of opening up two mysterious crates which he had taken with him — they contained the new A40 Devon and Dorset cars which he had designed to replace the 8, 10 and 12, production of which went on until the end of 1947.

As early as January 1947 Lord had told shareholders that he was not yet proposing to make a Mini car; that description seems first to have been applied to a small economy vehicle much earlier than has generally been imagined. He could not really have called the A40 a Mini, any more than Nuffield could have used the name for his famous Morris Minor. A car had to be very much smaller to be termed Mini, and it had to be revolutionary enough to become a cult before any title would stick. Rationalisation had to take place first. The big six car makers — Austin, Nuffield, Ford, Rootes, Vauxhall and Standard — were responsible for 90 per cent of all cars made after the war, and the number of basic models had been reduced from the 136 available in 1939 to 62 by 1948. Only in this way could the volume car makers hope to be successful. Sweeping away three old models and replacing them by one was the answer — hence the A40, designed for the home market, but in the first instance exported very successfully.

Like the A110 and A120, the A40 designation related to the power of the engine; in this case the new four-cylinder ohv unit of 65.48mm x 89mm (1,200cc) produced 39.5bhp at 4,400rpm. In view of the tendency to combine body with chassis on most British cars of 12hp and under, it is surprising that the A40 dropped the pre-war steel-platform design to revert to the more dated frame, all the main members of which were of box section, arc-welded from steel about 1/16in thick. Another major feature was the wish-bone type independent front suspension with its conical rubber articulation bushes and forwardly disposed steering linkage. The braking system also was unusual, the two leading shoe front brakes being hydraulically actuated, while those on the rear wheels were mechanically operated by standard Girling mechanism, the two being balanced by a floating lever.

In spite of the separate rigid frame and a very roomy body, the weight of the complete vehicle was kept very low. It was under a ton for the four-door Devon six-light saloon, which cost only £325 plus tax — £15 less than an Austin 10. Interior width was 4ft at both front and rear seats, and the luggage boot had a capacity of 7.5cu ft. Since the engine developed a maximum of 40bhp and gave a torque of 55 foot/lb over a considerable speed range, a lively performance resulted through the well spaced four-speed gearbox. A two-door version, the Dorset, sold for £315 plus tax; heaters were available at £6 extra and radios at £30. Body design, with built-in headlamps, was distinctly modern, doing away with running boards and altering the frontal appearance. Thermoplastic enamel replaced cellulose paint on the 8, 10 and A40 in August. It was sprayed on and baked, and being more flexible required no abrasive polishing which ensured a longer life. It was applied in mist green and portland grey colours to start with, being extended over the whole range by the end of the year.

A Devon prototype registered HOE 344, and a Dorset registered HOE 313, were taken to the Swiss Alps for extensive testing in June 1947 by George Eyston, the world-record-breaking driver. The two cars performed very well, doing 70mph and returning a fuel consumption of 40mpg. Lord had taken up another £2 million to improve production methods just before they went, and the investment went towards producing the A40.

As already mentioned, 8, 10 and 12 cars dragged on until the end of 1947 and Austin production for the year was about 62,544 made up as follows:

Model	No produced
8	16,000
10	30,000
12	3,000
16	3,000
A40	10,500
A110/120	44

Most of the cars went for export; for example, of the 30,000 A40s produced up to July 1948, 11,000 went to the US and only 1,000 were released for the home market. UK production was down slightly in 1947 to 287,000, of which 143,102 were exported, and Austin's finances showed a slight decline in the gross profits to £2,262,431, but the net profit rose to £707,156 and £416,929 was carried forward after payment again of a 40 per cent dividend on the ordinary shares. Morris increased their dividend from 17.5 per cent to 25 per cent, and Ford paid its highest dividend recorded so far at 7.5 per cent.

Government policy for 1948 was to increase UK car production from its 1947 target of 300,000 to 475,000. However although more cars were made than in the previous year the total only reached 334,815; more important, 226,911 were exported. Some 70 per cent of Ford output and 60 per cent of Austin's were sold abroad and, by June 1948, Austin had exported 100,000 cars since the war. In March all previous export records were broken when 5,722 vehicles, worth £2 million, left Longbridge; of the 1,200 cars sent to America in February, 1,053 were Austins.

At home, the basic petrol ration was reinstituted in the summer with a meagre allowance of 18-31 gallons a month, depending on engine size. More cars came back onto the roads and registrations rose to 2,000,000 again. About 1,000 non-productive workers were made redundant at Longbridge when work on the 8, 10 and 12 ceased, and the price of the A40s was increased by another £20. Lord announced that dividends would be pegged for a year at 40 per cent and he began an incentive scheme. Prize money was allocated based upon weekly production, lots being drawn for five prizes, the top one of which in the first week came to £75. It was a bad scheme and did nothing to placate the unions who were still worried about the redundancies; only five workers could benefit each week, by chance, on the efforts of 20,000. It brought criticism too from the Church's committee on gambling who judged it morally bad.

Two more new ventures started in 1948. In November 1946 an arrangement was made with Crompton Parkinson to produce electric vehicles. Austin-Crompton Parkinson Electric Vehicles Limited was formed, but nothing much was done until January 1948 when the new firm began marketing Morrison-Electricar vehicles through Austin dealers. The second venture resulted from Lord's interest in the development areas. He opened a factory at Tiryberth, Bargoed in South Wales where he employed sixty ex-miners suffering from silicosis and other complaints, under a resident doctor provided by the company. This non-profit-making scheme used scrap material, steel and leather left over from Longbridge to make two toy cars. One was called J40 Joycar; the other was an attractive replica of the twin cam racer, 4ft long and 2ft 6in high, operated by pedals. They cost £20 each, rather an expensive toy, and the author remembers saying at the time that they would be bought only by the very wealthy. A skilled man earned about £7 for a 48 hour week then, so a Joycar represented nearly three weeks' pay. Probably not many were sold in Britain, although by August 1949 when the Joy Roadster, the new name for the Joycar, cost £27 plus tax and the racing car, now called the Pathfinder Special, was reduced to £12 15s, 100 a week were being produced.

By mid 1948 the new FX3 Austin taxi, based on the 16 but without independent front suspension, was introduced. It was designed in conjunction with Mann & Overton with a pressed-steel body by Car Bodies of Coventry, being the first Austin cab with an enclosed driver's compartment. Such vehicles were quite luxurious and they ran as London taxis with great success for many years. Soon the 16 was going to get the new treatment and the announcement was made just before the first Motor Show at Earls Court for ten years.

The A70 Hampshire, styled on similar lines to the A40, used the 2,199cc 16 engine with a 6.8 to 1 compression ratio, tuned to produce 64bhp at 3,800rpm. Designed for export, it had the nasty steering-column gear shift and cost £475 plus purchase tax. Whereas the A70 looked like an overgrown A40, this cannot be said of the A90 Atlantic two-door four-seat tourer — called a convertible now to suit the American market — with its central spot lamp, flying A on each wing over the front lamps, and sweeping lines which did away for the first time with the frontal radiator appearance. There was no cowl on the bonnet cover, and the air intake was through the wide shallow grille under the lamps. Rear wings were completely cowled in, forming an integral part of the body. The 16 engine was bored out from $3\frac{1}{8}$in to $3\frac{7}{16}$in, giving a capacity of 2,660cc; a compression ratio of 7.5 to 1 produced 88bhp at 4,000rpm. It used the same chassis as the A70, but the engine had twin SU carburetters and the final drive ratio was 3.667:1 against 4.125:1. It cost £745 and caused a sensation. Everything was there for the Americans — power-operated hood, column change and top speed of 90mph. Even though the brakes were not much good, the Americans could not get this model quickly enough.

The Austin range of three basic vehicles now consisted of the A40 Devon, Countryman and Pick-up; the A70 and A90; and the A125 and A135. The 16 was retained for a while, with a price reduction of £20 to £535 for the saloon, there was also a Countryman version, and the long-wheelbase A125 Sheerline divided eight-seat limousine. For 1948 Austin production totalled about 62,000 vehicles made up approximately as follows:

Model	No produced
A40	42,500
A70	1,000
A90	500
A120/135	2,000
Commercials	16,000

Although the company had done better than in 1947, the gross trading profit fell to the 1939 level at £1,611,903, with a low net profit of £571,988. A disappointing result compared, for example, with that of Standard-Triumph who had just reported a trebled profit, but the reason for the low production was the dislocation caused by the three months that it had taken at the end of 1947 and beginning of 1948 to change over to the production of the new models. In December 1948 more ordinary shares were issued to capitalise another 2,071,556 units. For every 5 ordinary or A ordinary held, 4 new 5s ordinary shares could be taken up at £1 5s each, and balance being made available to holders of other classes of share. The issue was greatly over-subscribed.

After testing an A90 Atlantic at Montlhéry the previous winter Alan Hess — the new Austin public relations officer who had left the BBC to join Austins in February 1946 — Charlie Goodacre and Dennis Buckley, with Sammy Davis as pit manager, took an A90 over to Indianapolis in an attempt to smash all existing speed records for stock cars held, since 1928, by a Studebaker. An overheated engine halted the attempt after only 2,000 miles which were covered at an average of 77mph, a new one was put in and for seven days and nights the car tore along, covering in the end 11,875 miles at an average speed of 70.68mph. Surprisingly enough, the old 1928 Studebaker had averaged 68.58mph, but the A90 broke 63 records from 1km to 10,000 miles. A huge advertising campaign followed, Hess wrote a book about the attempt and the price of the car in the States was slashed by $1,000 — the biggest price cut in the history of motoring — to $2,975 (about £744). At home, although no Atlantics were available, the list price was reduced by £100 to £645. It did not do Austins much good and later Lord moaned: 'We went to Indianapolis to prove what the British car could stand up to, and I think we proved it. Now the question is — what benefit have we got in sales in America? I am afraid the answer is none. The response to the A90 has been disappointing.' Production of the convertible ceased in January 1951 by which time about 15,000 had been made; the sports saloon-version struggled on until September 1952.

Everything about the American market·was disappointing. Lord had

Lord's attempt to sketch his first idea for the Atlantic Convertible

decided to concentrate his maximum effort there, but sales were falling away and what sales remained were unprofitable. In June, July and August 1948, 7,000 Austins went to the States; in the same three months in 1949 exports there fell to 460. Lord said that in 1948-9 £150,000 had been lost on US business; only £205 was got in dollars for an A40, and the materials alone cost the company £203. About 1,200 cars, mostly A40s, were sent back from America in August. They had been in store for so long that they had deteriorated badly and needed modifications to bring them up to date. Exports were helped a little when the £ was devalued later that summer, rating it at $2.80, but even this had no lasting effect. Austins struggled on there for a while, but much greater demand was now coming from Canada and Australia, and this is where future efforts were concentrated.

At home the 100,000th A40 was completed in May 1949 and a new style was introduced, the MkII Devon, at £328 — £37 less than the existing car. It was a simplified version with a simplified bench-type front seat in leathercloth, no cover to the glove compartment, and no overriders, heater, sunshine roof, trafficators or spare tyre. The policy was to pare the car down as much as possible so that its selling price abroad could be reduced to a minimum. Lord said: 'Our market in America has simply dried up. We are out if our prices do not come down', hence the MkII A40. No mechanical alterations were made, except that the rear-axle ratio was raised giving 5.14:1 against 5.43:1 which increased the top speed by over 5mph.

Prices began to rise again in March 1949 after Morris put 10 per cent on some of his models; the A125 went to £1,150 and the A135 to £1,425. Other Austins followed suit on 3 August; the MkII Devon was increased by £22 to £350, there was £30 on the Countryman and £40 on the A70 bringing it to £515. All these, of course, were still taxed at 33⅓ per cent. Things were improving, the basic petrol ration was doubled that summer and more than 170,000 more cars were registered than in 1948. UK car production was up to 412,290 and, although the proportion exported was down, the total number was up to 257,922. Morris and his associated companies produced about 90,000 cars, Austin 116,996 (and 19,600 commercials) and Ford 78,725. Ford also made 39,000 commercials and 33,000 tractors which gave them a total of over 151,000 vehicles, a factor often overlooked, and certainly not appreciated as it should have been by either Nuffield or Lord. They should have got to work on the BMC merger much sooner than they did, instead of behaving like two spoilt children, and maybe the result would have been a dominant BL in the position that Ford is in today in Britain.

Approximately the 1949 Austin production breakdown was:-

Model	No produced
A40	90,800
A70	9,000
A90	15,000
A125/135	2,196

84,324 Austin cars and commercial vehicles were exported. In financial terms, the year to 31 July 1949 was excellent. Gross trading profit rose by about £½ million to £2,164,342, and net profit was up to £679,932, and there was still £563,126 to carry forward. Nuffield's results were disappointing that year, but Ford had a 25 per cent increase in trading profits; by paying only a modest dividend of 10 per cent they were able to carry forward nearly £5 million. Austins gave shareholders a much more generous 40 per cent,

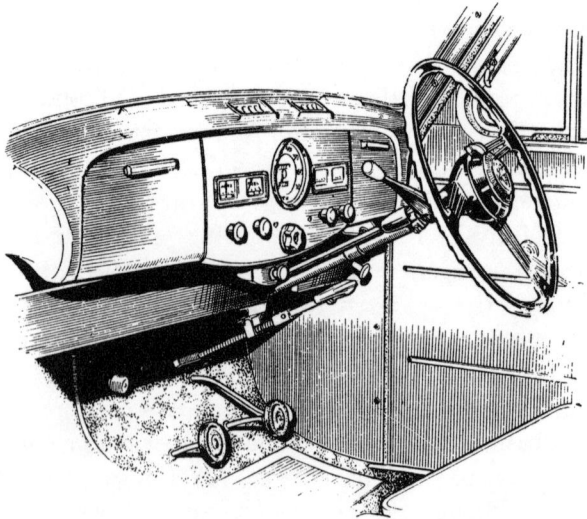

The A40 steering column and new fascia, October 1951

amalgamated the non-voting A ordinary shares into one class with the voting ordinary and also gave a 50 per cent share bonus of 2,330,500 5s ordinary shares on a one-for-two held basis by capitalising reserves of £582,625. This raised the issued capital of the company to over £4 million.

At the Motor Show, the new Rover 75 and the razor-edge Triumph Mayflower were the sensations, the Triumph being an odd-looking car, breaking away completely from the sweeping curves that were then popular. It was more traditionally British in appearance, and had a look of quality about it, but the right-angle edges caused accident repair problems, and aggressive cleaning removed the paint from the angles, causing serious rusting. Austins did not have very much new to offer for 1950. There was a long-wheelbase Sheerline limousine, a fixed-head sports saloon on the Atlantic chassis at £695, an altered rear axle on the Princess now priced at £1,375, the rear seats on the A70 were moved back to give easier entry, and the MkI A40 was given the MkII rear axle. A40s had swivelling front quarter lights and grained-finish fascia and door cappings.

Lord disliked the Labour government. They increased profits taxes from 25 to 30 per cent, and that was bad enough, but when they did something to hit his own pocket he was furious. After Sir John Black of Standard had been paid a fee of £25,000 in shares to bind him to the company for life, it was proposed that Lord should be given £25,000 in cash and 80,000 ordinary shares in return for an undertaking that he would not be involved in the motor business for the rest of his life if, for any reason, he were to leave Austins. Such payments were then free of tax, and there had already been a legal test case as the result of earlier problems but questions were now asked in the House, and the TUC asked the government to alter the law. Although Lord said he would rather not bother with the money than have all the fuss, the shareholders insisted after a vote in which holders of 600,000 shares were in favour with 100,000 against. He took the cash and the shares, but retrospective legislation was introduced in the April 1950 Budget, and he and Black had to pay surtax at 95 per cent.

16 The Great Merger - The British Motor Corporation: 1950-1952

Naturally, as time goes by, and models are changed, a certain degree of rationalisation will take place, but it will be done with the minimum of disturbance.

Leonard Lord on being asked when all BMC engines would be made at
Longbridge, May 1952

We have been in competition with Austins for a long time, and we shall remain in competition.

R.F. Hanks, director of BMC and vice chairman of the Nuffield Group,
June 1952

The year 1950 began with the introduction of the new Loadstar range of 2 and 5 ton trucks; basically the same chassis and engines were used as in the earlier trucks, but for export models the Perkins P6 diesel engine was available as an option. Cabs were redesigned and the front end was given car styling. Austin-Crompton Parkinson bought a controlling interest in ITD Limited, who made the well known Stacatruc industrial electric vehicles, and they were marketed without any great success by Austin-Crompton Parkinson. The Budget in April 1950 helped the industry by reducing by a half the double purchase tax on cars costing over £1,000, and by announcing an end to petrol rationing in May. There had to be a catch — for the first time purchase tax at 33⅓ per cent was levied on commercial vehicle chassis, and a further 9d a gallon was added to the petrol duty raising it to 1s 6d, which represented half the price of 3s.

Austins in 1950 had their most successful year so far. 142,723 cars and 23,000 commercials were sold. Approximately, the breakdown was:

Model	No produced
A40	110,000
A70	18,000
A90	12,723
A125/135	2,000

In general, the industry was very successful, more cars than ever being made — 552,515, of which nearly 400,000 were exported. Of the big six, Nuffield made 150,000 and Ford 185,000 cars, trucks and tractors; Standard 112,000 cars and tractors; Rootes about 90,000 cars and trucks; and Vauxhall 47,692 cars and 40,783 Bedford trucks and vans. Although Austin made more cars than anyone else in Britain, Ford actually produced more vehicles. Less than 7,000 British cars had been exported to the States in 1949, but there was a good revival in 1950, at over 20,000, but America was no longer top of the league. Australia and Canada absorbed over 76,000 each, Sweden 23,000, South Africa 19,000, New Zealand 16,000, Belgium 13,000 and India 10,000. Exporting was now much more profitable as a result of devaluation of the £, and the Austin results for the year ending 31 July 1950 were spectacular. The gross trading profit more than doubled to £5,080,870, the net profit trebled to £1,847,891 and £622,090 was carried forward — more than ever before; however, only a modest dividend of 35 per cent was paid on the ordinary shares.

Korea and the Cold War were in full swing, mass conscription in the form of National Service still applied to all males of 18, spending on defence increased and the rearmament programme was stepped up. Austins won a Ministry contract worth £1 million to supply a new light field car, the FV1800, which had been designed for the Fighting Vehicle Research and Development Establishment by Rex Sewell of Bentley and Lagonda and built experimentally at Nuffield Mechanisations Limited. They said at the time that they could not build it because there was no space to spare in the Nuffield organisation, but Austins leased back the factory at Cofton Hackett from the government who had been using it as a store since the war, and work soon began. Lord also won the contract to build the Rolls-Royce engine which had been chosen. He saw in this four-wheel-drive vehicle, with five speeds and a transfer box which enabled it to go as fast in reverse gear as in forward, a chance to compete with the highly successful Land-Rover, so he offered to pay half the tooling costs if he could use the tools and build a civilian version using the A90 engine. This was done, and it became the Austin Champ but, like the Gipsy which followed it in 1957, it never was a serious competitor to the Land-Rover. About 15,000 FV1800s were made. They were unloved by the services, difficult to service and repair, and most of them found their way into the reserve pools where they stayed until they were scrapped in the mid-1960s. Much of the two weeks' training of the Army Emergency Reservists of those days was spent in ferrying back FV1800s to depots in the back of Bedford 3 ton trucks!

George Harriman, one of the most charming men in the motor industry, was appointed deputy managing director of Austins in September 1950 at the very early age of 42. Another Coventry boy, he left Morris in 1940 to join Lord as his general works manager, succeeded Hannay as production manager in October 1941, was awarded the OBE in June 1943 for his war work, and became works director in September 1945. His sad tale that was to follow is given in detail by Graham Turner in *The Leyland Papers* published by Eyre & Spottiswoode in 1971 and is outside the scope of this book; suffice it to say that he was largely responsible for Austin's success from 1946 to 1952 and was awarded the CBE in 1951, an honour which no doubt would have gone to either Lord or Gibson Jarvie had they not made themselves so unpopular with the government. Gibson Jarvie retired in July 1952 at the age of 68 to concentrate on UDT business and Harriman took over as deputy chairman and managing director of Austins, a post which Jarvie had held since February 1946.

Three new Austins appeared at the October 1950 Motor Show. They were not to have the same impact as the two new Fords for 1951 – the 1.5 litre Consul at £415 and the six-cylinder Zephyr at £475 – but both the new Dagenham cars were built down to a price and were certainly not in the same class as the A70 Herefords which replaced the Hampshire. The body was restyled and enlarged, the chassis was 3in longer in the wheelbase and ½in wider in track and there were only four side windows which gave the car a much cleaner line. The only change to the engine was an increase in the oil-sump capacity from 10 to 11.75 pints, and hydraulic Girling brakes were used on both axles. Restyling of the body included a radiator grille extended upwards and combined with a horizontal grille at the foot. Push-button door handles, built-in air conditioning and heating and friction controlled ventilating louvres to the front doors completed the specification. The Hereford cost £545, and there was a two-door coupé version with power or manually operated hood at £690 or £670, very expensive and not very popular. It was discontinued in August 1952.

A40 Devons were the most successful Austins of their day, but how many people would pay £100 more than the £395 for a Devon with sliding head to get an open two-door sports A40? Quite a few did because it was a good little car; the chassis was basically the same as that used on the Devon, but by fitting twin SU carburetters the engine output was increased to 46bhp at 4,400rpm. A stiffened chassis and full hydraulic Girling brakes were an improvement, and apart from the flying A on the bonnet, it was difficult to see that it was an Austin with its American mouth-like air intake and straight-sided body. It appealed to the Americans in very much the same way as the MG had done.

For 1951, manufacturers were allowed to sell only 80,000 cars plus half of any production in excess of 460,000, at home. In spite of a 15-20 per cent cut in sheet steel supplies at the beginning of the year, which led to 4-day weeks at Cowley, Vauxhall and parts of Longbridge, the industry managed to produce 475,919 cars — less than in 1950, but 368,737 were exported. On the government's reckoning only 88,000 cars should have been released for UK sales, but their export statistics were notoriously unreliable and when the correct figures came out it was too late to discipline the manufacturers for having exceeded the quota by nearly 20,000! To make the allocation of new cars as fair as possible, the motor trade had sold them on the understanding that there should be no resale until after one year. This covenant was increased to a two-year period for 1951, and the scheme was controlled entirely by the retail trade. Second-hand car prices were already fantastic and the two-year covenant accentuated the shortage and put second-hand prices up even higher — an advertisement appeared in a national daily paper offering to exchange a 1939 car for a house. A 2-year-old car appreciated at about £250 a year, so an option was built into the two-year covenant to allow a trader to repurchase a car at its original price less an allowance for fair wear and tear. However, supply and demand regulated prices, and there was no way in which the trade could influence either, and second-hand car prices remained high until new cars were freely available again.

All Austin prices were increased in February, from £28 on a Devon and £30 on the new A40 sports to £100 on the A135 limousine. A further 6 per cent was added in August, to cover an average 16 per cent increase in steel prices. All the figures quoted are exclusive of the $33\frac{1}{3}$ per cent purchase tax, but the Budget in April doubled the tax, raising the price of an A40 from £537 to £655. With a further increase in petrol duty of $4\frac{1}{2}$d and an increase in company profit tax from 30 to 50 per cent, everything was being done to discourage the motorist from wanting the new cars that he was not going to get anyway. The government's argument was that the increases in taxation would discourage people from buying goods that should be exported, and free productive capacity for rearmament; the same results could have been obtained by quotas, but that would not have given them the extra revenue required by the ailing economy. Of course, second-hand car prices increased.

Lord had set three goals for Longbridge after the war. First, that the product must be a considerable advance on the pre-war vehicle, sound though he thought that was. Secondly, that the organisation first off the starting line with peace-time production would be very advantageously placed and, finally, that capacity at Longbridge would have to be very much greater than it was before the war — even two or three times as great — to ensure economic operation. He saw the results of his greatest achievement when he completed the new Longbridge car assembly building in July 1951. Lord wanted, for one thing, to free areas of the main factory for new development. He also wanted, by more uniform and quicker movement, to reduce stocks of materials, components and assemblies in order to economise in working capital. The result was by far the most modern and sophisticated plant in the world. It was built on the airfield as that was the only place which offered unrestricted space, but had the disadvantages of standing on higher ground than the existing buildings and at some distance from them. Minor units and bodies had to be moved from the shops to the new assembly building where they would travel along 16 miles of overhead conveyors, parts being fed in at 5 points and completed, tested cars coming out at the end. In order to feed the units to the line, a 1,000ft tunnel and covered way was driven up through the hillside and under the assembly building floor, most of the major parts being lifted automatically up through the floor and placed on the conveyor. Parts were marshalled into the correct sequence with the aid of a Hollerith punched card system. Cards to represent each car being produced were fed through the machine giving information to the stores, assembly line and other shops of the various parts that would be needed. Before all the parts were fed into the main assembly tunnel they were automatically marshalled in a holding area which provided a buffer stock to allow for staggered working hours in the different plants. Assembly along the four tracks could carry on non-stop, provided that sufficient components were built up in advance. Only three of the tracks were completed at the time, one being used for the A40, another for the A70, the third held for the new Austin 7.

Apart from speeding up the assembly process, and reducing the length of the assembly lines, the main advantage was in the reduction of the quantity of stock which had to be held during operations. Short, fast-moving supply lines with automatic marshalling meant that less stock was held in the pipelines, giving considerable savings. At the same time, handling costs and the chance of human error were reduced and, perhaps the most important feature, the plant could be adapted very quickly to any car model change. Given the steel, coal and a well-disposed government, with good home and export demand, Austins simply had to be successful — there was nothing to stop them — and their position was going to be even further improved with the introduction of their new small car, the AS3 or the A30. With a Morris Minor at £365 and the cheap out-dated Ford Anglia at £307, there was a need for another car in that price range, particularly in Europe where the new German Volkswagen was beginning to dominate. The new Austin was to cost only £325, but with tax it sold in Britain for £507.

At first, an attempt was made to call it the New Austin Seven; it had a small engine, it was a small car, but it had four doors and looked so much like a scaled-down A70 Hereford that the public never saw it as a true 'baby' car. Four doors only lasted until September 1953. After about 25,000 AS3s had been produced a new two-door body was brought out; the A35 followed the A30 and then there was another attempt to use the title 'Austin Seven' when the Mini came out in 1959. But I am straying into BMC history with its Austin Seven with one set of badges and Morris Mini Minor with another, where the title 'Mini' stuck much, I am sure, to the disgust of quite a few people at Longbridge.

Many components and arrangements were tried, including two-cylinder and four-cylinder engines, front and rear engine locations, and just about every known variation of power unit and suspension system. The basic problem was to be able to carry four people and luggage in the smallest body possible at the minimum cost. Rear-engine mounting was discarded because of the basic objection 'that luggage accommodation is bound to be curtailed unless overall dimensions are increased, since the space under the bonnet, restricted as it is by steering movements of the front wheels, is fundamentally less than that available at the rear'. It had been done on the VW, but for some reason British manufacturers of the day would go to almost any lengths to ensure that there was plenty of boot space. They seem to have had the idea that people only set out in a car when they were taking the family away on holiday with all the luggage. A roof-rack would have been the answer, and if the A30 had been given a rear-mounted engine and reduced boot space at the front, it might have been so successful that Issigonis would not have been given the opportunity to make the Mini, which solved the problem in a much better way by putting the engine sideways at the front end and driving direct to the front wheels.

It may have looked a larger car than it was because it so much resembled the Hereford, but the A30 was lower than the old Ruby and only a few inches longer at the front, and in fact there was slightly more room available inside the body of the old Austin 7 than in this new one, so long as the passenger at the back did not mind sitting over the back axle. No other similarities existed. Lord had gone back to the box-frame chassis structure with the A40 and the A70 after using platform chassis before, but this time the welded, stressed-skin pressed-steel structure served both as body and chassis — modern unitary construction. No chassis members were built into the floor and there were no sub-frames to carry engine and suspension; the heaviest section steel sheet used to carry the independent front suspension was only 16 gauge. Doors were made as simply as possible, from inner and outer pressings designed to avoid the use of wedge dies and to do away with interior window and sill mouldings. There was no upholstery on the doors — or anywhere else except on the seats — but the door-trim panel had simulated upholstery formed by painted and grained millboard sheets held in place by an extruded rubber section. Front windows lacked the conventional winding mechanism, and were held in the closed position by the interior door locks; rear windows did not open but there were both front and rear opening quarter lights for ventilation. With its plastic carpets, leathercloth trim and very basic finish, the A30 looked what it was, a car which had been built down to a price, with that austere look that went with utility furniture and cigarettes in paper packets instead of thin cardboard boxes. Nothing else about the car was unconventional, it used an 800cc engine based on the A40 power unit, weighed only 13¼cwts and performed and handled quite well. Quantity production did not begin until 1952.

Austin production in 1951 fell to about 121,500 cars and 20,000 commercials, the vast majority of which were A40s, now with the new A30 fascia with a central instrument panel and steering-column gear change, a feature not inflicted upon the A30. A40 bodywork was styled to conform to the A70 and A30 in February 1952, and it became the Somerset; 344,000 A40s had been made up until then, 265,000 of which had been exported. By the autumn things were not going well for the motor trade; in October, 2,500 Austin and 2,000 Morris cars were shipped back from Canada, the market there being depressed, but for Austins the year ending 31 July had been very good. A 45 per cent dividend was paid in spite of Gaitskell's threat to limit dividends for three years — the General Election came before he had the chance to enact the legislation — and in October a bonus of one week's wages was given to all workers who had been in full employment since 31 July. Turnover had been nearly £31 million, the gross profit over £8 million and the net profit nearly £3 million; 883,937 5s ordinary shares were offered at £1 5s each on the basis of one for every eight ordinary held to get as close as possible to the £5 million authorised capital, and after that there was to be a further issue of 10 million 5s ordinary shares so that the issued capital could be raised to £7.5 million. This proved unnecessary because the British Motor Corporation was about to be born.

As early as the summer of 1948, Lord Nuffield and Leonard Lord had a series of talks which resulted in their deciding, on 6 October, that

> there would be a constant interchange of information on production methods, costs, purchases, design and research, patents and all other items which would be likely to result in manufacturing economies. The object is to effect maximum standardisation coupled with the most efficient manufacture and, by pooling of all factory resources, a consequent reduction of costs.

Questions were asked in the House of Commons in November as to whether such a merger would be subject to the Monopolies Act, and if a merger between the two companies would operate against the public interest. Lord said that no financial merger was proposed and the Government decided that it had no reason to believe that any abuse existed or was likely. Roy Jenkins MP, writing in *Tribune* on 15 October 1948, gave a typical Socialist view:

> In so far as it holds out a prospect of greater efficiency it is to be welcomed; but in so far as it also involves a concentration of power greater than anything which has hitherto been known in the motor industry, it must be carefully watched.
> This is a dilemma which confronts private industry in many fields. If it does not amalgamate, it cannot be fully efficient; if it does, then the resultant unit is so large that it must come more and more under the supervision of the state. It is one which the motor industry can hardly escape.

In July 1949 the scheme was abandoned, preliminary investigations had been completed and 'the interchange of confidential information has ceased. No further steps will be taken with regard to the pooling of production resources, and no merger is contemplated'. This terse statement was not expanded, but the press were not slow to draw their conclusions; they remembered what Lord had said in 1936 when he left Nuffield: 'I am pig-headed and Lord Nuffield has his opinions.' Some thought the real object of suggesting a merger at the time was to stave off the Labour

Government's threat of nationalisation. By making the big six publicly owned, the motor industry would then be rationalised, and perhaps Lord and Nuffield felt by doing this themselves interference from the government would be less likely. Later, the industry formed its own standardisation committee which, covering all car makers, was even more effective than this initial Morris-Austin abortive attempt might have been. In the 1950 General Election, Conservatives and their supporters held 253 seats against Labour's 251, too narrow a majority to govern with, and in the following year – the year of the Festival of Britain – yet another election gave them 271 seats against Labour's 233. No one needed to fear any more plans for nationalisation of the motor industry for some time and, ironically, government interference eventually became necessary to keep the ailing car makers in business, rather than to nationalise them for the benefit of redistributing the handsome profits they made.

Details of the merger of the Austin and Morris companies were announced in December 1951. It all sounded very impressive with balance-sheet assets of £66 million involving makers of half the output of Britain's motor industry; the new group would be the fourth largest in the world, with a total of 42,000 employees. Austin's was the leading UK exporter of vehicles and had factories in Australia, Canada, the US, India and South Africa; Nuffield had a factory in Australia. It was stated that there was no question of producing a Nuffield-Austin car or of doing away with the separate Wolseley and Riley identities, and considering what Lord and Hanks were saying (two quotations are given at the beginning of this chapter) one might wonder whether the formation of British Motor Corporation was going to produce anything more than a holding company more suited to please accountants than production engineers. But this was not the intention; the joint enterprise would be able to dominate the home market, and would be in a stronger position to combat the US challenge in overseas markets when it came. All that the official statement said was that 'unified control would not only lead to more efficient and economic production, but would also further the export drive . . . amalgamation would be both in the national interest and to the advantage of the shareholders of both companies'.

Lord Nuffield was to be chairman, Lord deputy chairman and managing director; R.F. Hanks, vice-chairman of Morris Motors, and George Harriman, deputy managing director of Austins, were the only two other directors. Rather more Morris shares were issued than Austin, and of the £5 million capital in the new holding company which was to be in 20 million 5s shares, Austin shareholders were to be allocated 7,955,437 and Morris holders 10,600,000. At the announcement, Morris shares stood at 35s 4½d and Austin at 32s 6d, both yielding a little over 7 per cent on recent dividends. Rights of the existing preference and preferred ordinary stockholders were guaranteed both as regards capital and income, but on 29 February 1952 the rights were extended to embrace all classes of capital. As a financial journalist wrote in the *Investors' Chronicle* on 8 March 1952, it was a tidying up of colossal dimensions! The details of the formation of BMC are too complex to include here, but his article is strongly recommended to anyone seeking the full story.

Lord Nuffield was 74 at the time of the merger, and the story of the friction between Lord, Hanks and Nuffield; of Lord's final takeover of BMC and the resentment which he created between Cowley and Longbridge are covered brilliantly by Graham Turner in the already mentioned *The Leyland Papers*. I would like to close this book by just one short quotation from Mr Turner's book, which sums up the tragedy of the early days of BMC:

The fact was that Lord had fouled the atmosphere for the most important alliance in the history of the British motor industry to that point . . . The benefits of the merger were, indeed, never fully realised.

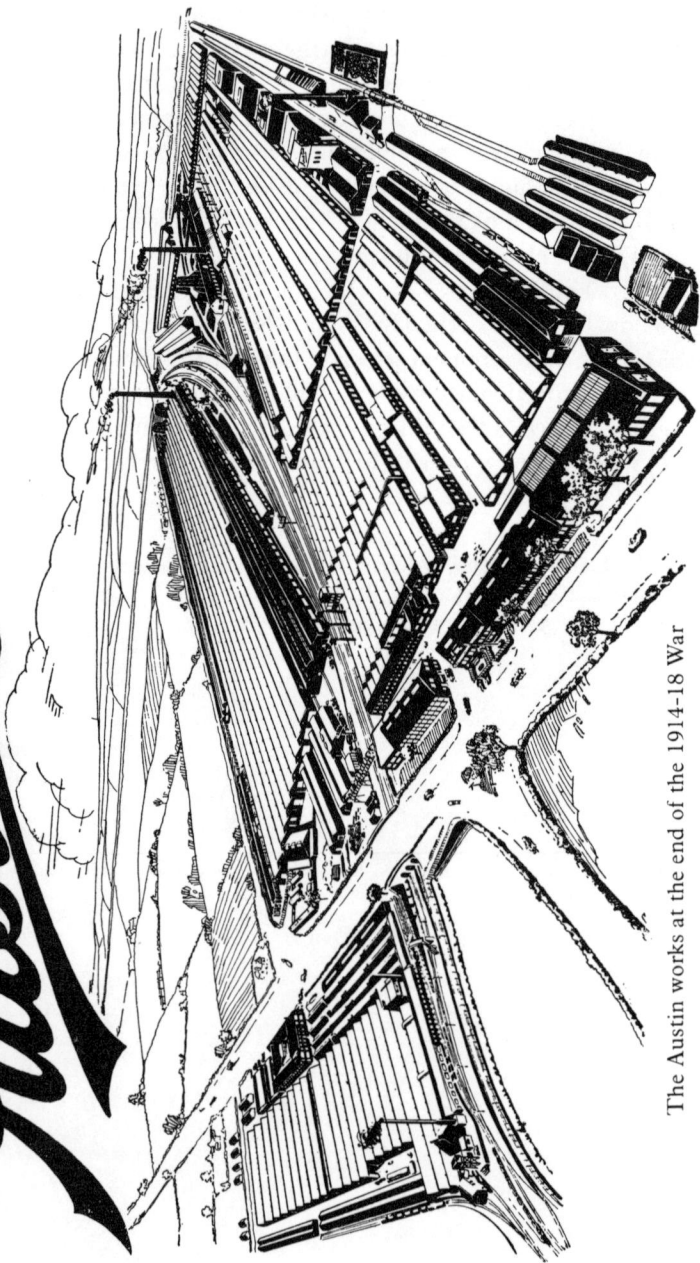

The Austin works at the end of the 1914-18 War

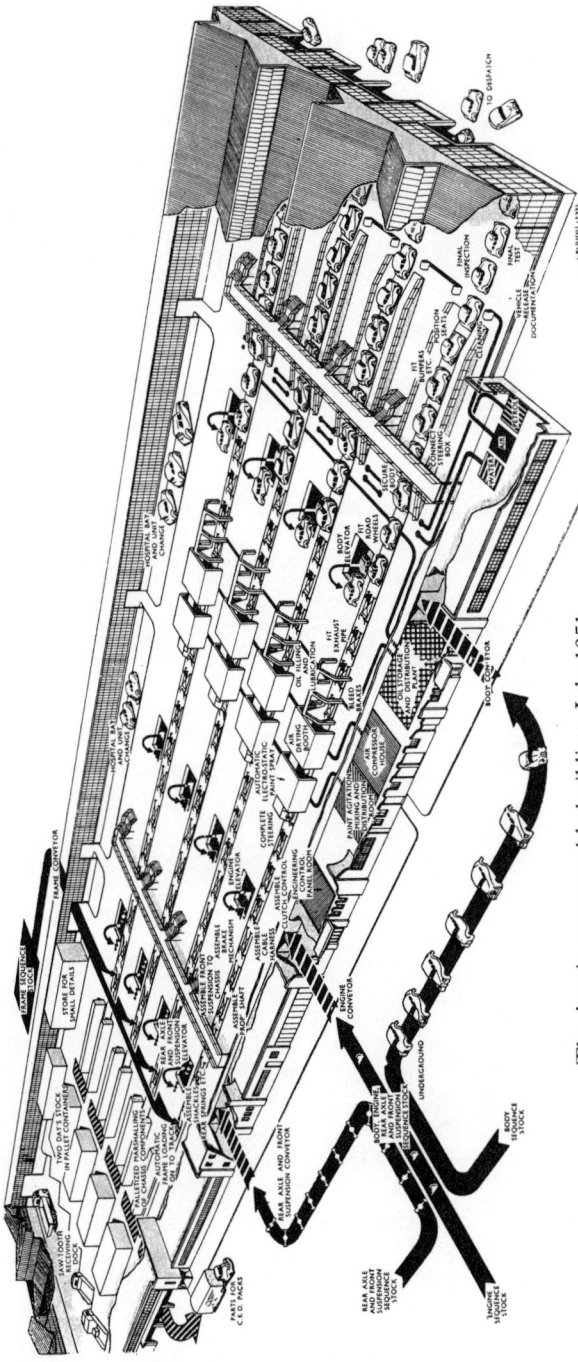

The Austin car assembly building, July 1951

Appendices

1 The 2-3 ton Lorry

It must have been towards the end of 1912 that Austin designed the 2-3 ton lorry chassis and a prototype was ready for testing during December of that year. The *Commercial Motor* published particulars in February 1913 and an official catalogue was published in July to coincide with the company's exhibit on Stand 28 at the Commercial Motor Show held at Olympia.

Heralded as a breakaway from the stereotyped layouts being produced at the time, the design was more eagerly accepted by technically minded theorists than by conservative vehicle users. To them, well-tried ideas meant more than novel designs. The really outstanding point about the vehicle was the way in which the 2ft 5in loading line was achieved. A dual propeller shaft drive was used, each shaft coming from a common differential unit housed behind the gearbox and driving each rear wheel through a separate crown-wheel and pinion. The wheels were carried on a tubular dead rear axle, but in order that the angled shafts could reach the wheels, at the same time retaining the low platform, the frame side-members were made of an open lattice section. Considerable depth was necessary both to avoid weakening and to enable enough up-and-down movement of the shafts to take place as the rear axle rose and fell.

Other dominant features included an inclined engine mounting which caused the crankshaft centre line to slope downwards towards the rear axle — this kept the crankshaft in line with the propeller-shaft's unladen angle. Apart from placing the starting-handle bracket above the front chassis cross-member - a somewhat doubtful advantage unless one happened to be over 6ft 9in tall — this positioning kept the sump high up in the chassis frame — a function made necessary by the fact that the front axle beam was positioned immediately beneath No3 cylinder. The four-cylinder 89mm x 127mm engine was of no particular interest being made up, largely, from parts used in the 20hp car unit.

In contrast with the rest of the vehicle, the archaic individually cast cylinders were noted as being the only ones of that type at the North of England Heavy Motor Exhibition held at Manchester in 1913. When later, in 1917, the 95mm x 127mm sports model 20hp engine replaced the smaller one, this still retained individually cast 'T' headed cylinders, and it was not until the introduction of the fabulous 20hp monobloc engine of 1919 that the old system was superseded. By that time, however, Austin lorry production had ceased.

Returning once again to novel features, inspection of the rear suspension will show the dual or Duplex springs, one mounted on top of the other, on either side of the axle tube. The catalogue tells us that this design 'provided for the transmission of either propelling or braking effort without imposing lateral bending action upon the springs'. Putting it in a different way, on vehicles in which the laden weight varies greatly from that when unladen, it was then considered evident by some designers that springs suitable under one set of conditions were insufficient, or too stiff, for another. Springs were thus understressed and the vehicle was unduly severe upon itself when running light – to the point, sometimes, of smashing itself to pieces on the roads of those days. Subsidiary springs coming into action on a laden vehicle were used in the form of Carey variable springs as fitted to the 1913 Aveling 5-ton steamers and the Duplex Austin springs seemed to have achieved a similar effect.

There were no other British commercial vehicle designs at that time using either a rear-mounted radiator or a centrally operated gear lever – a daring breakaway from the conventional undertaken about fifteen years before even British cars gave up the right-hand change.

In order that the point at which the wheel meets the road should be in line with the centre line of the king pin a most complicated arrangement of axle and stub-axle forging was employed, in which the king pin formed part of the stub-axle itself. It was good fun but quite unnecessary, because the same object can be much more easily attained by the more conventional method which Austin had employed previously.

It is interesting to attempt to visualise how contemporary users would have reacted to some of these features. Normally one can gauge the efficacy of a product from sales figures but, in this case, World War I started before any impact could be made upon the market, and by 1919 the one-model policy of the company had relegated the lorry to the history books.

Any attempt at ease of maintenance and simplification of control would, no doubt, have been welcomed, but there were two distinct points of view with regard to final drive. The shaft-drive advocates put chain drives as things of the past, they were more troublesome, more expensive to maintain than shafts and they absorbed more power. On the other hand, the chain-drive votaries argued that the introduction of a gear drive at that point was a waste of power, and anyway it involved the use of too much unsprung weight. The huge live axle casing caused rapid tyre wear and tyres were the major items in any bill for running expenses. By using two propeller-shafts, each chain was replaced by a separate shaft and the disadvantage of either system was, on the whole, overcome. It nullified also the objection to carrying an inordinate mass of unsprung weight behind.

Regarding tyre costs at that time, even on the Austin which was considered particularly economical, for an estimated 200 miles per week in 1913, £1 5s was allowed for tyre wear per vehicle – double the milage and you doubled the estimated cost. Against this a skilled driver could be hired for a mere £1 15s a week. Evaluating this with today's costs, a vehicle user would have to set aside some £50 per week for tyres per 200 vehicle miles, which would cause some enormous increases in freight rates.

The army's interest in these vehicles began in September 1913. No 4 Infantry Division was holding manoeuvres in the Midlands, and hired a 2-3 tonner from a contractor. The senior officers in the division were so impressed that they sent in a glowing report on its suitability.

We are fortunate in having, in lieu of users' recommendations and comments, a comprehensive War Office report on the functioning of some of the 2,000 2-3 ton Austins supplied on contract between 1914 and 1917. Conditions were atrocious;

inexperienced drivers, infrequent maintenance and Flanders mud, brought to light the weak features in any vehicle. The cross-member which took the weight of the power unit sub-frame was riveted to the side-members, and in almost every case these rivets were found to be loose. Much of the rigidity was lost at this point. Our old friends, the complicated stub-axles, gave trouble too. Bronze bushes were used for the front wheel bearings and, in the first consignment of lorries to arrive in France, nearly all the wheel bearings fractured in the same place, the flange breaking away from the iournal. The rear-mounted radiator led to 'complaints from the drivers as to the heat of the cab during hot weather, which was aggravated by the column of hot air passing through'.

Concerning the complicated differential unit and the three crown-wheels and pinions, the official view was that 'the amount of work necessitated in the adiustment and repairs to gears and shafts, constituted one of the most formidable operations of an overhaul. To maintain correct adiustment of the rear wheel bevels is a matter of some difficulty, however, in spite of the adiustable thrust washer provided. It was found in service that the accurate adiustment necessary for the correct working of the bevel gear was seldom obtained in the rear wheels, with the result that replacements to the gears were frequently necessary'.

By September 1917, in addition to the larger 3¾in bore engine, several other modifications had been introduced. The clutch was increased in width from 2½in to 3in, a stronger differential shaft was fitted, differential sun and planet wheels were redesigned, nickel-chrome steel gears replaced the case-hardened mild steel variety and a number of other variations were carried out to the chassis frame and the shafts and rear axle, to remedy the faults noticed by the War Office.

2 Austin Aircraft, 1909-1919

Herbert Austin first became interested in flight in the 1890s and in 1894 he sent drawings of his ideas for an aeroplane to Sir Hiram Maxim, who was then building his steam-driven flying machine at the Maxim Nordenfelt Guns & Ammunition Company's factory at Crayford in Kent. Sir Hiram had been working on powered flight for years and when he had been asked by a group of wealthy businessmen in 1887 if it was possible to make a flying machine he replied: 'Certainly, a domestic goose is able to fly and why should not a man be able to do as well as a goose'. Contrary to what one might think after reading that statement, Maxim was essentially a practical man. Of theorists he said: 'I think we might put down all of their results, add them together, and then divide by the number of mathematicians, and thus find the average coefficient of error'. So, in 1889 he had employed two American mechanics and begun his experiments at Baldwyns Park in Kent.

Unfortunately no copy of Austin's drawing has been preserved, but this letter from Maxim has:

H. Austin Esq

> Baldwyns Park
> Bexley
> Kent
> 12th June 1894

Dear Sir

Yours of the 4th inst is received, and I am free to admit that of the thousands of letters which I have received on the subject, yours is the most practical.

I have already found that the arrangement of the aeroplane which you have drawn out is the most practical of any, and that two thicknesses of cloth, one on either side, is the best form of an aeroplane, but the gas in between would not amount to anything.

My latest patent was for the arrangement so called 'venetian blind' after the manner of the drawing, as you can see we were both thinking in the same direction.

> Yours truly
> Hiram S. Maxim

An interesting reference in the letter concerns the introduction of a gas lighter than air between two thicknesses of fabric — a combination of a balloon with a heavier than air machine. The Venetian blind mentioned was probably some form of aileron for controlling the craft.

In 1897, when he was connected with Vickers Sons & Maxim Ltd, Sir Hiram approached Austin who was working with Wolseley and the result was that he designed and made many of the parts used in the steam-driven machine in the Wolseley factory. The two men must have met many times and they appear to have become good friends. But it was not until December 1909, when Austin was approached by an early enthusiast the Reverend J.Swann of Liverpool, that he built his first aeroplane at Longbridge. This solitary machine was powered by an FN engine, and the Reverend Swann took it away, but according to a contemporary report it 'jumped but never flew'. Austin did not make any more flying machines until World War I, when large quantities of aircraft were needed and the Royal Aircraft Factory at Farnborough farmed out work to factories all over the country.

Producing aircraft engines proved no difficulty to car manufacturers, drawings were provided and the engines were assembled from parts, some of which were made in the factory and others brought in from outside. During the war Austin made 2,500 engines of various types ranging from small rotaries to the RAF V8s and even including a 250hp V12 monster. Fifty-two RE 7 planes were made, the first of which was delivered in September 1915; later 300 RE8s were made and then a very large contract was placed for 1,550 SE5As. In one week in 1918 over 60 of these Scouting Experimental machines were accepted by the Royal Aircraft Factory after test flights from the Longbridge flying ground. H.P.Folland of the Royal Aircraft Factory was the SE5's designer and it was considered to be the best design to have come from the factory. It first appeared in France in the spring of 1917 to replace Nieuport Scouts as a challenger to the crack German Albatross, and although its top speed was only just over 130mph its ability to dive superbly at high speed made it a killer. Every newcomer to a squadron equipped with SEs was told to 'Dive and zoom, old boy'.

Captain Albert Ball, VC, DSO, MC, with 43 enemy aircraft to his credit — in one two-week period alone he accounted for 10 - was killed in 1917, a few months before his twenty-first birthday. His father was a director of Austins and in 1916 Albert Ball had devised what he considered to be an ideal single-seater fighter to combat the Fokker, called the Austin-Ball AFB1. In the following year he came home to Birmingham to discuss the machine with the firm's designer. Unfortunately the Air Board, with whom all decisions rested, were not impressed with the design, but Ball made a personal approach to the Director of Air Organisation which resulted in an order for two machines, and a promise for a substantial order if they proved successful.

Two Lewis guns were used, one to fire at targets above and the other firing through the hollow propeller-shaft, an advanced idea patented by Austin. The Austin-Ball was one of the first aircraft on which this idea was used, and the first British aeroplane fitted with a gun designed to fire forwards through the airscrew by means of a synchronising gear reached France on 25 May 1916. Austin's machine-gun designed to fire through the centre of the shaft was first patented on 3 December 1915, some six months before the interrupter gear made by Vickers was first used in action. The prototype Austin-Ball planes were not ready for testing until July 1917, two months after Ball's death, and by then the SE5s and Sopwith Camels had filled the gap so that, although the aeroplane's performance was described as startling and it would certainly have lived up to Ball's expectations, the Air Board turned it down on the grounds that: 'Its superiority over the other machines then in use was not considered great enough to iustify interference with existing production.'

Other experimental models followed. The Austin AFT3 or the Osprey was a triplane designed in 1917 as a competitor to the Sopwith Snipe; the prototype flew first early in 1918 and although it was not developed further continued to be used well into the summer of that year. The machine was made almost entirely of wood, and one of the most interesting features was the interchangeability of the six separate wing sections. Finally there was the Greyhound, a two-seater, intended to replace the Bristol Fighter, the last military machine designed by the company. Three were made and their equipment included camera, wireless, oxygen and heating apparatus. Had they been developed and not suffered from the unsatisfactory 320hp ABC Dragonfly rotary engine, they might well have gained the company government orders at a time when the demand for munitions was beginning to tail off.

All this experimental work and the skilled men which the manufacture of aircraft had brought to Longbridge — there were 130 aircraft carpenters and about 200 riggers and fitters — led to the introduction and subsequent manufacture of the Whippet.

Experimental prototype Whippets were made during the first half of 1919 under the direction of the company's chief aeronautical engineer, J.Kenworthy, who in his early days had worked with Geoffrey de Havilland at the Royal Aircraft Factory. During the war aeroplanes had become a familiar part of the military scene and Austin was not alone in thinking that a new era in flying had begun in which an inexpensive light single-seater machine would be in sufficient demand and attractive to sportsmen and ex-military flyers. Attempts to popularise this form of flying were made by the British Aerial Company in the form of the tiny little Crow, which weighed only 250lb and suspended the pilot below the wings in a wicker basket. There was also the Farman Sport which sold for only £380.

The amateur pilot, as well as knowing how to fly, had to be something of a mechanic in order to keep the machines of those days in a fit state to fly safely. The only other alternative was to employ a mechanic, and he would cost anything up to £3 15s a week. Most aircraft were made from wood covered with fabric with the whole structure held taut by bracing wires which needed constant skilled attention. In the Whippet an attempt was made to overcome this problem, and at the same time to cater for the non-mechanically-minded owner pilot, as no manufacturer had done before. Bracing wires were not used and the fuselage was made of steel tube, wood being done away with entirely.

Two other problems faced the owner pilot — space and cost. The Whippet had folding wings, and when they were parked the machine could be housed in a shed 18ft long, 8ft high, and only 8ft wide. Landing speed was as low as 30mph, and the idea was to land the aircraft in a field near one's home — about 150yd were needed for safety — fold the wings back and taxi down the road to the garage. As far as cost was concerned, with quantity production the Whippet was to sell for £450, about the price of a medium-sized car.

At the Aero Show in 1919 a prototype was exhibited fitted with a 2-cylinder horizontally opposed engine, but production models had 6-cylinder Anzani rotaries. The total dry weight was 500lb, the full wing span 21ft 6in and the fuselage was 16ft long. Air speed was from 30 to 95mph, rate of climb 5,000ft in 8 minutes, 10,000ft in 18 minutes and it was capable of flying for 2 hours without refuelling (about 180 miles). One machine at least was flown a lot during 1919 and 1920, and it was found to be very stable in flight, comfortable, reliable and very simple. A man could handle it alone by picking up the tail skid and pushing; an experienced RAF pilot remarked at the time that he could teach anyone to fly her in ten minutes.

Two Whippets were shown at the Olympia Aero Show in July 1920, by which time the price had been increased to £500. Captain N.D.Nares flew from Bristol to Farnborough, a distance of 90 miles, in 1 hour, later taking the aeroplane to Hendon where he gave demonstrations to potential customers. A few Whippets were sold, perhaps as many as seven — a production failure, not because the machine was in any way unsatisfactory or because of heavy competition, but because amateur flying simply did not catch on and people with money to spend in the immediate post-war period, even though they all seem to have disposed of it by the time of the slump which followed, certainly did not spend it on Austin aircraft.

One final fling was the entry of another Kenworthy-designed prototype called the Kestrel in the Air Ministry Trials held at Martlesham airfield near Ipswich in August 1920. Prizes totalling £64,000 were given to stimulate interest amongst manufacturers and the Kestrel came third in its class, winning £1,500 for the company. This two-seater was powered by a 200hp Beardmore engine. Again steel tubes were used, and with a top speed of 100mph it cruised for 4½ hours at 3,000ft at 80mph, giving 32mpg. Its landing speed was given as 35mph but the best it could do on these tests was 45mph and at that rate it needed 224yd in which to reach a standstill. Austin did not concern himself with flying machines again until Cofton Hackett was built, and all the spare Whippet wings were made into a rose pergola in Arthur Waite's garden.

3 The Austin Tractor

Motor tractors, although quite popular in the United States before 1914, were something of a novelty in pre-war Britain. Horses did a perfectly good job and on the few occasions when farmers did adopt mechanical ploughing, steam tractors or steam engines were used. There were one or two firms which specialised in the hire of steam drag-ploughing equipment, in which a steam engine at either side of a field would haul the plough along an endless cable. Most farmers, however, used horses for ploughing and reaping, and their traction engines for threshing. Farmers, conservative by nature, probably would have remained satisfied with the horse for some time but wartime circumstances necessitated a fresh approach to the problem. Their first difficulties were a shortage both of draught animals and of men to work the land. Large numbers of horses and farm workers had been sent to France during the early part of the war, the men mostly as volunteers prior to conscription in 1916, after which many of those remaining claimed and were granted exemption because of the vital nature of their work. Coupled with the shortage of manpower and horses our imports of food were down to a fraction of the pre-war level. After the navy's initial success in keeping the German Fleet within its home waters, the increasing toll taken by both German surface and submarine craft on our merchant shipping led to a shortage of food, resulting in widespread rationing and a nationwide food-production campaign.

With a view to increasing the production of food in England and Wales the government, in May 1916, approved a plan prepared by the Food Production Department of the Ministry of Agriculture for increasing the corn and potato acreage by 3 million acres by the 1918 harvest. This long-term plan was supplemented by immediate efforts to increase the ploughing of virgin land to grow more food for the 1917 harvest. In each county an Agricultural Executive Committee was set up to decide, with the aid of local farmers in subcommittees, which new land was to be cultivated. It also informed the Food Production Department of labour, machinery, horse and tractor requirements.

As early as June 1914 the Royal Agricultural Society of England had issued rules for conducting tractor-ploughing trials. These were so useful that the Food Production Department and the Agricultural Machinery Department of the Ministry of Munitions asked the society, early in 1917, to carry out further trials on a vehicle which had attracted much attention — the Ford tractor. As a result it was decided to manufacture large numbers of mass-produced standardised machines known as 'Ministry of Munitions' or 'MOM' tractors, Henry Ford having placed all his patents and some of his staff at the government's service free of charge. His only proviso was that the tractors should not be sold. All parts of these machines were produced in the United States and shipped to England for assembly at the government workshops in Manchester. There was, inevitably, some delay in implementing this decision and it was not possible to provide MOM tractors in time for ploughing for the 1917 harvest.

273

Selwyn Francis Edge, as well as being an important figure in the motor trade, was also a keen farmer with land in Sussex on which he had experimented with tractor ploughing as early as 1912, his favourite machine just before the war being the Ivel. He was, therefore, a natural choice for the post of Director of Agricultural Machinery, which he took up in January 1917. His department, working in conjunction with the Board of Agriculture and the Ministry of Munitions, controlled the entire agricultural machinery trade, the tractor-manufacturing side of which was not at first particularly active — nearly all motor manufacturers were employed in munitions production and only three or four firms still continued to make tractors. All these vehicles, together with imports from the States, were taken up by Edge and distributed to farmers through the County War Agricultural Committees.

As the imported vehicles arrived at the ports they were taken over by a team of engineers and drivers and delivered to the respective counties. Drivers were supplied by the MT section of the Army Service Corps; farmers were charged for their services and for the hire of the tractors. These imports from America provided the Agricultural Machinery Department with a supply of tractors until such time as the MOM machines were available and there is no doubt that they helped considerably in speeding up the ploughing programme. Most of the American vehicles which were not taken up by the ministry were handled by agricultural machinery merchants, motor dealers and manufacturers. Austin was amongst these, being glad to have the opportunity of selling American products because, at that time, his works were producing only for the Ministry of Munitions.

Some idea of the complexity of motor tractors, the American models in particular, can be gained from their advertisement. Such complicated mechanism combined with the lack of mechanical knowledge of the majority of farm workers contributed to lack of faith in the larger models. The Bates Steel Mule was the heaviest tractor marketed by Austin — a 4in x 5in 4-cylinder engine dragged its 2½ tons along the road at a crawl. With only one forward and one reverse gear its caterpillar tracks were driven by spur gear and final drive chains. This unstable vehicle, which cost £485, was renowned for a marked tendency to tip over without warning so, in April 1918, the Americans introduced a new version onto the market. Unfortunately this modified vehicle was not suitable for use on roads on which it left an appropriate trade mark, a furrow, made by its driving wheels.

The Killen-Strait was powered by either a 30hp petrol/paraffin engine at £500, or by a 40hp engine at £520. A single steering wheel was employed and caterpillar driving wheels. Capable of hauling a five-furrow plough, the Killen-Strait could also be used to haul 5 tons on the road. Perhaps the most interesting vehicle was the light car-type tractor — the Interstate. This, and the Omnitractor, were the predecessors of modern machines. It was powered by a 30hp Buda petrol/paraffin engine which made it capable of pulling a three-furrow plough. The clutch was hand-operated and the two-speed and reverse drive was taken through spur gears to the 60in diameter rear wheels. Another interesting feature was the centre-pivoted front axle. The Interstate cost £425.

During 1917 W.E.Walker, who had pioneered the Emerson tractor into this country before the war, joined the tractor department at Longbridge. He later became sales manager of the Vulcan Car Agency Limited, which took over the American tractor interests of the Austin company when Walker joined them. Austin gave up dealing in the American vehicles without regret because most of them were really quite unsuited to this country, and as late as 1919 he was still offering them for sale at greatly reduced prices.

The day of the light-weight tractor had come. Ideally suited as it was to conditions in Britain it set the pattern to be followed in tractor production for many years. The day of the awful complexity of the American vehicles making them too difficult to handle was over — the simple ploughman needed a simple tractor.

Although Herbert Austin had first become interested in tractors with the advent of the American monsters he must have noticed also a much smaller machine called the Wallis, the first tractor to be built on the frameless principle in which a large combined cylindrical crankcase, gearbox, transmission and rear-axle housing acted in place of a chassis. And before the Ford MOM tractor (built, incidentally, to the same design as the Wallis) was adopted, a committee had been formed to study the design for the best type of vehicle for use in Great Britain. Perhaps it is significant that Herbert Austin was a member of that committee because, in the middle of 1917, his company built a tractor which was almost an exact copy of the Ford MOM. During the winter of that year the vehicle toured Norfolk, Suffolk, Essex, Kent and Surrey, and was used for demonstrations until the middle of 1919. It was heralded as the 'first all-British tractor'. Production in quantity soon started; by July 1919 completed tractors were leaving Longbridge, and large numbers appeared on the market during the second half of the year.

The Society of Motor Manufacturers and Traders realised that a minor boom in tractors was approaching and organised a series of trials, the most important of which took place at South Carlton, near Lincoln, in September 1919. Some 10,000 people were able to watch tractors in action and the Austin was very highly praised.

By January of the following year one third of the company's output consisted of tractors and the production figures, for the week ending 12 June 1920 show the peak reached during the year: Austin 20hp cars — 134; Austin tractors — 66. In 1920 as a whole, approximately 1,500 tractors were built.

Between 1919 and 1922 the price of the Austin tractor fluctuated between £300 and £360, at which it compared favourably with Fordson. But all American vehicle imports were subject to 33⅓ per cent duty, and when the duty was removed the Fordson could be sold in this country for as little as £120. Austin slashed his price to £225 and then to £195 but the boom, as far as he was concerned, was at an end. Not that he minded because, by then, all the available factory space was required for the 12hp and 7hp cars.

Competition from the Fordson and the success of his new models led to a falling-off in tractor production from about 1922. They were still offered in catalogues as late as 1926, by which time the price had risen to £225 or £285 for the road-haulage machine.

Demand in the early years was particularly marked in France but French laws did not permit the free entry of foreign tractors into the country. Heavy duties had a serious effect upon sales so Austin decided to open up a factory at Liancourt,

Paris. These premises, taken over in August 1919, were soon capable of an output of about 2,000 tractors a year. French agricultural experts singled the vehicle out for special praise, and at the spring meeting of the Société Syndicale de la Motoculture at St Germain-en-Laye it was inspected and highly commended by M Poincaré, the French President. Doubtless this helped to make the tractor popular on the continent, and they were produced at Liancourt between 1919 and 1928 as agricultural and 20 ton road-haulage vehicles.

4 The Racing Austin 20

Felix Scriven, a Bradford businessman, ordered one of the new P3 models late in 1920. This was to prove an Austin 20 with a difference, for Scriven contacted Austins at the time of the Motor Show and asked them if they would produce a tuned-up Austin 20 capable of travelling at 70mph. When it came to the question of incorporating some of his own modifications the company refused at first but eventually agreed, on the understanding that they would not have to provide a guarantee that the car would reach any particular speed. Basically, it remained a standard Austin 20; its significance lies in the fact that, with the exception of the camshaft, inlet manifold and carburetter, all parts were taken from the production line. Utmost power was obtained from the 3.6 litre engine by careful assembly, balancing and tuning; the flywheel was lightened, an ⅛in machined from the cylinder head and a large-bore copper-induction pipe was used.

After it was delivered in March 1921 the car was taken for its first run at Brooklands track where it succeeded in lapping at about 70mph. As the inlet manifold failed to warm up sufficiently due to a combination of large water-pump, high-radiator frontal area and an enormous fan, Scriven made a copper water-jacket before entering the car for its first race.

At this period the engine was most efficient at about 3,500rpm, at which some 80bhp was obtained; Scriven was able to increase this to about 100bhp at 3,700rpm. Very short bursts on the track could be run at the limit of the revolution counter — 4,000. His own words about this: 'I always felt that revs in that neighbourhood were very dangerous and that anything might burst', explain why he was most happy with the engine running at about 3,500.

He entered the car for two races at the Easter Monday meeting at Brooklands. The first, in which he was the limit car with 1min 14sec start, was the Twelfth 75mph Short Handicap. These two laps, covering 5¾ miles, were driven at 70.56 and 75.30mph and the car won by, what at that time, was an unpreceder margin. Nothing more than 60mph had been expected by the handicappers so far too generous a margin had been allowed for the first race, which caused a stir at Longbridge where they intended to produce a works' racing 20 for themselves. For the next event, the Long Handicap, the start was reduced to 15sec. Even so, he was placed third, only just being beaten by André in a Marlborough and Hawkes in an AC. The final lap average speed was 83.5mph. Following a protest from another entrant in the first race the stewards asked Scriven to verify that the car's engine dimensions were still the original 95mm x 127mm. The cylinder head was removed and the protestor was satisfied that the engine was perfectly normal; it had not seemed possible that such a car could travel at speeds in excess of 80mph.

The car was not, to quote a contemporary press report, 'one of those racing machines which are wrapped in cotton wool and carefully towed to Brooklands'. Between track races, to which it was always driven down from Bradford, it was used for hill climbing as well as everyday motoring on the roads. Scriven's routine for getting from his home to Weybridge was made possible by the construction of the car's body, the rear half of which was detachable behind the seats so that either a streamlined pointed tail or a light section with two additional seats could be used. Wheels fitted with Palmer Cord racing tyres and the spare parts were packed into the detachable tail which was despatched by rail a few days before the race; the car, with it four seats, passenger and mechanics was driven down on the day prior to the event. Sometimes, however, they were not able to arrive beforehand, as was the case in May 1921 when excitement was caused as competitors were lining up in the Paddock for the Essex Club's Long Handicap. The Austin sailed in, dropped its passenger and spare wheels just in time to compete — and finish in second place.

By this time, the works' car was ready. Captain (later Colonel) Arthur Waite, Lord Austin's son-in-law, had been given the job of representing the company at Brooklands. *Black Maria*, as the car was called, was always entered in either Captain Waite's or Mrs Waite's name but usually driven by Lou Kings, Austin's chief tester. Its first race, in which Kings drove, was the Whitsun Senior Sprint Handicap at Brooklands on May 16 which it won at 72.12mph, a speed not likely to upset the handicapping. On the same day Scriven pushed his lap speed up to 85.57mph in another race.

Both cars were entered for the Long and Short 100mph Handicaps at the summer meeting in June 1921. Scriven failed to start in the Short race which the works' car won easily, achieving an average of 86.92mph in the second lap. In the other race Scriven's car went very slowly, but in one lap Waite obtained 91.38mph. Neither car was placed. This pattern continued with Scriven gradually increasing his speed in an attempt to catch up with the works' car, which was now lapping at over 90mph in each of its races — this was done eight times during eight different races at the 1921 August and autumn meetings. Scriven directed most of his attention to hill climbs that summer. At Holme Moss he came third in his class and was only beaten by Segrave and Campbell. At Tong Hill in Yorkshire the car made fastest time of the day in its class, beating 'the latest model 30/98 Vauxhall by $\frac{1}{25}$th second'.

These were not the only two large Austins to race at Brooklands in the twenties. There was one occasion on which, in addition to the works' entry and Scriven's car, a tandem two-seater, prepared by Austins for sand-racing, was entered also. This car first appeared under Mrs Waite's name at the last Brooklands meeting of the 1920 season on 24 September. Fitted with a special narrow white-painted radiator-cowling and discs on the rear wheels it managed to lap at over 91mph and gained third place in the 90mph Long Handicap. All three cars started in this race but Waite's entry retired. Scriven did not race at Brooklands again until Whitsun 1922 and, although the car did not excel itself it improved during the year, regaining some of its old form to win a 90mph Long Handicap in the August. The works' car had performed outstandingly at a similar race the Easter before, its second lap being officially timed at 98.04mph — the fastest BARC lap recorded for any Austin 20. The last works-entered car was raced at the Whitsun Meeting of 1923, but the much lower speeds attained suggest that this was not the car which did so well in 1922. From then on Captain Waite and the company concentrated on Austin 7 racing, and Scriven was left to increase his speed alone.

278

By the spring of 1924 Scriven's 20 was fast enough to win the 90mph Long Handicap and to lap at over 90mph for the first time. Another win was scored in August with a second lap speed of 93.97mph, and its final win in a BARC event took place at Whitsun 1925 when a lap average of 94.86 was accomplished. In order to reach these speeds additional tuning had been carried out to the engine and more cowling was placed around a much lighter body, which appears to have been made from fabric. A special extra-high-compression cylinder head was designed, and the final drive ratio altered from 3.93:1 to 3.48:1. About his speed in the later races Scriven remarked, 'on the Railway Straight I always exceed 100mph and was timed on one occasion, in this part of the track, to do 104'.

Many racing drivers of the period gave names to their cars; originally Scriven called his 20 *Felix the Cat* after the silent-film cartoon character. A model of this animal usually adorned the radiator cap. The name *Sergeant Murphy* first appears in the BARC records for the 1925 Easter meeting, but he must have used it first in 1924. In his own words, from a letter written in 1950:

In fact, as far as racing vehicles went in those days, it was by that time getting a little ancient. During this particular period there was a race horse called *Sergeant Murphy*, which in spite of its age continued to win good races and, so far as I can remember, won the Grand National [Mrs Sandford's *Sergeant Murphy* won the 1923 Grand National at 100 to 6] and so I called my car after it; afterwards, when the car got really old for those days, and it turned into more of a sports tourer, I had inserted (underneath the name) 'in mufti'.

Sergeant Murphy was still not worn out in 1925, and although he had another racing car, Scriven continued to use the Austin in trials and hill climbs. Unfortunately the car was broken up in the 1930s.

5 Notes on Production Statistics

It has proved very difficult to calculate accurately production figures for Austin cars. Over the years I have found many scraps, varying from the accurate set of records — since destroyed — of all models by type from the end of 1927 to 1935, sales figures, and chassis numbers from change registers and Service Journals, to production capability figures, sales potential statistics and details released to the press or given to shareholders. The Society of Motor Manufacturers and Traders did not publish individual company production figures until quite recently and even their early totals for the industry are only estimated. Books like Stone and Cox *Motor Specifications and Prices* and the *Motor Car Index* set out to provide information to assist insurance assessors in dating cars, and it is very fortunate that some editions contain details which have enabled me to arrive at accurate figures for quite a few years.

Manufacturers seem to have been reluctant to publish anything that could show their competitors how badly or how well they were doing — today a wealth of accurate detail is published each month — and unless early production records have been preserved, it takes a long time to arrive at figures accurate enough to be of much value. Figures given at AGM's were often incorrect; those provided to, or guessed at by, the press were often wildly inaccurate; and the very figures calculated by the company for their own internal use were sometimes wrong. When, in 1946, an attempt was made to work out exactly which car would be the millionth Austin, totals for each financial year from 1920 were available, and the total up to that year was recorded as 15,038. Attempts to be more accurate were made in 1954, the result then being 10,412, and in 1961 when it grew to 12,892. These were from records which even then were contradictory, and the figures I have arrived at are I think as accurate as they are ever likely to be.

Having studied Austin 7, 12 and 20hp models over the last twenty-five years, I am confident that figures given for them are substantially correct. Breakdown by types before 1919 must be very close; my worst figures are likely to be for the years from 1947 to 1951. Fortunately, microfilm statistics exist, so one day it will be possible for someone with a few more years to spare to count them up and provide the fine detail, and to correct any errors that I may have made.

After long weeks of juggling with chassis numbers, figures for calendar years, Motor Show years and financial years to arrive at the few columns of figures that follow, I leave willingly to some other hand the task of analysing the several thousand reels of microfilm held at BL Heritage.

6 Austin Identification by Chassis and Body Types, 1933 - 1939

Symbol	HP	Body Type	Commenced	Ceased
AAK	7	Tourer	Aug 1935	Jul 1935
AAL	7	Tourer	Aug 1935	Feb 1939
AC	7	Cabriolet	Aug 1934	Feb 1939
AP	8	Tourer	Feb 1939	
APD	7	2-seater Tourer	Aug 1934	Jul 1935
APE	7	2-seater Tourer	Aug 1935	Feb 1939
AR	8	4-door Saloon	Feb 1939	
ARA	8	2-door Saloon	Feb 1939	
ARQ	7	Ruby Saloon	Aug 1934	Feb 1936
ARR	7	Ruby Saloon	Aug 1936	Feb 1939
BRN	H12	Carlton	Dec 1933	Jul 1934
BRP	H12	York	Aug 1934	Apr 1936
BRT	H12	Berkeley	Dec 1933	Jul 1934
BRU	H12	Hertford	Aug 1934	Apr 1936
BTH	H12	Chalfont	Aug 1935	Apr 1936
BWN	H12	Westminster	Dec 1933	Dec 1934
BWQ	H12	Westminster	Feb 1935	Apr 1936
CRV	Big 7	4-door Saloon	Jul 1937	Feb 1939
CRW	Big 7	2-door Saloon	Jul 1937	Feb 1939
DJL	20	Ranelagh	Dec 1933	Jun 1934
DJM	20	Ranelagh	Jun 1934	Apr 1935
DJN	20	Mayfair Limousine	Apr 1935	Jan 1938
DJP	28	Ranelagh	Feb 1938	
DLL	20	Ranelagh	Dec 1933	Jul 1934
DLM	20	Ranelagh	Jul 1934	Jul 1935
DLN	20	Mayfair Limousine	Aug 1935	Jan 1938
DWM	20	Whitehall (10ft)	Dec 1932	Jul 1934
ERN	18	Carlton (10ft)	Dec 1933	Jul 1934
ERP	18	York (10ft)	Aug 1934	Apr 1936
ERT	18	Berkeley	Dec 1933	Jul 1934
ERU	18	Hertford	Aug 1934	Apr 1936
ERW	18	Hertford	Apr 1936	Jul 1937
ERX	18	York (10ft)	Apr 1936	Jul 1937
ERY	18	Norfolk (9ft 4in)	Jul 1937	
ERZ	18	Windsor (10ft 3in)	Jul 1937	
ETH	18	Chalfont (10ft)	Aug 1935	Apr 1936
ETJ	18	Chalfont (10ft)	Apr 1936	Jul 1937

281

Symbol	HP	Body Type	Commenced	Ceased
ETK	18	Iver (10ft 3in)	Jul 1937	
EWN	18	Westminster (9ft 4in)	Dec 1933	Dec 1934
EWQ	18	Westminster (9ft 4in)	Feb 1935	Apr 1936
FBC	12/6	Harley Standard	Dec 1933	Jul 1934
FBS	12/6	Harley de Luxe	Dec 1933	Jul 1934
FBW	12/6	Ascot	Dec 1933	Aug 1934
FBX	12/6	Ascot	Aug 1934	Jul 1936
FR	14	Goodwood	Jul 1936	Aug 1938
FRA	14	Goodwood	Aug 1938	
GC	10	Cabriolet	Dec 1933	Jul 1934
GCA	10	Cabriolet	Aug 1934	Sep 1934
GCB	10	Cabriolet	Sep 1934	Jul 1937
GR	10	Saloon	Sep 1933	Oct 1933
GRA	10	Saloon	Oct 1933	Jul 1934
GRB	10	Lichfield	Aug 1934	Jul 1936
GRK	10	Sherborne	Jan 1936	Jul 1936
GRL	10	Cambridge	Jul 1936	
HBC	Light 12/4	Harley Standard	Dec 1933	Jul 1934
HBS	Light 12/4	Harley de Luxe	Dec 1933	Jul 1934
HBW	Light 12/4	Ascot	Dec 1932	Aug 1934
HBX	Light 12/4	Ascot	Aug 1934	Jul 1936
HR	12	New Ascot	Jul 1936	Aug 1938
HRA	12	New Ascot	Aug 1938	
K2	Commercial	2 ton	Feb 1939	
K3	Commercial	3 ton	Feb 1939	
K30	Commercial	1½ ton	Feb 1939	

7 Vehicle Statistics, 1906-1952

Year	UK Production Cars and Lorries	Austin Car Production	Morris Production	UK Private Cars Registered
1906	*8,500*	31	-	23,192
1907	*12,000*	180	-	32,451
1908	*10,500*	216	-	40,902
1909	*11,000*	198	-	48,109
1910	*14,000*	579	-	53,169
1911	*19,000*	781	-	72,106
1912	*23,200*	1,107	-	88,265
1913	34,000	882	393	105,734

Year	UK Production Cars	Austin Car Production	Morris Production	UK Private Cars Registered	Cars and Chassis Exported	Cars and Chassis Imported
1919	*24,000*	*200*	360	109,715	-	-
1920	*50,000*	4,319	1,932	186,801	7,418†	-
1921	*32,000*	2,246	3,077	245,882	3,007†	-
1922	*55,000*	2,559	6,956	319,311	*2,000*	19,939
1923	71,396	6,417	20,048	389,767	*4,200*	22,067
1924	116,600	9,673	32,918	482,356	*12,500*	17,800
1925	132,000	16,429	53,582	590,156	*22,700*	40,800
1926	153,500	24,900	48,330	695,555	*25,000*	16,000
1927	164,553	37,520	61,632	800,112	*27,500*	25,000
1928	165,352	44,654	55,480	900,557	26,180	23,000
1929	182,347	46,029	63,522	998,489	33,808	21,520
1930	169,669	39,251	58,436	1,075,081	26,132	9,751
1931	158,997	39,676	43,582	1,103,715	18,682	2,118
1932	171,244	43,802	50,337	1,149,231	26,701	2,762
1933	220,779	57,741	44,049	1,226,541	41,334	3,619
1934	256,866	68,291	55,248	1,333,590	45,327	10,851
1935	325,192	73,562	96,512	1,505,019	51,209	13,563
1936	367,237	71,855	*95,000*	1,675,104	64,765	12,143
1937	379,310	89,175	*95,000*	1,834,248	78,113	18,560
1938	341,028	60,224	*95,000*	1,984,430	68,257	9,180
1939	305,000	57,367	*95,000*	2,073,404	67,033	-
1945	16,938	5,785	-	1,521,581	3,127	-
1946	291,162	*42,500*	-	1,807,067	86,492	63
1947	287,000	62,544	-	1,983,505	143,102	222
1948	334,815	*46,000*	-	2,002,201	226,911	221
1949	412,290	*116,996*	*90,000*	2,178,411	257,922	1,868

1950	552,515	142,723	90,000	2,307,379	398,302	1,375
1951	475,919	121,500	90,000	2,433,172	368,737	3,723
1952	448,000	118,000	-	2,564,686	309,832	1,876

Figures in italic are approximations
† Inclusive of commercial vehicles

8 Austin Production, Calendar Years by Types, 1906-1919

HP	25/30	15/20	18/24	40	60	15	7	50	10	15	30	10	20	Totals	2-3 ton Lorries
1906	27	4	-	-	-	-	-	-	-	-	-	-	-	31	-
1907	39	-	99	40	2	-	-	-	-	-	-	-	-	180	-
1908	1	-	150	47	8	10	-	-	-	-	-	-	-	216	-
1909	-	-	163	15	1	19	-	-	-	-	-	-	-	198	-
1910	-	-	357	16	2	184	15	5	-	-	-	-	-	579	-
1911	-	-	171	8	1	-	147	10	153	291	-	-	-	781	-
1912	-	-	578	15	-	-	-	5	214	293	2	-	-	1,107	-
1913	-	-	55	11	-	-	-	4	-	12	14	495	291	882	1
1914	-	-	2	-	-	-	-	-	-	4	128	269	142	545	164
1915	-	-	-	-	-	-	-	-	-	88	102	1,115	668	1,973	266
1916	-	-	-	-	-	-	-	-	-	-	179*	-	176	355	33
1917	-	-	-	-	-	-	-	-	-	-	-	-	14	14	386
1918	-	-	-	-	-	-	-	-	-	-	-	-	-	-	725
1919	-	-	-	-	-	-	-	-	-	-	-	-	-	8	463
Totals	67	4	1,575	152	14	213	162	24	367	688	425	1,879	1,291	6,861	2,038

* Armoured cars — another reliable source gives total production as 480

Model	RAC HP	Engine Dimensions (in)	Engine Dimensions (mm)	Number of Cylinders	1906 £	1907 £	1908 £	1909 £	1910 £	1911 £	1912 £	1913 £	1914 £
25/30	28.6	4½ x 5	114 x 127	4	(550-650)	(550-650)	-	-	-	-	-	-	-
15/20	27.0	4 x 5	102 x 127	4	(425-500)	-	-	-	-	-	-	-	-
18/24	27.3	4⅛ x 5	105 x 127	4	-	(450-525)	475	480	480	-	-	-	-
40	36.3	4¾ x 5	121 x 127	4	-	-	600	600	600	575	-	-	-
60	54.5	4¾ x 5	121 x 127	6	-	-	800	800	700	-	-	-	-
15	19.6	3½ x 4	89 x 102	4	-	-	-	305	325	-	-	-	-
7	6.8	4⅛ x 5	105 x 127	1	-	-	-	-	(150)	(150)	-	-	-
50	45.8	4⅜ x 5	111 x 127	6	-	-	-	-	650	650	650	650	-
10	10.1	2½ x 3½	64 x 89	4	-	-	-	-	-	240	240	-	-
15	19.6	3½ x 4½	89 x 114	4	-	-	-	-	-	330	330	330	-
18/24	30.5	4⅜ x 5	111 x 127	4	-	-	-	-	-	480	480	480	-
40	38.8	5 x 5	125 x 127	4	-	-	-	-	-	-	575	575	-
10	14.3	3 x 3½	76 x 89	4	-	-	-	-	-	-	-	260	260
20	19.6	3½ x 5	89 x 127	4	-	-	-	-	-	-	-	375	375
30	30.5	4⅜ x 6	111 x 152	4	-	-	-	-	-	-	-	550	550

( ) Price for complete car

10 Austin Car Production, 1919-1939

Year	20/4	12/4	7	16-18	20/6	12/6-14	Lt 12/4	10	Big 7	28	8	Totals
1919	200	-	-	-	-	-	-	-	-	-	-	200
1920	4,319	-	-	-	-	-	-	-	-	-	-	4,319
1921	2,246	-	-	-	-	-	-	-	-	-	-	2,246
1922	1,394	1,165	-	-	-	-	-	-	-	-	-	2,559
1923	2,064	2,417	1,936	-	-	-	-	-	-	-	-	6,417
1924	973	4,000	4,700	-	-	-	-	-	-	-	-	9,673
1925	886	8,500	7,043	-	-	-	-	-	-	-	-	16,429
1926	900	10,000	14,000	-	-	-	-	-	-	-	-	24,900
1927	1,000	14,000	22,500	10	10	-	-	-	-	-	-	37,520
1928	927	13,714	22,709	6,401	903	-	-	-	-	-	-	44,654
1929	378	8,759	26,447	9,136	1,129	-	-	-	-	-	-	45,849
1930	-	6,889	23,826	7,560	976	-	-	-	-	-	-	39,251
1931	-	-	21,282.	5,558	705	9,529	-	-	-	-	-	39,676
1932	-	2,602.	20,121	3,839	605	6,309	1,867	8,609	-	-	-	43,802.
1933	-	2,452.	20,475	2,788	629	2,896	7,020	20,937	-	-	-	57,741
1934	-	2,996	22,542.	2,954(16) 2,630(18)	491	2,008 2,331(15.9)	8,252	24,149	-	-	-	68,291
1935	-	2,934	27,280	2,052(16) 3,280(18)	555	1,313 2,830(15.9)	6,915	27,377	-	-	-	73,562.
1936	-	1,960	23,500	4,000	505	4,100	12,000	27,000	-	-	-	71,855
1937	-	750	23,000	3,400	380	5,950	15,500	35,000	5,500	-	-	89,175
1938	-	445	8,500	2,583	156	2,750	11,000	18,238	16,414	138	-	60,224
1939	-	445	1,000	370	51	2,649	9,100	22,000	1,600	152.	20,000	57,367

11 Austin Production, 1946-1951 (approximate)

Year	8	10	12	16	A40	A70	A90	A110/135	Totals	Commercials
1946	17,000	19,000	3,000	3,500	-	-	-	-	42,500	7,500
1947	16,000	30,000	3,000	3,000	10,500	-	-	44	62,544	15,500
1948	-	-	-	-	42,500	1,000	500	2,000	46,000	16,000
1949	-	-	-	-	90,800	9,000	15,000	2,196	116,996	19,600
1950	-	-	-	-	110,000	18,000	12,723	2,000	142,723	23,000
1951	-	-	-	-	100,000	12,000	8,000	1,500	121,500	20,000

12 Net Turnover and Profit, 1905-1913

Year Ending	Net Turnover*	Profit†
	£	£
Oct 1906	14,772	
(11 months)		
31 Oct 1907	84,930	
30 Sep 1908	119,744	
(11 months)		
30 Sep 1909	169,821	
30 Sep 1910	209,048	
30 Sep 1911	276,196	39,174
30 Sep 1912	354,209	55,745
30 Sep 1913	425,641	41,130
31 Dec 1913	102,870	

* Net turnover, after deducting commission on sales
† Profit after depreciation, but before charging directors' salary, tax, interest, bank charges and national insurance contributions

13 Austin Finances, 1914 - 1951

Year Ending	Issued Capital £	Gross Profit/Loss £	Net Profit/Loss £	Carried Forward £
30 Nov 1914	650,000	70,940		413
(14 months)				
30 Nov 1915	650,000	63,909		
30 Nov 1916	650,000		227,177	176,125
30 Nov 1917	650,000		262,642	380,267
31 Dec 1918	650,000		358,272	591,081
(13 months)				
31 Dec 1919	1,650,000		237,866	13,995
31 Dec 1921	3,350,000	dr 381,923	dr 2,333,846	dr 1,883,601
(2 years)				
31 Dec 1922	3,350,000	198,835	18,564	dr 1,805,037
30 Sep 1923	3,350,000	381,640	176,334	dr 1,599,578
(9 months)				
30 Sep 1924	3,350,000	470,902	161,174	dr 1,438,404
30 Sep 1925	3,350,000	748,890	447,852	dr 1,717,446
30 Sep 1926	3,350,000	648,415	330,508	dr 1,386,938
30 Sep 1927	2,150,000	962,477	406,469	10,639
31 Dec 1928	2,150,000	861,299	243,025	59,664
(15 months)				
31 Dec 1929	2,150,000	1,297,446	559,789	71,452
31 Jul 1930	2,150,000	858,137	384,342	279,820
(7 months)				
31 Jul 1931	2,150,000	1,376,244	489,232	270,489
31 Jul 1932	2,150,000	1,078,145	390,387	319,220
31 Jul 1933	2,150,000	1,188,440	506,798	357,497
31 Jul 1934	2,150,000	1,502,212	661,280	362,933
31 Jul 1935	2,622,459	1,469,144	623,923	370,842
31 Jul 1936	2,622,459	1,496,696	553,793	373,955
31 Jul 1937	2,622,459	1,665,125	555,577	303,330
31 Jul 1938	2,622,459	1,282,828	362,158	303,447
31 Jul 1939	2,622,459	1,609,580	344,720	312,290
31 Jul 1940	2,647,361	1,530,787	232,480	356,047
31 Jul 1941	2,647,361	1,760,993	220,635	311,595
31 Jul 1942	2,647,361	2,342,792	338,230	378,964
31 Jul 1943	2,647,361	2,164,530	258,976	319,067
31 Jul 1944	2,647,361	2,137,505	214,149	326,107
31 Jul 1945	3,591,641	2,077,400	257,043	349,234
31 Jul 1946	3,591,641	2,249,370	625,369	368,688
31 Jul 1947	3,591,641	2,262,431	707,156	416,929
31 Jul 1948	3,591,641	1,611,903	571,988	444,473
31 Jul 1949	4,096,041	2,164,342	679,932	563,126
31 Jul 1950	4,682,666	5,080,870	1,847,891	622,090
31 Jul 1951	4,682,666	8,254,142	2,840,989	872,002

Index

INDEX